POTENT MANA

POTENT MANA

MANA

Lessons in Power and Healing

WENDE ELIZABETH MARSHALL

Cover image: Taro fields in Kauai's Hanalei River Valley, Hawaii;
courtesy of iStockphoto/Jim Kruger

Published by State University of New York Press, Albany

© 2011 State University of New York

For information, contact State University of New York Press, Albany, NY
www.sunypress.edu

Production by Diane Ganeles
Marketing by Michael Campochiaro

Library of Congress Cataloging-in-Publication Data

Marshall, Wende Elizabeth, 1961–
  Potent mana : lessons in power and healing / Wende Elizabeth Marshall.
    p. cm.
  Includes bibliographical references and index.
  ISBN 978-1-4384-3435-3 (hardcover : alk. paper) 978-1-4384-3434-6 (pbk.)
  1. Hawaii—History—1959– 2. Colonization—Psychological aspects.
  3. Self-determination, National—Hawaii. 4. Hawaii—Colonization.
  5. Hawaiians—Ethnic identity. 6. Hawaiians—Social conditions.
  7. Indigenous peoples—Ethnic identity. 8. Indigenous peoples—Government
relations. I. Title.
  DU627.8.M37 2011
  996.9'04—dc22

                                                                2010018155

10 9 8 7 6 5 4 3 2 1

For

Adelaide Austin
1906–2003

Bunch Hammond
1930–1989

Julie Adelaide Marshall
1940–2007

CONTENTS

ACKNOWLEDGMENTS/GENEALOGY

An author's opportunity to acknowledge the support that made book writing possible is not simply about public recognition and gratitude. Acknowledging is also an enactment of genealogy, a statement of origins, and a record of familial, political, and academic kinship.

I hoped to write a book that honored my kinship ties, as well as the lessons I learned from my Kānaka Maoli teachers. It helped to imagine that I was writing a love poem that, although filtered through the particulars of my training and experience, would be worthy of my Hawaiian guides and expressive of my profound solidarity with the project of decolonization in Hawai'i. In the community of Wai'anae, I was blessed by many wise teachers, in particular Ho'oipo DeCambra, Puanani Burgess, and Pōkā Laenui. They invited me into their offices, classrooms, and homes and trusted me to interpret the work of their lives and their love for Hawai'i. Their tremendous faith in the project of decolonization has remained a great source of my inspiration as a scholar and as a community organizer. I am grateful for the guidance of Kaimi Chung, Kamana'opono Crabbe, Palama Lee, Randall Like, Vicky Milles, Mari Ono, Dixie Padello, Jim Winters, and others who I cannot name because of concerns with confidentiality. I hope that *Potent Mana* contributes in some small way to the struggle for decolonization and the powerful resurgence of Kānaka Maoli.

I wanted to explain decolonization and the struggle of Native Hawaiians in a way that made sense for people who were not aware that such a struggle existed in the fiftieth state, so, I conjured up various mothers of my many students and explained Hawaiian decolonization to them. For trusting me to teach their children and to summon their spirits as collective muse, I thank Lynnette F. Hammond, Barbara Ann Miller, Caroline Sahni, Karen Shaw, Marti Snell, Ruth Stewart, Kiljai Taylor, Doris Thomas, Mayra Y. Vargas, and Mariel York.

I am grateful for the community of graduate and undergraduate students, as they are my primary interlocutors. I thank current and former graduate students Helen Chapple, Holly Donohue-Singh, Ann Githinji, Abby Holeman, Anjana

Mebane-Cruz, Matthew and Marlo Meyer, Yadira Perez, Mieka Brand Polanco, Will Schroeder, Claire Snell-Rood, Anne Stachura, Lisa Stewart, David Strohl, Todne Thomas, and LuAnn Williams. I also thank current and former undergraduates Naseem and Shereen Alavian, Omid Akhavan, Mark Brewster, Mary Elizabeth Bruce, Seth Croft, Jeremy Davis, Liam Del Rios, Stephanie Dewolfe, May Gallanosa, Katie Gillespie, Vicky Jones, Camilo Kohn, Caroline Kuo, Timothy Ly, Kimiknu Mentore, J. T. Roane, Stephanie Shaw, Kevin Simowitz, Preyasha Tuladhar, Jalan Washington, and Ruthie Yow. Last, for sharing their wisdom and ceaselessly urging me on, I especially thank Ayla Fahire Ayvadas and Christin Taylor.

I am the product of good mentoring. For engaging with me and my work through thick and thin in a multitude of productive ways, I thank my formal mentors Ellen Contini-Morava, Adria LaViolette, and Susan McKinnon at the University of Virginia, and Dede Yow, now retired from Kennesaw State University. I also thank Lawrie Balfour, Eve Danzinger, Wendi El-Amin, Karen Hall, Julie Lassetter, George Mentore, Norm Oliver, Geeta Patel, and Kath Weston, all at the University of Virginia, for believing in me and my work.

In my life before Virginia, I also received committed mentoring and training. In 1986 I graduated from the Center for Third World Organizing's (CTWO) Minority Activist Apprenticeship Program. I was trained at CTWO by Gary Delgado, Alfredo DeAvila, Francis Calpatura, and Rachel Sierra, who shaped my views on the world in profound and unalterable ways, and who grounded me in an epistemology of community organizing. For her firm guidance and inspiration, I thank my ancestor, the Reverend Marilyn Adams Moore. I learned theology from James Cone and Delores Williams at Union Theological Seminary and anthropology from Vincanne Adams, Rena Lederman, Emily Martin, and Kay Warren at Princeton. Kim Blankenship at Yale's Center for Interdisciplinary Research on AIDS taught me how to apply insights from public health literature to my humanities work on HIV. Hector Carrillo, Barbara Marin, Olga Grinsted, and other faculty of the Collaborative HIV in Minority Communities Program, at the Center for AIDS Prevention Studies, University of California, San Francisco (UCSF), patiently mentored the social scientist in me, as did Sheldon Fields, David Malebranche, Lois Takahashi, Mark Padillo, and Nelson Dias-Vargas, my colleagues in the program.

In Charlottesville I was fortunate to belong to a community committed to the work of social justice. They reminded me to honor my debts to the ancestors and to focus my work on issues that are relevant to ordinary people. For this inspiration I thank Karen Waters, Joe Szakos, Harold Foley, Joy Johnson, and Holly Edwards. The circle of friends, those who have nurtured me over the years, includes Quinton Hosford Dixie, Nia Mason, Rima McCoy, Sally Noland MacNichol, Tanquil Jones, Hanan Sabea, and Claire Yoo. For their support and kinship I thank my uncle, John Morris, my sister, Holly Marshall, and Jon Paul Hammond, whose presence in my life is a lesson in love, faith, and healing.

I am very grateful for the insights of two anonymous reviewers, for the Hawaiian language copyediting skills of Aggy Stevens-Gleason, and for the support of Gary Dunham, executive director of State University of New York Press. For allowing me permission to cite from his private papers in chapter 2, I thank Pōkā Laenui. Thanks as well to Calyx Press for granting permission to cite lines from Haunani-Kay Trask's poem *Sons* in the final chapter, and to Mountain Apple Records for permission to cite lyrics from Israel Kamakawiwoʻoleʻs song "Hawaiʻi '78" in chapter 5. Grants from the Ford Foundation Minority Dissertation Fellowship, Harvard University, the National Institute of Drug Abuse (National Research Service Award), Princeton University, and the University of Virginia enabled the research and writing for this book.

INTRODUCTION

Ethnography of Decolonization in Hawai'i

The term *decolonization* was applied, after the Second World War, to the achievement of independence and recognition of indigenous national governments by former colonial rulers. Decolonization, in this sense, was synonymous with formal national liberation and was understood as an achievement in the public domain of politics, often at the behest of the colonial power (Flint 1983, 390; Nkrumah 1970, 101–103).[1] But in the late twentieth century, decolonization took on different meanings. Rather than being understood as a formal event initiated at the center of colonial power, decolonization was perceived as a process internal to the colonized that promised "the fuller redemption and realization of a people" (Nkrumah 1970, 105).[2] In Hawai'i, at the turn of the twentieth century, this deeper meaning of decolonization was occurring at the intimate level of the body and soul and collectively at the level of community.

Canonical works on the trauma of colonialism (Nandy 1983; Fanon 1963, 1967; Memi 1965) thoroughly explored the wretchedness of being colonized but did not necessarily theorize the means of achieving decolonization or explore practices that might lead to healing. The stories told in *Potent Mana: Lessons in Power and Healing* move this conversation about the healing of the colonized forward by exploring the theories and practices of Native Hawaiians engaged in creating the real means to achieve decolonization.

Potent Mana explores Kanaka Maoli, or the Native Hawaiian, cultural, and political struggle against American neocolonialism in the late twentieth century. This book focuses on the broad array of efforts used by Native Hawaiians in the mid-1990s that stressed healing the wounds and transcending the shame of colonialism. For Kanaka Maoli (Native Hawaiians) being colonized was—is—a violent process that for over two centuries disrupted Hawaiian life and health.

1

Being colonized meant that the very possibility of Hawaiian existence—the possibility of specifically Kanaka Maoli ways of being and knowing—was deliberately erased. Being colonized meant foreign penetration deep into the psyches, souls, and cells of indigenous Hawaiians. It meant death and disease on both the structural level of community, as well as at the personal level of bodies and souls.

For Native Hawaiians decolonization depended upon recognition of the potency of ancestral knowledge as a guide for contemporary well-being. Haunani-Kay Trask, a poet and political scientist, described the centrality of ancestral knowledge for Hawaiians in the late twentieth century:

> We face our past: *ka wā mamua*—the time before. The past holds our wisdom and our *kūpuna* (elders') knowledge. As our culture tells us, we are guided in the present on the path so well followed by our ancestors in the past. (Trask 1996, 912)

At its most fundamental, decolonization was about overcoming the shame of being colonized. It meant that the ways in which Hawaiians had internalized the degradation of colonialism had to be confronted and overcome. It required a process of remembering the traditions of ancestors and reinterpreting and rewriting histories that had only been told from a colonial point of view. Decolonization was about challenging Western interpretations of Hawaiian culture and history and reinterpreting from a Native point of view to meet the needs of indigenous Hawaiians in the twenty-first century.

Decolonization meant healing. One of the most important domains of decolonization practice involved the reemergence of healing methods and ways of perceiving health and disease that derived from ancestral knowledge. It meant a reinvigoration of specifically Hawaiian epistemologies for understanding the connection between humans, the environment, and the divine. It meant a return to specifically Hawaiian methods for achieving health that were outlawed and suppressed by colonial rule. It meant dreaming, imagining, and seeing before and beyond the times of Western rule. At the most profound level, decolonization was the recognition of the potent mana of Hawai'i.

POTENT MANA

Mana, according to Clifford Geertz, was a favorite term of anthropologists (*tabu* and *potlatch* were others) that seemed to provide a conceptual key to unlocking the mysteries of other cultures (Geertz 1983, 157). As a reified Polynesian term rendered intelligible to the West through scholarly debates, the meaning of mana generated a great deal of literature.

In the early twentieth century, Marcel Mauss explicated mana as a "magical force," as "the talisman and source of wealth that is authority itself," and as a sign of "social superiority" (Mauss 1990[1925], 38, 8, 75). In *The Gift* (1925), Mauss made the Polynesian concept of mana central to his argument about gift exchange and reciprocity.

> To be first, the most handsome, the luckiest, the strongest, and wealth-iest—this is what is sought after, and how it is obtained. Later, the chief gives proof of his *mana* by redistributing what he has just received to his vassals and relations. He sustains his rank among the chiefs by giving back bracelets for necklaces, hospitality for visits, etc. In this case riches are from every viewpoint as much a means of retaining prestige as something useful. Yet are we sure that it is any different in our own society, and that even with us riches are not above all a means of lord-ing it over our fellow men? (Mauss 1990[1925], 75)

Mauss's glossing of mana, along with Durkheim's (1965[1915]), was later chal-lenged by anthropologist Raymond Firth. Firth (1940) argued that the term had become merely theoretical, a heuristic device for Western scholars seeking to understand the intricacies of "primitive religion." Based upon ethnographic data from his study of the Tikopia in the southwestern Pacific, Firth doubted that the term as deployed by Mauss and other Western scholars bore much resemblance to the term's use in "native phraseology"(Firth 1940, 487). According to Firth:

> A Tikopian chief is regarded as having a peculiar responsibility towards his people. He is considered to be able through his relations with the ancestors and gods to control natural fertility, health and economic conditions. . . . Success or failure in theses spheres are symptoms of his *mana*. (Firth 1940, 490)

As opposed to Mauss, who viewed mana as an expression of social superiority and high rank enacted through reciprocity and gift exchange, Firth understood mana as a sign of the successful rule of a chief who fulfilled "his duty to his people and *deserv[ed] their praise*" (1940, 497, emphasis added). Mana, among the Tikopia as mediated by Firth, was an expression of a core cosmological prin-ciple that acknowledged the profound imbrications and codependence between the human, natural, and divine worlds that produced a society marked by fecun-dity, health, and well-being (505).

The notion that mana was the result of a balance between land, humans, gods, and ancestors was omitted from some Western scholarly debate in the decades following Firth's essay (see Elbert 1957, 268; Oliver 1989[1961], 72).[3]

Following Firth, Keesing argued that mana was "a quality of efficacy manifest in visible results" (Keesing 1984, 149). Western scholars misconstrued its meaning, Keesing argued, by translating it into the Western concept of power as quantifiable. Mana, in Keesing's view, was not a quantifiable substance but a quality or "a *relationship*, always contextual and two-sided" (1984, 150, emphasis added). Valerio Valeri's analysis of mana in "ancient Hawai'i"[4] further stressed relational reciprocity between humans and the divine as central to the meaning of the term. He posited that mana derived from mutual feelings of love and sympathy between humans and the divine constitutive of a relationship of reciprocity (Valeri 1985, 99). Recognizing the centrality of the concept of 'ai[5] to Hawaiian cosmology, Valeri hypothesized that "god is clearly treated as a commensal who eats with his worshippers and is fed by them as they are fed by him" (104). Mana was coproduced by humans and the divine: "for both man and god having mana *depends* on their relationship. It is their *relationship*, therefore, that truly causes their ownership of mana" (Valeri 1985, 104, emphasis added).

Following Valeri, Bradd Shore (1989) posited that the Polynesian concept of mana was based upon "the possibilities of exchange" between the world of humans and the world of the divine. Mana, Shore argued, was central to a Polynesian worldview (1989, 142), and throughout the Pacific the meaning of mana was "linked to generative potency, [and] to the sources [of] organic creation" (140). Shore imagined that pre-contact Polynesia was based upon an "economy of *mana*" in which humans sought to appropriate and harness the creative power of the gods "in the service of human needs: biological reproduction, fecundity of the land and sea, and the reproduction of the social forms that gave shape to human relations" (143). Mana, then, was a relationship, a "generative potency," linked "to the two primary sources of human life: food and sex" (165).

However, the mana literature also reflected what Mignolo and Tlostanova (2006, 206) have characterized as an "epistemology of imperial expansion," in which a privileged analyst makes "the rest of the world an object of observation." Through this imperializing lens, mana was cast as an artifact of the past, and scholarly attention focused on the concept's linguistic status and former relevance in pre-contact Polynesian society. As the object of Western scrutiny, the epistemology of mana was demoted to the status of primitive relic. Much less scholarly work concerned the meaning and currency of mana in late-twentieth-century Polynesian societies,[6] and until recently the perspective of indigenous scholars on the significance of mana did not circulate in the Western political economy of academic knowledge. Late in the twentieth century, however, Hawaiian scholars writing from an epistemology of decolonization reinterpreted the meaning of mana and demonstrated its relevance in a neocolonial context.

Following Greg Dening's (1980) work in *Islands and Beaches*, the historian Lilikalā Kameʻeleihiwa put the concepts and metaphors central to the worldview of Hawaiians in the time before the arrival of Westerners at the core of her historical analysis (1992, 6). In *Native Land and Foreign Desires*, she explored the privatization and commodification of Hawaiian land that occurred in the mid-nineteenth century (see chapter 1) as a pivotal, catastrophic moment for Native Hawaiian culture and health, and as an economic and cultural victory for the West (Kameʻeleihiwa 1992, 8, 11). In particular, she analyzed the clusters of meaning around the Hawaiian conception of ʻāina (land), and she demonstrated that decentering European metaphors created the possibility for different interpretations of contemporary Hawaiian life.

According to Kameʻeleihiwa, the concept of mālama ʻāina signified the social imperative for humans to serve one another and to care for the land (1992, 32) in the time before the arrival of Westerners.[7]

> In practical terms, the [common people] fed and clothed the [ruling chiefs], who provided the organization required to produce enough food to sustain an ever-increasing population. Should a [commoner] fail to cultivate or [care for] his portion of [land], that was grounds for dismissal. By the same token, should a [ruling chief] fail in proper direction of the [common people], he too would be dismissed—for his own failure to *mālama.* . . . Hence, to *Mālama ʻĀina* was by extension to care for [the common people] and the [ruling chiefs], for in the Hawaiian metaphor, these three components [land, ruling chiefs, and common people] are mystically one and the same. (Kameʻeleihiwa 1992, 31)

As a central sociocultural metaphor, mālama ʻāina describes the intimate relationship between humans and the environment and marks a critical distinction between the worldview of Hawaiians and those who came to colonize the islands (Patterson 2000, 230). While Kameʻeleihiwa was most concerned with the concept of pono, which she defined as the (social) harmony that derives from the reciprocal relationship between elder siblings and younger siblings to love, protect, and feed (Kameʻeleihiwa 1992, 25), her exegesis of mālama ʻāina is nevertheless relevant to the meaning of mana I explore here as a relationship productive of a healthy society. In a Western frame, these clusters of meanings might be grasped as an ethos, and as a set of principles or protocols to guide social relations (Patterson 2000, 230).

Kameʻeleihiwa's history closes with the observation that pre-haole[8] Hawaiian metaphors and meanings attached to mālama ʻāina "still survive" (1992, 317). Haunani Trask, whose work explores contemporary Hawaiʻi, further asserted the relevance of pre-haole metaphors to the struggle for Hawaiian sovereignty (Trask 1993, 117). In the preface to her book of poetry, *Light in the Crevice Never Seen*, Trask wrote:

> My people have lived in the Hawaiian Islands since the time of Papa—
> Earth Mother—and Wākea—Sky Father. Like many other native
> people, we believed that the cosmos was a unity of familial relations.
> Our culture depended on a careful relationship with the land, our
> ancestor, who nurtured us in body and spirit. (Trask 1994, xiv)

But Trask does not leave us to imagine that mana is a remnant of the ancient
past. She expressed the centrality of mana to the practices and aspirations of a
people engaged in decolonizing.

> Part of the beauty of Hawaiian decolonization is the re-assertion of
> *mana* in the sovereignty movement as a defining element of cultural
> and political leadership. Both the people and their leaders understand
> the link between *mana* and *pono*, the traditional Hawaiian value of bal-
> ance between people, land, and the cosmos.
>
> In this decolonizing context, *mana* as an attribute of leadership is
> at once a tremendous challenge to the colonial system which defines
> political leadership in terms of democratic liberalism . . . as well as a
> tremendous challenge to aspiring Hawaiian leaders who want to
> achieve sovereignty. (Trask 1993, 117)

Trask's interpretation of the political and cultural significance of mana as a challenge to neocolonialism illuminates the profound, enduring connection between
contemporary Native Hawaiians and ka po'e kahiko (the people of old, the
ancestors of Native Hawaiians). Reclaiming mana as ontology is crucial for
decolonization and is an exigency for the survival of indigenous Hawaiians. This
book is called *Potent Mana* because the meaning of mana—historically and in
the present—holds relevant lessons for others who struggle with the shame and
injustices of colonialism. The title is meant to suggest that meanings and
metaphors that were effaced in the process of colonization can be recovered, and,
that once reclaimed, can illuminate the path toward decolonization.

HEALTH, CULTURE, AND POWER

The healing methods and epistemologies of the body derived from the knowledge of elders posited a relationship between health, culture, and political
power. By developing healing methods that exceeded scientific ways of knowing, evolving solutions to the health crisis affecting indigenous Hawaiians challenged Western ideas about the origins of disease in individual, temporal,
organic bodies.

The healing practices and epistemologies of late-twentieth-century Native Hawaiians invigorated and applied methods and ways of understanding illness from the ancestral past. Healers, health activists, and those who had been healed challenged biomedical and scientific wisdom on the meaning of health, as well as social scientific and epidemiological understandings of disease. By expanding the meaning of health to include the impact of politics, economics, and culture on the bodies of the colonized, health and political power were decisively linked.

At a 1994 conference on Native Hawaiian health, I was introduced to the Kanaka Maoli analysis of health and disease that combined ancestral knowledge with social epidemiological insights challenging biomedical and scientific understanding and insisting that health, culture, and power were inseparable. Speakers at the conference argued that health must be a central concern of the sovereignty movement, and that improving the health of Native Hawaiians meant dealing with the questions of poverty, homelessness, and inadequate schools. In a speech at the conference, Kuʻumealoha Gomes, a public health scholar, said that health depended upon "no more homeless Kānaka Maoli." She referred to the work of Brazilian philosopher Paolo Freire (1989) to illuminate the connection between health and political empowerment, and she challenged "classical western liberalism" and the "western medical tradition," arguing that they failed to recognize the crucial role of poverty in the production of disease. Gomes and other speakers repeatedly underscored the exigency of access to the land for the health of Native Hawaiians. Pointing to the neocolonial uses of land in Hawaiʻi, Gomes's remarks drew enthusiastic applause when she compared access to golf courses with the difficulty of procuring poi, a Hawaiian staple dish made from mashed, fermented taro root. "Now it's hard to get poi and easy to play golf," she said, "but we can't eat golf balls" (field notes).

Debates about the meaning of history, culture, power, and health were not confined to scholars. In a year and a half of ethnographic fieldwork in Waiʻanae, Hawaiʻi, I participated in community-wide conversations that occurred in public places. In a shopping mall, a beauty salon, a health clinic, and a beach encampment, and in programs, group therapy sessions, and conversations at a mental health and substance abuse treatment center, Waiʻanae Hawaiians were engaged in lively debates about these issues. They deliberated about the importance of historical reinterpretation from indigenous points of view and considered the relevance of indigenous Hawaiian culture to contemporary struggles for health. They agreed that an imposed disconnection between Kanaka Maoli and ʻāina was a certain route to disease, and they debated the priority of the demand for sovereignty and independence from the United States. Most importantly they engaged in collective processes of imagining alternative futures based on lessons from Hawaiian culture and history that countered neocolonial realities of military and tourist control of the land.

I learned profound lessons about the relationship between colonialism and well-being from Hawaiians who were marginalized by the political-economic realities of neocolonialism. One of my first lessons occurred at an encampment of homeless Hawaiians on the beach at Mākua. After spending the morning talking-story[9] with two encampment leaders, David Rosa and Leandra Wai, Wai suggested that we go—fully clothed—into the ocean. As we floated in the calm, clear waters, Rosa and Wai told stories about swimming with a school of dolphins and about the tremendous healing energy of the sea. Rosa pointed to a shallow pool of water formed by the rocks and told me that when women had premenstrual syndrome they would go and sit in the pool in order to feel better. He said that people with disabilities came to live at Mākua and were healed, physically and emotionally. When reporters come to Mākua, Rosa said, they end up telling the beach people their troubles. "We tell them to go into the sea to hoʻohakahaka [to make an open space], and wash out the shit and stress of western living." David described the settlement on Mākua Beach as outside of Western time and Western space (field notes).

In "Mākua: To Heal the Nation," a video documentary about the encampment, Wai described the settlement at Mākua as a "sanctuary, a place where many come to heal. . . . A common reason for coming down here [is that] life had shattered one way or another." At Mākua, she said, "We are healing our past of torment and destruction." Another encampment resident called Mākua "a healing place." He said that

> people that come here, they have all these problems but they don't know why it starts working out [when they get here]. . . . A lot of them used to be drug addicts. . . . Now they can get high off this place, the ocean, the mountains . . .
>
> No matter how violent or angry they might be out living in the concrete jungle when they come out here there is a more relaxed feeling . . . the true person starts coming out.
>
> Where do we go if we make a mistake . . . ? Unless something is set up like this for us to come to, a city of refuge type thing. . . . What [is happening at the beach] now is [the] practicing of sovereignty. [We] are not waiting for it, [we] are doing it now. (Nā Maka o ka ʻĀina 1996)

In the early 1990s, a movement that defined American rule in Hawaiʻi as illegitimate and that demanded sovereignty was gaining ground. The goal of the Native Hawaiian sovereignty movement in the 1990s was the return of Hawaiian land and the recuperation of a Hawaiian nation. The movement was comprised of various cultural and political organizations, parties, and practices. As part of a larger movement for cultural revitalization, the focus on sovereignty, which included the most militant and politicized people and organizations, involved smaller (but growing) portions of Hawaiians. The movement for cultural revitalization was more widespread and diffuse and was clearly centered on the Hawaiian body. Feeding the body poi (mashed taro root), lau kalo (stewed taro leaf), and ʻopihi (limpet) in an effort to improve Hawaiian health via a return to traditional foods; adorning the body with tattoos in the form of Polynesian symbols; wearing kīhei (cape) and malo (loincloth) at protests and other Hawaiian cultural events; moving the body in the hula kahiko (traditional hula) in waʻa (canoes) and in kuʻi a lua (traditional martial arts)—all of these were common expressions of Hawaiian cultural pride in the late twentieth century. The revitalization of Hawaiian culture was further evident in the resurgence of the Hawaiian language, the institution of schools in which Hawaiian was the sole language of instruction, and the keen popular interest in Hawaiian history, particularly in regard to the overthrow of the Hawaiian monarchy. An interest in health, healing, and the meaning of disease cut across these domains of the sovereignty and revitalization movements. The demand for health was connected to politics and power, to a return to culturally specific ways of eating, dressing, and performing, and to disputes over access to the land and water.

The health status of Kanaka Maoli was perceived as a barometer indicating the negative impact that colonization and American statehood had on indigenous bodies and souls. In the late twentieth century, Native Hawaiians were experiencing higher morbidity and mortality rates than other ethnic groups in the Islands and in the United States. Trask argued that the fact that Hawaiian women suffer from the highest rates of breast cancer in the United States was directly "traceable to Americanization of our country, including theft of lands where we once grew healthful Native foods," and to enforced participation in a supermarket system of food distribution. She argued that the "high infant mortality, low life expectancy, [and] high adolescent suicide rates" among Native Hawaiians directly resulted from "colonialism and the subsequent loss of control over our islands and our lives" (Trask 1996, 911). Significantly, the struggle for health was also a bellwether of political and cultural movement, since achieving health was viewed as an impossibility under contemporary neocolonial conditions.

LESSONS ON POWER AND HEALING

The story of the oppression and colonization of Hawaiians is not widely known in the United States. A vital cultural revitalization and decolonization movement received little attention from the U.S. mainstream media and remained inaccessible to Native Americans, African Americans, and others waging similar struggles in the United States. *Potent Mana* was written because lessons from Hawaiʻi are relevant and crucial to similar struggles of other oppressed communities in the United States, and around the world. The lessons I explore here began as academic questions that were rethought and reformulated as I learned from Hawaiians. Questions that emerged from the field were transformed into notes and interviews, into a dissertation, and eventually into the substance of this ethnography. Many of my "informants" were intellectual mentors with whom I learned to understand the many themes that cluster around decolonization, as theory and as practice. This ethnography extends those face-to-face lessons into a wider sphere.

I follow Whitaker (1996, 1) in arguing that ethnography "should be approached contingently, as a form of learning, rather than absolutely, as a form of representation," and that the goal of ethnography is to further communication "between the parties" involved (Whitaker 1996, 7). The parties that *Potent Mana* involves include Native Hawaiians, Native Americans, African Americans, and other oppressed groups. Anthropologists and other scholars who are allied with the struggles for justice are also interested parties, as are any readers who want to learn about colonialism, neocolonialism, and decolonization.

Potent Mana distills important lessons I learned in Waiʻanae, Hawaiʻi, in the late 1990s. There are other perspectives on the colonization of Hawaiʻi and on the struggle for decolonization. But for me, the practices, theories, interpretations, and dreams of Native Hawaiians comprise a story that needs to be told. Clearly, the 1990s decolonization movement was not a simple, unified expression of cultural or racial pride. It was a complex mass movement fraught with internal critiques, debates about strategy and meaning, and divisions both shallow and deep. But the focus here is on how a specific group of Hawaiians in a specific time and place approached the problem of decolonization. Critiquing these lessons is another project, for another scholar, or another time. Although there are certainly other ways of exploring social movements, I offer the wisdom and clarity of those who struggled for decolonization in Waiʻanae as a critique of colonialism, the imposition of Western culture, and the effect of these on health.

There are, perhaps, particular aspects of who I am that allow me to explore the decolonization movement in Hawaiʻi with tremendous empathy and respect. It is not only my doctoral training in sociocultural anthropology at Princeton University that prepared me to write *Potent Mana*—I have been learning lessons all of my life. I am African American, the great-granddaughter of slaves. I worked as a community organizer in Central Harlem, New York City, with poor women and children. I have a master's degree in religious studies from Union Theological Seminary, where I studied black liberation theology under the direction of James Cone and Delores Williams. I spent the equivalent of three years as a postdoctoral fellow pursuing training in public health. My theological background and my work as a community organizer prepared me to grasp the spirituality of Hawaiians and to understand how spirituality and political struggle are inextricably linked. My ancestry, my experience as an organizer, and my scholarly training have shaped the deep hermeneutic of suspicion with which I approach official histories and orthodox knowledge production and have led me to understand the conditional nature of any epistemology. These biographical facts are not incidental to the ultimately anthropological analysis presented here.

From my perspective, the health crisis of indigenous Hawaiians is mirrored by crises affecting the bodies and souls of Native Americans, African Americans, and others in the United States. The many lessons that can be learned from an analysis of how Native Hawaiians in the late twentieth century struggled to achieve well-being are urgently relevant. One of my goals for this book is to insert the lessons I learned about health, culture, and power into U.S. debates on health disparities. As articulated by mainstream media and many scholarly journals, the issue of health disparities is reduced to problems of access and education, and to solutions that do not challenge the fundamental relationship between social, political, and economic injustice and the unequal distribution of disease. Native Hawaiians add the significant dimension of culture to critiques of biomedical and Western scientific constructions of disease that privilege politics and economics. The insight that the suppression of indigenous knowledge and other forms of colonialism create and sustain disease is mostly neglected by otherwise committed scholars using race, class, or gender as key analytics in the analysis of health inequality. Lessons on healing and power from Hawai'i illuminate the contradictions inherent in scientific and biomedical epistemologies, and the dangers of commodifying land, water, and health. My hope is that *Potent Mana* will contribute to a scholarly literature and encourage more community organizing that recognizes the important relationship between indigenous knowledge, power, and health.

THE HAWAI'I LITERATURE

Anthropologists once conceived of Hawaiians as a people without culture (Kroeber 1921, 129–37), and historians imagined that there was little resistance to American colonial intrusions (Ralston 1984, 21–40; Silva 2004). The anthropology of Hawai'i and other Pacific Island places has been centrally concerned with questions of authenticity and tradition (Linnekin 1983a; Keesing 1989), and the history of Hawai'i has been conceived of as a narrative arc moving inexorably toward incorporation by the West. But as the scholar NoeNoe Silva (2004, 2, 16) has argued, Hawaiian resistance to foreign intrusion, which began with the first landing of Europeans, was evident throughout the nineteenth century, and it continues today. Through a careful exegesis of the Hawaiian language press from the mid-nineteenth to the mid-twentieth century, Silva brought to light the history of Native Hawaiian written resistance to American conquest. From the moment of the first encounter with British and American foreigners, the struggle for Hawaiian political and cultural integrity has not ceased. The form of struggle changed with historical circumstances, since the violent structural and cultural realities of being colonized meant that resistance was often expressed indirectly. Clearly, however, the resurgence in political and cultural activism that was evident in Hawai'i in the late twentieth century was in a historical tradition of resistance.

When I first studied the anthropological literature on Hawai'i, I found little that answered my questions about neocolonial Hawaiian life. It seemed as though, for anthropologists and historians, Hawai'i and Hawaiians were frozen in some "ancient" past or had been incorporated into the logic of Western modernity. Research on the historical anthropology of Hawai'i was rich and detailed. Western scholars (see Barrére 1975; Davenport 1969; Linnekin 1983b, 1985, 1987, 1990; Sahlins 1981, 1985, 1994; Valeri 1985) wrote about ancient kingship and ritual, the impact of religious transformations on nineteenth-century Hawaiian culture, the cultural and economic effects of the relationship between Western traders and Hawaiian royalty, and the role of women in mid-nineteenth-century Hawaiian land transformations. The twentieth century was sparsely covered, and work such as Linnekin's (1985) *The Children of the Land* explored a Hawaiian community in terms of its relationship to tradition and not in terms of the relationship of tradition to twentieth-century struggles for political and cultural integrity. Alan Howard's 1974 ethnography of a Hawaiian community, *Ain't No Big Thing*, while providing a cogent analysis of Hawaiian life after statehood, was concerned primarily with the question of "Americanization," and not with Hawaiian resistance to colonial and neocolonial impositions.

The historical literature on Hawai'i (Daws 1968; Day 1960, Fuchs 1961; Kent 1993[1983]; Kuykendall 1965, 1967; Okihiro 1991; Takaki 1983) also failed to provide answers. This literature was preoccupied with the experience of Asian immigrants and plantation history in Hawai'i to the extent that the existence of Hawaiian communities in the twentieth century was simply effaced. It seemed to me that the scholarly literature on Hawai'i worked to reinforce the notion that there were no more "real" Hawaiians—that they had simply withered away.

However, recent work by Native Hawaiian scholars challenged the (neo)colonial and nonindigenous perspective of the literature and changed the terrain of Hawaiian studies. Scholars such as Haunani-Kay Trask (1987, 1991, 1993) and Lilikalā Kame'eleihiwa (1992) produced critical work that was politically committed to the goal of sovereignty and deeply grounded in the culture of Hawai'i. Their work first informed me about the contemporary movement for Native Hawaiian sovereignty, about the condition of late-twentieth-century Hawaiians, and about the history of colonialism. In the path blazed by Trask and Kame'eleihiwa, a cohort of younger Native scholars—including Kauanui (1999, 2002), Meyer (1998a, 1998b, 2001), Osorio (2002), Silva (2004), and Tengan

(2005, 2008)—is producing highly significant work that redefines the history and anthropology of Hawai'i (Tengan 2005, 249).

METHODOLOGY

The burgeoning challenge in Hawai'i to American neocolonialism drew me to the Islands for field research. From the vantage point of a graduate student at an East Coast university, I imagined that I would study the relationship between nationalism and healing, political power and health. My original field proposal argued that clinics where suffering Hawaiian bodies were treated were likely places for the instantiation of nationalist ideology. Following the academic fashion of the time, I was influenced by such scholars as Anderson (1991), Chatterjee (1986, 1993), and Fox (1990), and I planned to observe the recruitment of marginalized Hawaiians into a larger nation-making process under the direction of an indigenous intelligentsia elite. During my preliminary research trip to Hawai'i in the summer of 1994, I met with Hawaiians living in Honolulu who were committed to the revitalization of Hawaiian culture and the restoration of Hawaiian sovereignty. And then I spent a few days on the Wai'anae Coast, where Kanaka Maoli community leaders and their allies articulated theories that connected health to colonial and neocolonial oppression and were actively engaged in creating practices toward the goal of decolonization.

I arranged for my primary field site to be a Native Hawaiian substance abuse treatment center on the leeward side of the island of O'ahu, in the community of Wai'anae. Once in the field, there were many scholarly assumptions that I abandoned. Learning from Wai'anae Hawaiians meant cutting through scholarly categories that had defined the project as an academic exercise. As I learned from Wai'anae Hawaiians about their present, their past, and their dreams for the future, I realized that the concept of nationalism did not adequately describe the cultural revitalization movement, the demand for sovereignty, or the daily practices meant to heal the wounds of colonialism. As I learned about the centrality of the notion of *decolonization,* I began to understand its multiple dimensions. Decolonization was an epistemological standpoint, a way to critique the West. Decolonization was a set of practices meant to heal the physical and psychic wounds of colonialism. And, most importantly, decolonization was an aspiration, a goal that defined demands for cultural integrity and community well-being.

Wai'anae is a working-class community on the western edge of the island of O'ahu. With a population of 38,000 in 1994 (DBEDT 1995, xx), a significant proportion of whom were Hawaiian or part-Hawaiian, Wai'anae was a center of Native Hawaiian cultural and political struggle. In the lexicon of Wai'anae movement leaders, decolonization was a process that occurred primarily in the bodies and souls and the cells and psyches of Hawaiians, rather than externally in the public space of politics. Decolonization was seen as a process that required remembering and recreating the ways of Hawaiians in the times of ka poʻe kahiko before they had been inundated with English, Christianity, and the morality of land and water as private property. In Waiʻanae, decolonizing meant rejecting the shame and self-loathing endemic to colonized people; it meant transforming that shame through powerful processes of dreaming, of remembering, of pulling from the past that which was libratory, redemptive, and exemplary of viable Hawaiian ways of being and knowing. In the mid-1990s Waiʻanae Hawaiians were relearning Hawaiian—as a language, a worldview, and a way of healing.

In fifteen months of fieldwork, I spent my days volunteering for a Native Hawaiian-run drug treatment program called Hoʻo Mōhala. Because of many Native Hawaiians' suspicions about outsiders, and especially of the role of researchers in the community, I began working primarily with Hoʻo Mōhala's administrative program, writing grant proposals and reports and compiling data. Initially I was not permitted to involve myself in the day-to-day workings of the clinical program, but working in the administrative program allowed me to meet people in the larger Waiʻanae community and to become acquainted with other programs and activities that were similarly committed to decolonization and Hawaiian cultural revitalization. The period of time I spent working primarily with the administrative program also allowed me to build relationships with counseling staff and clients. Eventually Hoʻo Mōhala's board of directors granted permission for me to have access to some aspects of the clinical program, and I began working as a volunteer with counselors, clients, and their families. I was permitted to accompany the intake assessment counselor on recruitment trips to Oʻahu prisons, to interview clients and their families, and to participate in group sessions and in outdoor activities. Some clinical activities remained off limits, including participation in a Native Hawaiian men's group and observation of hoʻoponopono (therapy sessions) led by counselors for clients and their families.

I conducted informal, open-ended interviews with administrators, counselors, clients, and family members at Hoʻo Mōhala, with administrators and counselors at other programs, and with other community members and leaders in Waiʻanae involved in other decolonization efforts. The open-ended format of my interviews helped me gain insight into the various interpretations of what was occurring at Hoʻo Mōhala, in Waiʻanae, and in the sovereignty movement, and allowed me to elicit people's memories and dreams. I learned important lessons about how closely tied dreaming and remembering are to any process of decolonization, since reliance on official, Western sources of knowledge defeats the purpose of displacing neocolonial reality.

PLAN OF THE BOOK

Chapter 1, "Ka Poʻe Kahiko: The People of Old," tells the story of American colonization in the nineteenth and twentieth centuries with a focus on the ways in which American (mis)interpretations of Hawaiian bodies and Hawaiian ways of being and knowing contributed to an enduring sense of shame among the colonized. Native Hawaiian historian Jonathan Kay Kamakawiwoʻole Osorio (2002) argued that late-twentieth-century Hawaiians were "still a beleaguered race," and that the problem was not just "poverty and homelessness" but also "a lingering sense that our 'failure' is the result of our own inadequacy as a people." Osorio posited that the sense of failure was the result not only of political oppression but also stemmed from

> an insidious discourse that portrays . . . Western conceptions of government, economics, education and ideals as the only proper and "realistic" models for contemporary societies. This discourse, this language, was woven into the cloak of the colonizers in Hawaiʻi. To reject that colonization necessarily entails rejecting the discourse as well. (Osorio 2002, 259).

Chapter 1 explores the history of colonial intrusion and the "insidious discourses" that justified the theft of land and resources in Hawaiʻi since the eighteenth century. British and American colonizers deployed a variety of practical and discursive methods that worked to invalidate Hawaiian life and knowledge. The imposition of the English language, as well such ideologies and practices as land alienation, cash economies, and forms of Christianity, along with the introduction of deadly diseases and the massive death of Hawaiians, occurred against a Euro/American interpretive framework that conceived of Hawaiians as sinful, diseased, pathological, and disgraced. From the Calvinist theology of New England missionaries to ideologies that equated ownership of private property with moral righteousness, the experience of being colonized rendered Hawaiians undeveloped, benighted, and destined to wither away on both discursive and structural levels. Western theories of liberty and democracy that did not extend humanity to Natives and other non-Europeans and scientific ideas that elided the relationship between social structure, political power, and health blamed Hawaiians for their state.

In Hawaiʻi, the efficacy of Western methods of healing physical, psychological,and social distress was contradicted by the massive deaths that occurred after the first contact with Europeans and Americans. Epidemic diseases that Hawaiian bodies were unprepared for decimated indigenous communities. The disease of Hawaiians has continued up to the present neocolonial moment, despite triumphalist rhetoric about the superiority of Western healing methods. At the turn of the twentieth century, Native Hawaiians demonstrated poorer health and greater susceptibility to chronic and infectious diseases, and still Western science and medicine failed to ensure their physical and social health.

Chapter 2, "Wai'anae: A Space of Resistance," explores the community that was the site of my field research in the mid-1990s. Wai'anae had the largest concentration of Native Hawaiians in the Islands at the end of the twentieth century. As a place remote from Hawai'i's metropolitan centers in the nineteenth century, Wai'anae became known as an outpost of Hawaiian culture and tradition, and of resistance to colonizing and missionizing. In the late twentieth century, although Wai'anae could no longer be considered remote, the tradition of resistance continued. Chapter 2 considers the narrative history of Wai'anae as a place of resistance to the incursions of the West, and the ways in which this history of resistance took on new meaning in the second half of the twentieth century. Wai'anae became a crossroads, a place of intersection, between traditions and modernity, and precisely because of this intersection, it became a fertile ground for resistance and the development of decolonizing processes.

Chapter 3, "Mana: What the Data Hide," explores the existential condition of Native Hawaiians in the late twentieth century and the meaning of the health and social statistical data that purport to describe it. Hawaiians were represented in statistical data as poor, diseased, pathological, and criminal. Following Zuberi (2001), I argue that the collection of vital and social statistics forms the basis of Western explanatory models that see the origin of disease and dysfunction in the raced bodies of the oppressed. In the late twentieth century, data showed that Hawaiians controlled little wealth, owned few businesses, were employed predominantly in unskilled service jobs, had the highest rate of unemployment, and had the lowest incomes in the state. Native Hawaiians had shorter life spans and higher rates of chronic and infectious diseases, in addition to higher rates of suicide, infant death, and teenage pregnancies, than other ethnic groups in the Islands. They occupied a third of all prison cells in the state. Fewer than half of Hawaiian teens graduated from high school, and they had high rates of robbery, vandalism, drug abuse, gambling, and running away. Hawaiians comprised only 5 percent of the student body at the University of Hawai'i-Mānoa, and only 2 percent of those who succeeded to graduation.

According to the logic of the West, the meaning of this disease, deviance, and criminality was completely self-evident and indicated a problem essentially rooted within Hawaiians themselves. But for Native Hawaiians in the late twentieth century, reinterpreting the Hawaiian history of colonialism also meant challenging neocolonial explanatory models that rendered them diseased, dysfunctional, and criminal in the first place. Rather than accept Western notions of pathology and deviance, the Hawaiians I worked with interpreted a sick body/mind/soul as a symptom of colonization, implicating both Western culture and Western rule. An exigency of such reinterpretation involved re/membering and re/creating specifically Hawaiian practices that allowed for the possibilities of decolonization.

Chapter 4, "The Stench of Mauna Ala, Colonialism, and Mental Health," begins with the story of a mid-twentieth-century Hawaiian woman who "became crazed with the pain of being unable to be Hawaiian in her Hawaiian land." Her story anchors a discussion of how the mental health care system in much of the twentieth century served colonial interests. The establishment of a modern, rationalized mental health system occurred in the years following annexation by the United States. The Territorial Hospital for the Insane was under the leadership of an Australian psychologist, who was inspired by Francis Galton's (1892) theories of hereditary genius and the imperfectability of non-Europeans. Colonial psychology located the source of mental illness and social deviance in the racialized bodies of both indigenous Hawaiians and imported Asian plantation labor and sought their rehabilitation. The mental health apparatus represented Native Hawaiians and other non-haole (non-white) people as self-consciously mentally inferior, unable to cope with a higher grade of civilization, and seeking refuge in self-destruction. This chapter also describes the successful civil rights suit brought against the Hawai'i Department of Health in 1976. The U.S. Department of Health, Education, and Welfare found the state of Hawai'i in violation of the Civil Rights Act of 1964 for failing to provide adequate services to non-whites. Chapter 4 ends with a discussion of the first attempts to establish Native Hawaiian-run clinics and specifically Native Hawaiian healing methodologies.

Chapter 5, "Ka Leo: Remembering Hawaiian," is a discussion of the processes of relearning and recreating specifically Hawaiian ways of knowing and being that occurred in Wai'anae in the late twentieth century. It explores the ways in which Wai'anae Hawaiians learned and relearned the Hawaiian language and found the courage to transcend the shame of being colonized. A ubiquitous discourse in Wai'anae concerned the need to heal and recover from colonialism. Physical and mental disease, shame, and family dysfunction were viewed not as symptoms of organic illness and social inadequacy but as signs of being colonized and the unhealthiness of Western living. Feelings of shame about being Hawaiian were thought to ramify in families and across generations and were supported by mainstream discourses that portrayed Hawaiian neighborhoods as crime-infested areas filled with single mothers on welfare. But in Wai'anae, Hawaiians attempted to deal with these existential and discursive issues by treating shame as a source of disease, and by translating and reinterpreting traditions that had been driven underground and almost forgotten into a basis for healing and recovery.

Chapter 6, "Dreaming Change," is a discussion of a specific effort to heal the bodies and souls of Native Hawaiians at a drug treatment center in Wai'anae.

This chapter centers on the life and work of Meipala Silva and traces her political and cultural awakening as a Native Hawaiian woman. Her work to create healing spaces for troubled Hawaiians, many of whom were remanded to drug treatment centers by the courts in lieu of incarceration, is explored as an example of decolonizing practices.

In the Conclusion, "'Ropes of Resistance'[10] and Alternative Futures," I place Native Hawaiian efforts to decolonize in the larger political economic framework of globalization and neoliberalism. By the turn of the twentieth century, haoles (whites) had become the single largest ethnic group in the Islands, largely as a result of their in-migration. Development pressures meant a severe decline in affordable housing and the concomitant rise in homelessness for Hawaiians and other people of low wealth in the Islands. Neoliberalism poses a new set of challenges to efforts of resistance and decolonization by Wai'anae Hawaiians. The Conclusion argues that Hawaiian decolonization is made even more crucial and relevant in a global era of neoliberalism. Following Trask (1994) and Ho'omanawanui (2004), I argue that the dreaming and planning practices of decolonization become the "ropes of resistance" for "unborn generations," who will continue to celebrate Hawaiian ways of being and knowing even against great odds.

A NOTE ON TERMS, THE USE OF
HAWAIIAN LANGUAGE, AND FORMATTING

For clarity I use the terms "Hawaiian," "Native Hawaiian," "indigenous Hawaiian" and "Kanaka Maoli" interchangeably. In Hawai'i, where the population is considerably racially mixed, any easy distinctions are problematic. The vexed question of who is Hawaiian and who is not, and how Hawaiian-ness is measured, is a debate that raged within the Islands. "Blood quantum," or percentage of Hawaiian "blood," is used to limit certain entitlements such as entrance to a school funded by endowments left by Hawaiian elites or access to Hawaiian homelands. But blood quantum was not an issue for most of the Hawaiians with whom I worked. The majority were ethnically mixed (i.e., Hawaiian-Chinese-Portuguese, Hawaiian-Haole, etc.), although culturally they strongly identified as Native Hawaiian.

A glossary that appears at the end of this book defines key Hawaiian terms, with their English translations. I use italics to distinguish the voices of my collaborators and informants (in English) derived from taped and transcribed interviews and from field notes.

I use the phrase "in the time of ka po'e kahiko," following the nineteenth-century historian Samuel Kamakau, to refer to what is mistakenly referred to as "ancient Hawai'i." I object to the connotation implicit in the term "ancient

Hawai'i" because it obscures the reality of the intense connection that late-twentieth-century Hawaiians felt with the past, and it obscures the short duration of two centuries marking the time since the coming of Europeans and Americans. The notion that before 1778 Hawaiians were living in ancient times reflects what Briggs (1996, 449) called discourses of modernization that posit a decisive gulf between "tradition" and modernity and serve to support the hegemony of Western historical narratives. "In the times of ka po'e kahiko" is a poetic phrase that recognizes the endurance of ancestral ties and distinguishes the present neocolonial era from what Stannard (1989, 70) refers to as "pre-haole-Hawai'i."

Potent Mana is an ethnography of decolonization in Hawai'i. It is not as much a story of what was as it is a story of what may be possible. Now, in the twenty-first century, Native Hawaiians still struggle with the lasting effects of colonialism and the continuing injustice of neocolonialism. This ethnography focuses on Native Hawaiian *aspirations* for decolonization in a specific time and place (Wai'anae in the mid-to-late 1990s), and since struggles against oppression are rarely linear, we do not yet know what the ultimate results of these aspirations will be. What we can be sure of is that during the 1990s there was a great deal of thinking and acting by Wai'anae Hawaiians about what it might mean to be decolonized. This book explores those dreams and activities.

My hope is that *Potent Mana* will do two things—first, that it will demonstrate that through memory, practices of healing, and struggles for land, water, and cultural integrity the voices of ka po'e kahiko reverberate through time; and, second, that the voices of the Native Hawaiians whose daily practices and scholarly work inspired and taught me will reverberate across space and influence the struggles of others.

1

KA POʻE KAHIKO

The People of Old

In order to understand efforts toward decolonization in the late twentieth century, it is necessary to understand what colonialism meant from the perspective and experience of the colonized. This chapter tells the story of ka poʻe kahiko—the ancestors of Native Hawaiians, or the people of old—who experienced the trauma of Western "discovery." Anthropologist and historian Greg Dening wrote that "giving the dead a voice, letting their signatures on life be witnessed," motivated his history writing. But it is not only the dead to whom history gives voice. Dening knew that

> [t]he living need history, too. Not to be made to feel guilty for a past they are not responsible for or cannot change. The living need a history disturbing enough to change the present . . . disturbing in the sense of awakening a consciousness that brings resolve to change. It is the present made by our past that we are responsible for. It is our own banality that needs to be disturbed, our presumption that we are disempowered by the very structures and systems which we make ourselves and sustain with our moral lethargy. If my history, my story and reflection, shows that things can be otherwise, then I think it fulfills a need. (Dening 1996, 87)

Dening makes clear that what is at stake in different historical accounts is the production of present possibilities and alternative futures. This is a crucial insight, since throughout the twentieth century, histories of Hawaiʻi were written as if American colonization were inevitable, and as if the descendants of ka poʻe kahiko had not survived.

The history that I present here draws heavily on recent scholarly work by Native Hawaiians. It is written from a perspective that expresses a genealogical connection with Native Hawaiians in the present and with their ancestors, ka poʻe kahiko. It is written to answer vital questions about the present struggles of Native Hawaiians that can only be understood from a perspective centered on the integrity and humanity of those who were colonized. Unlike histories centered on the experience of Europeans and Americans, which tend to justify the oppressive relations of colonialism and neocolonialism, this history suggests alternative trajectories and opens the possibilities for other futures.

Walter Rodney (2005) wrote that to be colonized is to be removed from history.

> The removal from history follows logically from the loss of power that colonialism represented. The power to act independently is the guarantee to participate actively and *consciously* in history, a striking illustration of the fact that colonial Africa was a passive object, as seen in its attraction for White anthropologists, who came to study "primitive society." Colonialism determined that Africans were no more makers of history than were beetles—objects to be looked at under a microscope and examined for unusual features (116).

Hawaiians, too, were made the passive objects of anthropological and historical study. The writing of new histories centered on the experience of and resistance to colonialism is essential to the creation of decolonized futures. The historical summary that I present here provides the reader with a sense of the violence of colonization and the trauma of being rendered a passive historical/anthropological object. This summary provides a context for understanding Native Hawaiian cultural and political efforts to transcend neocolonialism in the late twentieth century.

KA PAE ʻĀINA

Ka pae ʻāina (the islands of Hawaiʻi) rise from the depths of the dark blue waters of the mid-Pacific, 4,000 miles west of Japan, and 2,500 miles from of the western edge of North America. These islands are the most isolated on earth. In the poetic language of the Kumulipo, the Hawaiian origin story, ka pae ʻāina emerges from the heat of the earth, the unfolding of heavens, and the eclipse of the sun by a round, bright moon. In the Kumulipo, ka poʻe kahiko (who would become known as Hawaiians after contact with Westerners) were born from a "deep darkness, darkening" (Kameʻeleihiwa 1992, 1–2).

Ka poʻe kahiko, the ancestors of Native Hawaiians, were self-governing, self-sufficient, and complete. Before the British, before the sandalwood and whaling trades, and before the onslaught of Western settlers and the spread of Western disease, the islands overflowed with geo-theological significance. In the world-view of ka poʻe kahiko, the ʻāina was comprised of conscious elements that communicated and interacted in relationships of mutuality, reciprocity, and familiarity across a spectrum of divinity, humanity, and nature.

> In traditional Hawaiian thinking nature and land are considered sacred and animate. The world is a conscious entity and people can communicate with all species in nature and interact in a mutual relationship of rights and responsibilities. The Kumulipo (creation chant) implies that the universe is alive and conscious and that its evolutionary development comes from within. This evolution explains how man is related and is kin to nature. . . . *Akua* (gods) are conscious spirits . . . [who] take animal, plant and other natural forms, even in more than one place at a time." (Minerbi 1994, 103)

A pantheon of deities was in direct communication with the highest aliʻi (chiefly class) through the mediation of various orders of kāhuna. Kāhuna were holders of expert knowledge and specialists in ritual matters. Knowledge of health and healing practices was controlled by kāhuna lapaʻau (Valeri 1985, 136, 137), who could "see all the hidden things of the gods" (Kamakau 1991, 27).[1] Chiefs (both male and female) mediated the relationship between the makaʻāinana (populace, common people), the gods, and the land. Despite elaborate hierarchy in the times of ka poʻe kahiko, society was organized to ensure that the common people thrived. According to Kamakau, "the well-being (pono) of the kingdom was in their hands" (Kamakau 1991, 8) A host of ʻaumākua, ancestral guardian spirits, shared the islands, communicating directly with the common people, who lived their lives according to the principles of lōkahi, a practice of spiritual, cultural, and natural balance with the elemental forces of nature. This balanced life in the times of ka poʻe kahiko meant that disease was a rare occurrence. Kamakau (1991, 98) noted that the specialized knowledge of kāhuna lapaʻau was rarely needed, since "destructive and contagious diseases and epidemics" were infrequent and the "native diseases . . . were few."

The common people lived on ahupuaʻa, divisions of the earth into vertical sections running from the mountains to the sea. Ahupuaʻa[2] were self-sustaining land divisions that extended from the upland section of the mountains to the sea. Ahupuaʻa consisted of diverse natural resources, including an upland forest that produced the timber for house production and the raw material for canoes, weapons, and tools, agricultural zones for farming and coastal zones for fishing, and streams. Sweet potatoes grew in the uplands, as well as breadfruit, bananas, and coconut in the lowland and midland areas (Mueller-Dombois and Wirawan 2005, 293–94; Kirch and Sahlins 1992, 19). Freshwater streams were modified by human-made ditches for the irrigation of taro on alluvial terraces. Such sophisticated land use practices enhanced the natural ecosystems through conservation (Mueller-Dombois and Wirawan 2005, 309–10). Ahupua'a, in the times of ka po'e kahiko, contained both natural places and human structures that were endowed with mana, or spiritual power. These mana-infused spaces expressed the faith in and relationship of ka po'e kahiko with the gods and the 'aumākua. These wahi kapu, or sacred spaces, included temples and shrines, pond fields, and terraced slopes for growing taro, and pu'uhonua, or places of refuge and sanctuaries for forgiveness and rebirth (McGregor 1996, 20–23; Minerbi 1994, 99–106).

Ka po'e kahiko imagined a cosmos that resulted from the mating of Papa (Earth-Mother) and Wākea (Sky-Father). They created a teeming universe in which the land, the rocks, the wind and the water, the trees, the birds, and the fish were conscious, communicating, familial beings, related to both humans and the divine (Kame'eleihiwa 1992, 19–27; Blaisdell 1996, 170). The world of ka po'e kahiko was a "spiritual ecology" in which borders between the "manifest and unmanifest worlds" were fluid and permeable (Herman 1999, 82–83). Hawaiian origin stories stress this close kin relationship between the gods, the land, and human beings. Indeed, the intimate relationship between ka po'e kahiko and the environment marked a critical distinction between ka po'e kahiko and those who came to colonize the islands.

They developed a hierarchical political system based on the power of chiefship and a system of surplus agriculture (Sahlins 1972, 146–47; 1968, 26–27) characterized by terracing and irrigation. Although the land was "held" by the supreme chief, the chief did not own it but served as a trustee to the deities Kāne and Lono. Although there was an elaborate hierarchy, the common people had gathering rights and access to means of sustenance. Land use was not defined on the basis of discrete individuals and discrete space; rather, it was fluid and diffuse, defined by need, such as "grass areas for thatch, forest areas for timber and medicinal herbs, beach access and other resource areas" (Herman 1999, 81).

Like other Polynesian people, ka po'e kahiko were once navigators who traversed the Pacific between ka pae 'āina and Tahiti, and there is evidence that foreigners visited the islands before the late eighteenth century (see Finney 1991; Dixon 1932; Bushnell 1993, 17, 18). But it was not until British ships weighed anchor off the coast of Hawai'i in the late eighteenth century that ka po'e kahiko encountered Europeans en masse. Especially in comparison to colonialism in the Atlantic world, the beginning of colonization was relatively recent and began in full force only in the early decades of the nineteenth century. Set against the eons of Hawaiian cosmology—the infinitude of the Kumulipo—the brevity of the colonial epoch (and its neocolonial aftermath) is important to keep in mind. Although in the process of colonialism Hawaiians were decimated, dispossessed of the land, and deprived of cultural integrity and political autonomy, the relative brevity of Euro/American rule in the Islands would, in the late twentieth century, enhance the possibilities for indigenous memory to counter the force of colonial hegemony.

METEORIC TRANSFORMATIONS

Anthropologists described the meeting between indigenous people and Europeans as a "colonial encounter." Although the encounter metaphor points to possibilities of dialectical exchange, and the production of a synthetic "culture" that reflects both the colonized and the colonizer, it also obscures the asymmetrical power constitutive of being conquered. The "encounter" might better be described as a meteoric impact that set off a disastrous chain reaction over hundreds of years. This colonial meteor first exploded in Hawai'i in 1778, when Englishmen anchored offshore. They arrived in two ships that weighed 450 tons and carried four cannons and twelve swivel guns each. Under the aegis of England, a successfully imperialist maritime nation, the public objectives of these foreigners were to collect natural specimens, to describe the disposition of any people, and to cultivate their alliance and commence trade (Beaglehole 1966, 233–34). There were other, secret orders to secure a base that would allow England to control trade in the Pacific (194–95, 253).

More than any other factor, the privatization of the land—the opening of the possibility that foreigners could own and control it—was a requirement for the successful colonization of the Hawaiian Islands. Two fundamental structural transformations occurred within the first forty years of European arrival that would ease the way toward this Euro/American goal of land privatization. First, the centralization of state power and the creation of a nation occurred with the advice and technology of Euro/Americans. This was followed by the ending of the 'aikapu, the religious law that governed the highest-ranking elite. Both transformations were catalyzed by Euro/American intrusion and were significant steps toward the commoditization of the land.

Before Europeans, the chain of islands that later became Hawai'i was not conceived of in geo-political terms as a nation or a single unit (Herman 1999, 76). Political control was dynamic, and chiefdoms were "constantly expanding and contracting, consolidating and collapsing," so that the endurance of any particular hereditary chiefly line was unpredictable. The sacred power of a paramount chief was not infallible, and reassignments of the divine mandate occurred via coup or victorious invasions (Davenport 1969, 3, 7). The political and geographic fluidity that was characteristic of the Islands sharply contrasted with European notions of stability, continuity, and boundedness. The structural impermanence of rule challenged Western notions of power and order. From a European perspective, congress with such an unstable entity was impossible.

Thus containing the Islands in a territorially marked nation-state with stable rule was imperative (Jolly 2007, 100). European ideas about political permanency, coupled with European weapons and counsel, had a transformative impact on the political life of ka pae ʻāina. The use of stones, clubs, and daggers and the martial art of lua (Kolb and Dixon 2002, 517) ended with the arrival of Europeans and their guns (Seaton 1974, 195). When this became apparent to a paramount chief named Kamehameha, he established a monopoly over the arms trade and recruited American advisors to train his army in the use of firearms (Davenport 1969, 14). With these advantages, Kamehameha forced rival chiefs to recognize his supremacy and succeeded in creating a unified, centralized nation-state.

The subversion of the ʻaikapu[3] was the second profound structural change to occur. Although it is sometimes grasped as the state religion, there was no separate realm of civic society in ka pae ʻāina. The ʻaikapu formed the basis of the social order (Ohnuma 2008, 368); it marked distinctions between genders and between those of high and low rank. Women and men did not eat together, and women were forbidden from eating foods ritually offered to the gods. The kapu, or set of prohibitions, delineated modes of practice that persons of low rank were required to observe in the presence of superiors (Davenport 1969, 10; Kameʻeleihiwa 1992, 23). According to Davenport, violations of the kapu were strictly enforced. But in the time between the death of a supreme chief and the installation of a successor, the kapu was circumvented. Symbolizing a temporary suspension of the divine mandate and the peopleʻs grief, the kapu could be openly defied. During this period of opening, the successor was removed to avoid ritual contamination. Upon reentering society, the first act of the new supreme chief was to reinstate the ʻaikapu and thereby assume the divine mandate to rule (Davenport 1969, 10). The ʻaikapu[4] as a formal system of religious law ended in 1819, after Europeans had been in Hawaiʻi for forty years. Because the religious law was transformed before the arrival of the first Congregational missionaries from New England, there has been confusion about the role foreigners played in promoting the change. It has been argued that the changes reflected dissent within the ranks of highest chiefs (Kuykendall 1967, xx) or "social staleness . . . [and] culture fatigue" (Kroeber 1948, 404) of a world order that was no longer relevant. What is clear, however, is that it is impossible to imagine that the impact of foreigners was insignificant, although changes in the religious law also may have been beneficial to the interests of some high-ranking elites.

Kamehameha, the first Hawaiian chief to centralize power across the islands, upheld the kapu. But the ʻaikapu did not survive beyond his reign. When he died, his successor Liholiho was joined by Kamehamehaʻs wife Kaʻahumanu as kuhina nui, co-ruler. Kaʻahumanu was a prime instigator against the ʻaikapu. She led a group of ʻainoa, or "free eaters," who challenged gender-segregated eating and the restriction of certain foods for high-ranking women. When Liholiho returned from the proscribed period of the ritual of seclusion that preceded his ascension to power, he did not act in the expected way by asserting his divine authority to reinstate the kapu (Davenport 1969, 15). This transgression of the established ordering of things signified the end of the ʻaikapu as a formal system.

The overthrow of the ʻaikapu was not uncontested. Supporters of the religious law attempted to overthrow the new chief. But by controlling Western ships and weapons, Liholiho defeated his opponents (Davenport 1969, 18). A Western analyst likened the end of the formal religion to "displacing the keystone of an arch," resulting in the collapse of the whole structure (Alexander, cited in Seaton 1974, 197). While this might describe the ways in which the elite were upended by the transformation, it is important to note that for the majority of common people, the worship of ʻaumākua continued (Johnson 2003, 342).

Although it is possible that the abolition of ʻaikapu was the result of changing practices among the highest chiefs, and triggered by Kamehameha's rise to centralized power, it is certain that the presence of foreigners contributed to the erosion of this system. Dening has argued that European presence disrupted strict observance of forbidden practices among the Enata of the Marquesas, a Polynesian society comparable to Hawaiʻi. The customs of the foreigners were an affront to the structural integrity of the ʻaikapu (Dening 1980, 126–27). Women traveling from the beach to European ships in the first forty years of contact who ate and drank with the sailors were engaging in behavior that was kapu on the Islands. Europeans failed to properly observe the ʻaikapu-driven veneration of the highest-ranking chiefs by coming into physical contact with them. These repeated violations of the kapu may have bred skepticism and a sense of exception that triggered a crisis of legitimacy for the ʻaikapu (126–27; Sahlins 1981, 36–37).

In Kameʻeleihiwa's analysis, the ʻaikapu was a perfect expression of the social and theological ethos of ka poʻe kahiko, and its subversion destabilized Hawaiian society. The upheaval caused by the constant influx of foreigners and foreign ways undermined the efficacy and legitimacy of the aliʻi and disrupted the lives of common people. Along with the destruction of the social and religious order came massive dying from epidemic diseases introduced by foreigners. In this context of death and social disruption, "Christian salvation and the promise of life after death" was alluring (Kameʻeleihiwa 1992, 141, 142; see also Kashay 2008, par. 29, 40[5]).

The ʻaikapu formally ended before the arrival of Calvinist missionaries. It was not until 1824 that Calvinist Christianity was declared the state religion. Kameʻeleihiwa argued that new religion was intelligible to Hawaiians through the symbols and metaphors upon which the old religious law had been based (Kameʻeleihiwa 1992, 154). The "generative scheme" of the ʻaikapu remained an implicit customary norm (Bourdieu 1977, 20, 16; see also Sahlins 1981, 31–32). The new religion did not end the determination of the ruling chiefs to seek mana. Kameʻeleihiwa pointed out that the Hawaiian term *ʻai* translates into English as "eat" as well as "to rule" (Kameʻeleihiwa 1992, 146). The ruling chiefs, she wrote,

> were determined to *ʻai* (consume and rule) the physical manifestations of the foreigner—his goods, his food, and his "sparkling water" (liquor). Such a display fed the *mana* of the [elite] and made it grow in the eyes of the people. The [ruling chiefs] were accustomed to having the best of everything and to ruling all aspects of their society; that tradition had no need to end. (Kameʻeleihiwa 1992, 146)

Although the infectious greed of capitalism originated in the West, Hawaiians were not immune to its seduction. Undermined, in part, by implicit Hawaiian norms recast in the new Western religion and economics, they were "[c]aught in the entangling net of capitalist economy and foreign domination" (Kameʻeleihiwa 1992, 317).

Anthropologist Robert Redfield concluded that changes to indigenous religious systems "occurred on the margins of the expanding white man's civilization" (Redfield 1959, 129). It is clear that European personnel, weapons, goods, and customs played a critical role in the transformations that began with the violent centralization of Hawaiian rule and continued through the privatization of the land in 1848.

In the Hawaiʻi before Europeans, the ʻaikapu formed the center of the social structure. When it was overthrown, Hawaiian political and social life was destabilized. The political vacuum created by the abolition of the ʻaikapu made it easier for Europeans and Americans to dispossess Hawaiians of their land (Kameʻeleihiwa 1992, 316). Kameʻeleihiwa has argued that the Hawaiian term *pono,* meaning necessity, goodness, morality, and perfect order, was a central metaphor for ka poʻe kahiko. She posited that pono between the commoners and the chiefly class was achieved through the ordering of the ʻaikapu. No new specifically Hawaiian system of establishing pono evolved in place of the ʻaikapu. Instead, Calvinist missionaries, foreign merchants, and foreign investors were able to use the instability of this period of social transformation to further their colonizing agendas. What evolved was a Hawaiian monarchy under a coercive system of ordering that facilitated European and American expansion.

TRADE: SANDALWOOD AND WHALING

European capitalist imperialism depended upon the opening of new markets for production and investment, monopolies on resources and trade, control of labor, and a powerful military to protect these investments from competing states (Boswell 1989, 180). In Hawaiʻi, foreigners saw the potential for the extraction of great wealth and an outpost in the Pacific of great strategic advantage with which to protect this process of extraction. Thus foreigners coveted the islands with fierce desire, and by the mid-nineteenth century, Hawaiʻi was entangled in the sandalwood and whaling trades. Hawaiians were at a great disadvantage in their relationship with foreign traders. Americans and other foreigners set the terms of trade so that they controlled the new market and ensured that any surplus generated accrued to them. Hawaiians became, in Kameʻeleihiwaʻs phrase, enmeshed in "capitalist cycles of never ending debt" (Kameʻeleihiwa 1992, 170–71).

The commencement of the sandalwood trade in 1810 opened up the Hawaiian Islands to the "large-scale exploitation of the environment for profit" (Herman 1999, 84). Although the trade was short-lived, ending before the 1840s, it was extremely lucrative for foreigners and had a devastating impact on the Hawaiian people. Kamehamehaʻs centralization of state power demanded an arms buildup, and he used the income from the sandalwood trade to procure ships and ammunition (Seaton 1974, 195). But the costs of arming the nation exceeded the income generated by sandalwood, establishing a pattern of indebtedness to foreigners that would continue under subsequent ruling chiefs, and that drove their further involvement in trade (Cook et al. 2003, 12). The great demand for sandalwood displaced the subsistence activities of commoners. Obliged by relations of reciprocity to render service to high chiefs, commoner men were sent to upland forests to harvest sandalwood and haul it to the shore, which left their subsistence plots unattended (Ladefoged 1993, 123; Davenport 1969, 17–18). Inglis (2005, 238) noted that the inability to care for subsistence plots resulted in a diminishing food supply and a growing problem of malnutrition, which in a biomedical sense left the immune systems of commoner Hawaiians less able to fight disease. The demand for great quantities of sandalwood exhausted the supply and effectively ended the trade by 1829.

The whaling trade succeeded sandalwood. If the British controlled the sandalwood trade, then whaling was decisively American—nearly 80 percent of whaling vessels were American owned. Whaling was the fourth largest industry in the New England state of Massachusetts, and profits from the industry were used to seed investments in shipping, cotton, textiles, and railroads (Moment 1957, 263). Whaling also enriched the American merchants established in Hawaiian ports. It was estimated that each of the 1,000 whaling vessels in 1841 spent an average of $700 or $800 when docked in Hawaiʻi (Freidel 1943, 380). Whaling, too, brought fundamental changes to Hawaiʻi, as commoners were increasingly drawn into cash economies as workers and sailors (Ladefoged 1993, 123; Kent 1993[1983], 21).

WESTERN DESIRE FOR HAWAIIAN LAND

After denuding the land of sandalwood and the sea of whales, Western business interests pressured the Hawaiian kingdom to provide land "in fee simple" for large-scale plantation agriculture. In the earliest decades of the nineteenth century, Western landholding was contained by a specifically Hawaiian system of use. Westerners coveted large parcels of land for development as agricultural plantations but were forced to abide by the conventions of a system of land use in which access to land was under the control of Hawaiian chiefs. Americans petitioned the Hawaiian government, but the land grants bestowed by the ruling chief were revocable, and the land so granted could not be sold (Banner 2005, 283–84). Concerned about protecting and advancing their investments, European and American investors portrayed the Hawaiian government as "feudal [and] despoti[c]." An American advisor to the king argued that

> . . . the present system of landed tenures . . . rests upon the nation like a mountain, pressing and crushing them to the very earth . . . remove it, and the fettered resources and depressed energies of the nation will rise, and cover the land with prosperity and plenty. Unless the people— the real cultivators of the soil, can have an absolute and independent right in their lands—unless they can be protected in those rights, and have what they raise as their own—they will inevitably waste away. (Lee 1847 n.p., cited in Banner 2005, 294–95)

In contrast, Kame'eleihiwa has argued that a central metaphor for pre-contact Hawaiian society was mālama 'āina, or caring for the land. Mālama 'āina expressed the bonds of love and honor between the common people and the ruling chiefs, a relationship always mediated through the gods.

> Ali'i Nui [highest-ranking chiefs] were the protectors of the maka'āinana, sheltering them from terrible unforeseen forces. Should an Ali'i Nui neglect proper ritual and pious behavior, surely a famine or calamity would ensue. Should a famine arise, the Ali'i Nui was held at fault and deposed. Alternatively, should a Ali'i Nui be stingy and cruel to the commoners, the cultivators of the 'Āina, he or she would cease to be pono, lose favor with the Akua and be struck down, usually by the people. . . . A reciprocal relationship was maintained: the Ali'i Nui kept the 'Āina fertile and the Akua appeased; the maka'āinana fed and clothed the Ali'i Nui. (Kame'eleihiwa 1992, 26)

This reciprocal relationship of mālama 'āina was impossible for Westerners to comprehend. The Hawaiian system of land use was perceived by Westerners through a cultural lens that conceived of land as a commodifiable resource to be exploited for the production and extraction of wealth. Misconstrued by Westerners as feudal, the Hawaiian system of land use based on conceptions of mālama ʻāina came under relentless attack. Under cover of the trope of the oppressed Hawaiian serf, Western businessmen pressed their interests in expanding their investments and encouraged the settlement of Americans and Europeans in the Islands. Until land could be freely bought and sold as a commodity, the future of Western investment was uncertain.

THE MĀHELE

Māhele in Hawaiian means to portion or divide. The Māhele was the 1848 legislation proposed by Westerners that introduced the concept of land as private property and conferred upon them the legal means to fully control and profit from it. New England Calvinist Missionaries deplored the Hawaiian land use system because they believed that it encouraged "licentious, indolent, improvident and ignorant" behavior among commoner Hawaiians (Wylie, cited in Kameʻeleihiwa 1992, 202). But it was not just the Christians whose sermons equated the use rights of the Hawaiian system of land tenure with ignorance: the major issue for American businessmen was communal land rights. In the *Polynesian*, a commercial newspaper that began publication in 1840, the foreigners' campaign to privatize the land dominated the news. The paper's Boston-born editor argued throughout the 1840s that capital investment in the kingdom was thwarted by the lack of permanent land titles. In the years leading up to the Māhele, the newspaper argued that private land ownership would bring prosperity and would "preserve" the Native population by providing them with an "incentive" (in Chapin 1996, 32–33).

A travel account from an American visitor to Hawaiʻi in the late 1840s diagnosed the problem with prescience when he claimed that land in fee simple would result in the "preponderating influence" of foreigners, such that "the land [would] slip like water through the hands of the chiefs" (Wise 1849, 374–75, cited in Banner 2005, 286). The Hawaiian king, Kauikeaouli, was also clear on the dangers of allowing foreigners to own Hawaiian land. In Privy Council Records from 1846 on the subject of a land dispute with a foreigner, the king is recorded as saying, "[W]e indeed wish to give Foreigners lands the same as natives and so were granted, but to the natives they are revertible and the foreigners would insist that they have them forever" (Privy Council Records 15, in Banner 2005, 285).

Kameʻeleihiwa has argued that by the mid-1840s the Hawaiian kingdom faced increasing threats of foreign military invasion and the loss of sovereignty (1992, 188–90). The French had forced the queen of Tahiti to agree to

Protectorate status, and had threatened to take all her lands if she did not acquiesce to French demands (O'Brien 2006, 118). The Hawaiian king wrote a sad note to the Tahitian queen. He said that he was sorry about "the death of [her] Government," but that he could not help because he did not have "the power [*mana*] within [him]" (cited in Kameʻeleihiwa 1992, 189).

Under threat of the loss of sovereignty, the Hawaiian king set in motion the process of the Māhele in 1848. All lands became alienable, and in 1850 legislation permitted foreigners to buy and sell land in fee simple. Commoner Hawaiians voiced their opposition to the ownership of land by foreigners. A petition from 300 citizens of the island of Hawaiʻi urged the king to refuse both land and citizenship to foreigners. "If the Chiefs are to open this door of the government as an entrance way for the foreigners to come into Hawaiʻi," the petition argued, "then you will see the Hawaiian people going from place to place in this world like flies" (Petition 1845a, cited in Kameʻeleihiwa 1992, 331). Another petition from 301 citizens of Lānaʻi begged the king to protect the independence of the government, to refuse to appoint foreigners to government positions, to refuse land to foreigners, and to prohibit them from citizenship. "We are afraid," they wrote, "that the wise will step on the ignorant, the same as American and other lands,—and you on us" (Petition 1845b, cited in Kameʻeleihiwa 1992, 333). A third petition from 1,600 citizens of Maui predicted that allowing foreign land ownership would cause "troubles" for the "government, [and for] ourselves even to the first and third generations after us" (Petition 1845c, cited in Kameʻeleihiwa 1992, 338).

The petitioners were prescient: the damage of the Māhele was sure and swift. The greatest obstacle to the investment of foreign capital had been overcome. While commoner Hawaiians were eligible to file land claims based on traditional use rights, only 12,000 filed at a time when the population was 72,000. The low number of claims can be attributed to the fact that many commoners lived in remote areas and were not aware of, or did not understand, the need to file a claim, while others simply missed the deadline (Linnekin 1987, 27). But even the minimal land holdings of commoners that accrued as a result of the Māhele were soon lost, since without access to an entire ahupuaʻa, as provided by traditional land tenure, the small plots that commoner Hawaiians controlled could not provide subsistence (Herman 1999, 85; Levy 1975, 857). These plots were soon purchased by foreigner plantation owners (Levy 1975, 861), producing an abundance of landless and impoverished Hawaiians. Landlessness, and the inability to grow subsistence crops, created widespread malnutrition, which exacerbated the spread of multiple epidemics (see Inglis 2005, 238).

At the time of the Māhele there were less than 2,000 Europeans and Americans combined living in the Islands (Levy 1975, 848). By 1862, with their numbers steadily increasing, foreigners owned half of the land. By 1896, census figures showed that only 12.8 percent of Hawaiians owned any land at all (Spitz

1967, 477). Merry has argued that the Māhele transformed land use that was based on the reciprocal relations between the commoner Hawaiians and the ruling elite. In place of this relationship based on genealogy and rank, the Māhele substituted relations of inequality based on property ownership and the market. Although they acquired the right to own land, the vast majority of Hawaiians were impoverished. The Māhele transformed an agricultural people into an "increasingly displaced, mobile population migrating to the towns . . . or struggling to survive in more remote, isolated valleys" (Merry 2000, 95).

DISEASE AND ITS INTERPRETATION

In addition to weapons, and the atmosphere of terror and coercion they produced, the foreigners arriving in Hawaiʻi in the late eighteenth century brought with them a variety of infectious diseases. The economic, sociocultural, and sexual intercourse between the people of Hawaiʻi and these foreigners would result in deadly processes. The sociocultural transformations catalyzed by the imperialist exigency of controlling trade in the Pacific, coupled with the diseases introduced by Europeans, laid waste to the bodies and souls of ka poʻe kahiko. But in tandem with the epidemics were foreign interpretations of Hawaiian culture and society. Refracted through the cultural logics of the West, the dying bodies of ka poʻe kahiko became the basis for a powerful ideology of Hawaiian infirmity that justified American colonialism (see Scheper-Hughes and Lock 1986, 137).[6]

In *Health and the Rise of Civilization*, Cohen (1989) argued that the introduction of epidemic disease on subjugated populations gave the subjugators a powerful advantage, not only in terms of health but also in terms of politics. As a "major weapon" of advancing civilization, disease harbored by invading Europeans eliminated the indigenous in large numbers. It demoralized them and "convinced them of the superiority of the . . . colonizing system." Thus epidemic disease was both a biological and an ideological weapon that proved the "superiority of civilization and its gods" (Cohen 1989, 54). But it was not (or not only, as Cohen argues) the colonized who became convinced of the superiority of civilization and its gods—Europeans and Americans themselves, whose twin ideologies of Hawaiian infirmity and Western superiority, became a symbolic weapon to further imperial goals.

The social transformations that occurred in Hawaiʻi in the first 100 years after the arrival of Europeans and Americans must be understood in the context of a demographic catastrophe of horrific proportions. From 1778 to 1893 (the year that the United States officially occupied Hawaiʻi), the indigenous population declined from upward of 800,000 (Stannard 1989, 44–52; Kameʻeleihiwa 1992, 81, 141) to 40,000, a decline of 95 percent. The vastness of the Pacific

Ocean had protected Pacific Island populations from deadly pathogens until the arrival of Europeans and Americans in the late eighteenth century. Once introduced, the diseases tore through island populations, and the constant influx of foreigners meant "wave after wave" of epidemics (Igler 2004, par. 41–43). Furthermore, the diseases introduced by Westerners did not just affect death rates. As Inglis (2005) argued, epidemics were also sites of cultural transformation. Pre-haole Hawaiians viewed disease as the result of social and cosmological disorder, but Western theological and scientific theories influenced Hawaiians to place the blame for disease on individual sin and other improper behaviors (250, 254, 256).

In an epidemiologically informed study of nineteenth-century global Pacific exchange networks, Igler suggested that the "dialectic of trade and disease" proved to be greatly beneficial to Europe and America. In Hawai'i, traders spread disease, which weakened and diminished the Native population and gave Europeans and Americans a decisive advantage in emerging trade practices (2004, par. 39). The spread of disease gave foreign traders an advantage precisely where they needed it most. As the hub of global trade in the Pacific, Hawaiian ports had more traffic than any others, so "by 1850, the microbes of Europe, Asia and Africa" were decimating the Hawaiian population (par. 40).

The British were the first Europeans to arrive in Hawai'i, and they brought with them syphilis, gonorrhea, tuberculosis, and influenza (Stannard 1989, 70). In their wake, epidemics hit the Hawaiian population with searing strength and caused widespread female infertility and death. In 1804, an epidemic known as ma'i 'ōku'u (variously identified as cholera, the bubonic plague, typhoid fever, bacillary dysentery, or yellow fever in a biomedical lexicon) spread through the population of O'ahu (Kamakau 1992, 189, 236; Kuykendall 1965[1938], 49; Bushnell 1993, 103; Ii 1993[1959], 16, 33).[7] According to Kamakau, ma'i 'ōku'u "was a very virulent pestilence, and those who contracted it died quickly. A person on the highway would die before he could reach home. . . . The body turned black at death" (Kamakau 1992, 189). A series of epidemics followed ma'i 'ōku'u. Leprosy entered the Islands in the early 1800s. Inglis argued that leprosy, in particular, "had an overwhelming impact on the social fabric of Hawaiian society" (2005, 228). Hawaiians suffering with the disease were "arrested" and banished, by order of the Board of Health, from their families, community, and land. "With the introduction of each new epidemic," Inglis wrote, "Hawaiian lives were lost." But it was not just Hawaiian lives that were lost. The removal of sick Hawaiians to the leper colony at Moloka'i opened up further opportunities for haole to claim the land. Leprosy, among other epidemics, exacerbated depopulation, but it also intensified the dispossession of Hawaiians from the land (228).

Other epidemics occurred throughout the nineteenth century. In 1826, an outbreak of "cough and bronchitis" (Kamakau 1992, 274) and "congested lungs and sore throat" caused the death of "thousands, especially in the country districts." A ship arriving from Valparaiso in 1839 carried the dead body of the captain, who had died at sea, and "brought a pestilence from which many died" (236). An epidemic of "colds, dull headaches, sore throats and deafness" occurred in 1844 (237). In 1848, "an American warship brought the disease known as measles," accompanied by dysentery, to Hilo. "It spread and carried away about a third of the population" (236–37, 418). In the following year, according to Kamakau, the disease spread to Maui, Lāhainā, and eventually Oʻahu (411).

In 1853, a deadly epidemic of smallpox ravaged Honolulu. The virulence of the epidemic was described by Kamakau:

> The small pox came and dead bodies lay stacked like kindling wood, red as singed hogs. Shame upon those who brought the disease and upon the foreign doctors who allowed their landing! . . . [T]he disease broke out like a volcanic eruption.
>
> From the last week in June until September the disease raged in Honolulu. The dead fell like dried *kukui* twigs tossed down by the wind. Day by day from morning till night horse-drawn carts went about from street to street of the town, and the dead were stacked up like a load of wood, some in coffins, but most of them just piled in, wrapped in cloth with head and legs sticking out. . . . Death spread to ʻEwa, to Hālawa, to Waimānalo, until it surrounded Oʻahu. Some large tracts were entirely denuded, some had but a few survivors. Not a family but bore its loss. (Kamakau 1992, 416–17)

Actions by Boards of Health to contain the disease and heal the sick were ineffective, particularly in regard to the smallpox epidemic. Kamakau's chronicle clearly distinguishes between care for the sick in "Honolulu and places in its vicinity" and the rural districts of Oʻahu and other islands. According to Kamakau, "[o]n Maui there was not a member of the Board of Health who did anything to care for the sick, as they were cared for by the government in Honolulu"(1992, 417). But even in Honolulu, care for the sick was ineffective. The principal means of epidemic control involved removal of the dead and the burning of "infected houses" (Kuykendall 1965[1938], 411–13).

Efforts to care for those infected with smallpox were sidetracked by American political maneuvering. A public meeting in 1858 became an occasion for an American attack on Hawaiian sovereignty. Although convened to discuss strategies for coping with the epidemic, American businessmen turned the meeting into a "political demonstration" against the Hawaiian king that "secured the adoption of resolutions bitterly condemning" Hawaiian government officials, "accusing them of being responsible for the smallpox epidemic" (413).

Inoculations for smallpox had been developed as early as 1721 in England (McNeill 1989[1976], 220),[8] and vaccinations were offered in Honolulu during a smallpox outbreak in 1858. Writing about Native Hawaiians and the epidemic in ways that belittled their suffering, historian Gavan Daws described attempts to provide vaccinations. In Daws's interpretation, although many Native Hawaiians were inoculated, others refused.

> The Hawaiians had never given much attention to Western ideas about medical treatment, and in this instance they paid a terrible price. At Honolulu many natives were vaccinated or inoculated, and if they were lucky the vaccine took. Thousands of others refused to be helped. Some scratched their arms, simulating vaccination marks, rather than submit to the white physicians and their volunteer helpers. Others went to native medical kahunas for aid. The dreadful consequences were plain. Hawaiians fell sick everywhere. Some were abandoned and died alone, their bodies left to rot. Others were buried where they lay, without coffins, in graves so shallow that wandering pigs and dogs could unearth them. Some native families nursed their sick at home, devotedly and uselessly, and carefully laid the dead under the dirt floors of their thatch huts or in their house yards, following their old burial practices and condemning themselves to follow the dead into the grave. (Daws 1968, 140)

But Hawaiians paid very close attention to the ways in which Western ideas about healing were different from their own, and they did not accept their dying as inevitable. In response to the scourge of sexually transmitted diseases, King Kamehameha IV and Queen Emma secured funding in 1859 for a hospital to treat impoverished Hawaiians. In 1860, they presided over the passage of an "Act to Mitigate Evils and Disease Arising from Prostitution," which provided a system for examining and treating sick Hawaiian women (Chapin 1996, 69–70).

A Board of Health was established in 1855 to address the massive dying of Native Hawaiians, particularly the epidemic of cholera (Inglis 2005, 106). However, after 1863, the haole-influenced board's main focus was isolating the predominantly Hawaiian victims of ma'i Pākē, or leprosy. A law passed in 1865 criminalized "any person alleged to be a leper" and provided that such persons be arrested and "condemned to a [life] of virtual imprisonment" on the geographically isolated and perpetually underfunded Makanalua peninsula on the northern shore of Moloka'i (Inglis 2005, 94–98, 124, 112; Kuykendall 1982[1953], 72–75). The Board of Health and the few Western physicians reviled the practices of traditional Hawaiian medicine. A physician for the Queen's Hospital described the "poor natives" as "[i]gnorant and superstitious, accustomed by his ancient kahunas [sic] to view only a supernatural agency in disease and remedy," and thus unable "to easily reconcile himself to the sober, unpretentious working of a scientific method in curing disease" (Kuykendall 1982[1953], 72).

Medical science, however, was no more effective in stemming the waves of epidemic diseases that swept away the lives of Kanaka Maoli than conversion to Christianity. The Board of Health's criminalization of Hawaiians with leprosy and its public antipathy toward Hawaiian healing methods rendered it ineffectual. The board also was charged with the regulation of kāhuna; in their view, "great evils arise to the Hawaiian nation from the . . . want of regulation for Hawaiian practitioners of medicine" (Chun 1994, viii). Regulation by the board included a $10 licensure fee and a requirement for the keeping of records. Kāhuna were expected to record types of diseases, medicines used, number of cures and deaths, and the name, sex, and places of residence of any patients (viii). Records were subject to inspection by the board, and failure to comply with the regulations concerning record keeping could result in fines up to $100. Practicing without a license could result in fines from $20 to $100.

In the mid-nineteenth century, few foreign doctors were available in the Islands, especially in rural districts. Western medicine was a cash commodity and was "rare and expensive" (Chun 1994, iii). The actions by the Board of Health to demote Hawaiian healing knowledge, to criminalize Hawaiians suffering with leprosy, to constrain kāhuna by charging exorbitant fees, and to monitor those who sought treatment exemplify the ways in which colonialism debased the bodies, souls, and culture of Kanaka Maoli. Furthermore, the Board of Health did not stop the dying.

As a response to the injudicious actions of the Board of Health, a group of Native Hawaiian men on Maui organized in 1866 the ʻAhahui Lāʻau Lapaʻau (Conference on Traditional Medicine). Their goals were to study Native medical practices and "to search for the means to continue our race upon our own land" (Chun 1994, xxxvii). This they intended to do "with or without the government's board of health" (iii). The ʻAhahui refused to accept the twin ideologies of Hawaiian infirmity and Western superiority, or the inevitability of Hawaiian depopulation and death. In a speech delivered to the committee, J. W. Kauwahi explored the "problem of depopulation." He argued that

> . . . depopulation has robbed parents of their children, men and women of their friends. It has destroyed families and the concept of community life. It has emptied schools, where once they were full of school children and students. It has emptied churches, where once they were swelled with people, and also the fields [are emptied]. Depopulation has affected the royal families down to the commoners, and many have died. . . . Shall we just stand by and watch in despair and cry? Is it not worth the effort to investigate, experiment, and to test for whatever can help our people? (Chun 1994, xxx)

The ʻAhahui Lāʻau Lapaʻau contradicted Daws's assessment of Hawaiian reaction to the smallpox epidemic. Their work demonstrated an understanding of disease that was far more sophisticated than the views of many Americans, especially those influencing the actions of the Board of Health. In the view of the ʻAhahui, neither sin nor ignorance caused the spread of disease. Rather, Kauwahi argued that the illnesses reflected a disjuncture between Hawaiian and Western ways of living.

> [T]he Hawaiian people have mixed the new and old ways together and in doing so they have become more susceptible to those illnesses familiar and new to them. Therefore, the mixing of these two new types of illnesses internally has developed into a hybrid, that is [one made up of] the traditional illnesses contracted due to their way of living and the food they ate, and the introduced illnesses which are contracted due to the change of clothing and improper health care. These types of illnesses mixed and become deadly because there are no doctors or traditional practitioners who know the medicines to treat these hybrid illnesses. (Chun 1994, xxxii, brackets in original)

The expense of Western medicines was noted and compared to the cost of traditional remedies, "which [could] be grown in no time at home, or sought after without much difficulty as they grow all over" (Chun 1994, xxxvi).

Noting with alarm the increase in the population of foreigners, Kauwahi predicted that "[s]oon they will over populate our islands" (xxxiv). His analysis of the difference between Hawaiian and foreign birth and survival rates focused on the methodology of Western medical and scientific research efforts to maintain Westerners' health.

> I have seen the medicines they use, what they eat, what their personal habits are, and I know that their scientists have sought to understand the nature and use of proper medicines to cure themselves. Therefore, their birth rate has dramatically increased and their families swell into the doorways. (Chun 1994, xxxiv)

The ʻAhahui posed a series of research questions that they hoped would lead to solutions. Much of the discussion revolved around the power of the Board of Health, doubts about its ability to help Hawaiians, and a critique of "modern medicine" when compared to traditional Hawaiian healing (xxx–xvii). The main project of the ʻAhahui was to interview traditional healers, to catalogue their knowledge "in the pursuit of the betterment of public health," and to distinguish between "quacks" and authentic kāhuna (v, xxxi).[9] The ʻAhahui recognized the danger that the loss of Hawaiian healing traditions posed in the midst of a continuing series of deadly epidemics, and they called for the training of traditional practitioners. They also called for government "to situate [foreign] doctors in all districts" and "to build a school where people [could] be trained [in Western medicine] for future generations" (xxxv). Kauwahi argued that "the first priority of the government should be to take care of its people's welfare," but he was not optimistic. The Board of Health "has done very little," he said, "and still it does not much, and it is not expected to do little more in the future" (xxxv). Notwithstanding Kauwahi's call for the health of the indigenous to be a governmental priority, the resources of Hawaiʻi were distributed not to ensure the health and well-being of Hawaiians but to facilitate the profit of foreigners. Haunani-Kay Trask wrote that "the world of ka poʻe kahiko collapsed from the violence of contact: disease, mass death, and land dispossession; evangelical Christianity; plantation capitalism; cultural destruction, including language banning; and, finally, American military invasion in 1893 and forced annexation in 1898" (H. Trask 1996, 906).

In just over 100 years, between the first landfall of Europeans and the American-led coup that overthrew the Hawaiian monarchy, Native Hawaiians were dispossessed from their lands, culturally marginalized and denigrated, and politically disenfranchised. Relentless processes of epidemic disease and massive depopulation occurred throughout the 100–year process. The result of these forces, collectively, was genocide. "As the twentieth century dawned," H. Trask wrote, "we were but a remnant of the great and ancient people we had once been" (907).

What happened to Hawaiians also occurred elsewhere between the fifteenth and nineteenth centuries, as Europeans sought political and economic domination of the world. The ideologies of imperialism gave Westerners a sense of righteousness expressed as cultural superiority, white supremacy, and the reserved right to usurp all resources. Trask argued that European notions of cultural superiority have been "thoroughly repudiated . . . as . . . matter[s] of imperial policy masquerading as historical fact" (Trask 1993, 39). But into the twenty-first century, notions of cultural superiority are clearly evident in Hawaiʻi and in the rest of the (neo)colonized world.

The historical record is replete with European and American justifications for colonizing Hawaiʻi in the nineteenth century. From the very beginning, foreigners misinterpreted the culture, religion, and politics of ka poʻe kahiko. Various metaphors were employed by Euro/Americans beginning in the early nineteenth century to devalue Hawaiian life and culture, and to justify the colonial theft of Hawaiian land and resources. Beginning with the Calvinist theology of the New England missionaries, Hawaiians were written about as essentially sinful, vice-ridden, ignorant, disorderly, and deviant, and destined to wither away. Throughout the nineteenth century, the metaphors characterizing Hawaiian life and culture shifted from an early focus on sin, licentiousness, and disease to later notions about ignorance, criminality, and deviance. Although the epistemological grounding of this interpretation of Native life and culture shifts from theology to science and medicine, from Christian eschatology to the gospel of modern progress, the interpretations form a circular chain of logic, relying on and implying each other. Thomas Szasz (1958b, 185) argued that in societies founded on religious principles, there is no difference between "sin" and "crime" and that "the concept of 'illness,' as a purely medical notion, exists only in a rudimentary form, since all types of misfortune and suffering tend to be regarded as divine punishment." Indeed, into the twenty-first century, such logic is echoed in discussions of Native Hawaiian disease, social pathology, and criminality.

In *Dark Vanishings: Discourse on the Extinction of Primitive Races*, Patrick Brantlinger argued that "extinction discourse" rose from the ideologies of imperialism and racism and occurred wherever Europeans and Americans encountered indigenous peoples (2003, 1). As a performative discourse that "acted on the world" as much as it described it, extinction discourse served as a key ideological justification for the Indian Removal Act of 1830 in the United States (4). Extinction discourse denied coevality between the colonizer and the colonized, representing the indigenous as "creatures of the past . . . always already dead because they are futureless" (66, 52). The discourse of extinction was ubiquitous, largely unchallenged within the West, and its stress on the inevitability of indigenous death contributed to its lethality (190).

In Hawai'i, the extinction discourse began with a British lieutenant on the first European ship. He conjectured that there were 400,000 inhabitants, a serious underestimation, according to Stannard (1989), who carefully demonstrates the possibility of upward of 800,000 inhabitants at the time of European arrival (27, 50–55). Subsequent conjectures, as equally unfounded as the first, put the indigenous population at 200,000 to 300,000. Indeed, as Stannard argued, representing the land they coveted as underpopulated served the myth that the land bases of indigenous people were "patiently waiting Western penetration and conquest" (xvii).

By the time the first New England missionaries arrived in 1819, the population of Hawai'i had already suffered a series of epidemics. Recognizing sin and licentiousness when they saw it, the missionaries steadily created a discourse of extinction based not on the spread of disease but on the very natures of the savages they were meant to redeem. Everywhere the missionaries looked they saw something called "unrepentant sin," a category of physical and spiritual behavior that was loathsome to them. Missionary women who were charged with the education of Hawaiians, in their letters home to Massachusetts and Connecticut, expressed shock over the Hawaiians' lack of culture. "This people," one of the first missionary women wrote, "were in a state of nature. . . . Both men and women were . . . allowed to move around in public in a state of perfect nudity"

(Thurston 1921[1882], 90). Another woman wrote about her perceptions that Hawaiians were "sunk to the lowest depth of sin and depravity." Another observed that "language cannot convey to you a just idea of their stupidity" (Grimshaw 1983, 478, 498). American women were deeply shocked by what they considered the lack of purposeful and productive labor on the part of Hawaiian women. Rather than noticing that in a society in which "material wants were easily satisfied" work was not reified as a sign of goodness, missionary women were incensed to find that Hawaiian women spent "many precious hours in sleep," a behavior they deemed indolent (499–500). The mothering techniques of Hawaiian women were scrutinized and deemed severely lacking. Hawaiian mothers, one wrote, existed in evil, and their children were "plunging into sin" (503).

Missionary misinterpretations of Hawaiian life stemmed from the sixteenth-century theology of John Calvin.[10] The Reverend Hiram Bingham, head of the first company of missionaries that arrived in 1819, described Hawaiians as personifications of "unrighteousness, fornication, wickedness, murder . . . deceit, [and] malignity." Guided by his theology, Bingham saw Hawaiians as ". . . haters of God . . . , inventors of evil things . . . , without natural affection, implacable [and] unmerciful" (Bingham 1855, 23).

The arrival of the missionaries coincided with epidemics that were causing massive Hawaiian death. In a time before scientific knowledge would posit germs as the origin of disease, the missionaries sought to explain indigenous affliction. Missionary William Ellis (1979[1825]) blamed the "dark mind[s]" (202) of those he hoped to convert. Ellis described a meeting with a sick chief on Maui, "who was afflicted with a pulmonary complaint, and almost reduced to a skeleton." He recommended that the chief "fly to Jesus, the great physician of souls." The chief at first resisted, indicating to Ellis the enveloping nature of the "darkness of paganism" (202). Inveighing against the "priests, and the incantations of sorcerers," Ellis promised the chief "the prolongation of his mortal life." At this, the chief agreed, saying he "would do anything to live" (201), and Ellis "pray[ed] for him to Jesus" (201).

But since the civilizing influence of Calvinism was clearly unable to save Hawaiians, other explanations were in order. Reverend Artemas Bishop, another of the earliest Congregational missionaries, wrote in 1838 that, "[I]t is not civilization, but civilized vices that wither the savages. [. . .] He drinks into them like water, without knowing that their attendant diseases are cutting the tendrils of his heart, and drawing away his life's blood" (in Bushnell 1993, 228–29). As a variant of extinction discourse, Bishop's view defined indigenous Hawaiians as only capable of assimilating the vicious underbelly of civilization—the sins and vices that disciplined Calvinists had transcended. Since the Native was unable to achieve similar transcendence, the missionaries theorized that Natives would simply wither away.

Americans focused intensely on Native use of intoxicants. The narrative of the Natives' penchant for drinking and dancing was support for the larger discourse of the Natives' inability to make the transition to civilization and was viewed as a cause of further physical degeneracy. The spread of foreign intoxicants in the Islands and into Hawaiian bodies is a persistent undercurrent in the historiography of nineteenth-century Hawai'i. From Liholiho's[11] drinking binge prior to ending the 'aikapu to public discussion of King Kalākaua's drinking in the foreign press ("The New King" 1873, 9), the monarchs were represented as heavy drinkers. Kuykendall wrote that

> [b]eside their other gifts to the Hawaiians, the foreigners initiated them into the use of alcoholic liquors and tobacco, taught them the art of distillation, engrafted upon the primitive social order some of their own vicious habits, *and were the means of bringing in diseases which started the Hawaiian people on a toboggan slide down the slope of depopulation.* (Kuykendall 1965[1938], 28, emphasis added)

And, according Holt, the spread of alcoholism was particularly acute, since Hawaiians, already "warmly disposed to hedonism . . . took to alcohol with a fatal and giddy determination" (Holt 1971, 23).

The theological language underpinning the discourse of Native extinction shifted in the course of the nineteenth century toward a more secular, political, and historical idiom. British traveler Isabella Bird argued in the 1870s that white settlers had liberated Hawaiians from their own dark ages.

> However many causes for regret exist; one must not forget that only forty years ago the people inhabiting this strip of land between the volcanic wilderness and the sea were a vicious, sensual, shameless herd, that no man among them, except their chiefs, had any rights, that they were harried and oppressed almost to death, and had no consciousness of any moral obligations. Now, order and external decorum at least prevail. (Bird 1906, 67)

Toward the latter half of the nineteenth century, the language of the extinction narrative shifts away from theology toward the "perishing nation." Bird wrote that

> [i]n riding through Hawai'i I came everywhere upon traces of a once numerous population. . . . This nation, with its elaborate governmental machinery, its churches and institutions, has to me the mournful aspect of a shrivelled [*sic*] and wizened old man dressed in clothing much too

big, the garments of this once athletic and vigorous youth. Nor can I divest myself of the idea that the laughing, flower-clad hordes of riders who make the town gay with their presence are but like butterflies fluttering out their short lives in the sunshine. (176–77)

Sereno Bishop, a missionary descendant, writer for the *New York Independent*, and advocate of American annexation, wrote that

[We] look upon the Hawaiian as a very "sick man." He is weak and wasted. He cannot direct or save himself. . . . It is as hopeless any longer to entrust the natives with sovereignty, as to leave a debauched spendthrift without a guardian to save the remnant of his estate. (Bishop 1893, cited in Tate 1962, 250)

Bishop predicted that an American-style republican government led by whites was the inevitable "nature of things."

. . . [W]e cannot fail to distinctly perceive that in the nature of things it is wholly impossible that their unprecedented distinction of being the ruling race with a native sovereign can be permanent, or that in the rapid decrease of their numbers and growth of the white race, a Hawaiian throne can long continue, even under the most favorable circumstances. The base of the throne is decayed, and no severe shock will be awaited to topple it over. . . .

As in due time the native sovereignty comes to its natural end, whether by the decay of the native people, the lack of chiefs, or a general end of its usefulness . . . [r]epublican government will be the natural, fitting and obvious arrangement. (cited in Kuykendall 1967, 277–78)

Bishop's argument, that "nature" would eventuate the overthrow of Hawaiian sovereignty, was based on an organic metaphor of growth and decay. However, despite the effects of cultural, economic, and biological disruption on Native life and culture, Hawaiians held political power through huge majorities in the legislature and were the largest voting bloc in the Islands up until the mid-1880s. Euro-American men did not become the decisive factor in Hawaiian politics until a group of Americans forced the Hawaiian king to accept a constitution that enfranchised them and placed property requirements on legislators in 1887. Despite the rhetoric of the colonizers, there was nothing "natural" about U.S. occupation of Hawaiʻi: it was American political conspiracy, and not Hawaiian sin or disease, that toppled Hawaiian sovereignty.

2

WAIʻANAE

A Space of Resistance

To resist is to retrench in the margins, retrieve what we were and remake ourselves. The past, our stories local and global, the present, our communities, cultures, languages and social practices—all may be spaces of marginalization, but they have also become spaces of resistance and hope. (Smith 1999, 4)

Before I moved to the working-class community of Waiʻanae on the leeward coast of Oʻahu in early 1996, I stayed briefly in Honolulu at the University of Hawaiʻi. In casual conversations I learned an important distinction about the community I planned to study. Waiʻanae, I was told, was "dangerous," "rough," and "really, really local." A Korean graduate student in biostatistics worried about my safety and wondered what I might learn in a place like Waiʻanae. When I visited a family friend, an elderly drag queen who had once been a performer in Waikīkī, she said Waiʻanae was dangerous and that I should stay put in Honolulu. A taxi driver (who appeared "Asian" to me) asked, "Where are you from? You look like a local girl." I replied that I was African American, an anthropology graduate student, and in Hawaiʻi to do research in Waiʻanae. "You don't look African American," the taxi driver said. "You look Hawaiian-Portugee. But, ho, Waiʻanae's rough, it's really, really local."

My experience as a community organizer in Central Harlem, New York City, in the mid-to-late 1980s prepared me to interpret these outsider warnings about the difference of Waiʻanae. In Harlem I learned to suspect academic studies that portrayed poor and working-class communities as socially and biologically pathological (Jackson 2001, 4, 190; Mullings 1996, 78, 117, 165). I learned, also, that the popular and media narratives of fear and loathing about poor communities like Harlem emanated mostly from the (sometimes politically

45

motivated) imagination of outsiders (see Reeves and Campbell 1994). Non-Harlemites imagined all sorts of crime and mayhem lurking on the streets, although for the most part these fearful outsiders had not been there to see for themselves.

But the messages about Harlem as a wild, dangerous place came from within as well. As an organizer, I went door to door through Central Harlem to speak with neighbors about joining forces to improve the conditions of their lives. Many people initially refused to join the community association because they feared their neighbors. People told me, "Everyone around here is on crack." Although it was never the case that everyone was using crack, the single greatest obstacle to building viable tenants' associations was tenants being suspicious of their neighbors.[1] Central Harlem residents internalized the negative messages that emanated both from within and from without, and they allowed these representations to immobilize and shame them (Bourgois 1995, 264; see also Kardiner and Ovesey 1972; Fanon 1963, 1967). When they joined the community association, however, they learned to see themselves and their neighbors in a new light. As Gaventa (1980, 213, 257) argued about power and powerlessness in an Appalachian mining community:

> As actions upon perceived limit situations[2] were successful, more participation occurred, leading to further action. In a concrete situation an interrelationship begins to be seen between participation and consciousness, so that one becomes necessary for the development of the other in the process of community change. . . . The powerless must be able to explore their grievances openly, with others similarly situated. They must develop their own notions of interests and actions, and themselves as actors.

In working collectively, people in Central Harlem began the process of defining themselves.

The experience of being a community organizer in Harlem prepared me to better understand the term *local* from the perspective of Honolulu dwellers. "Local," I gathered, indicated rural/urban, periphery/metropolitan, and lower-class/upper-class distinctions. It carried negative connotations suggesting backwardness, provinciality, and poverty. I eventually understood these stories as warnings that I was about to transgress a fortified border in the imaginary landscape of city folks. Indeed, the most memorable warning came from a self-described kama'āina[3] haole woman. She told me that she had once walked her dog, a black standard poodle, on a beach in Wai'anae. She claimed that a group of "local boys" had hurled insults at her such as, "Haole, go home." She was not so much afraid for herself, she said, as she was for her dog. Earnestly, she said to me, "[They] eat black dogs, you know."[4]

THE MEANING OF "LOCAL"

The meaning of "local" has complicated inflections, rooted in histories of colonialism and capitalism in Hawai'i. "Local" mediates the varied experiences of colonized indigenous Hawaiians, primarily Asian Pacific imported plantation labor,[5] elite haole descendants of the earliest colonizers, and other haole more recently arrived.[6] Recent scholarship has explored the meaning of "local" identity within and against a prolific public discourse on Hawaiian racial harmony (Rohrer 2008), in the context of the marketing of "aloha" by the tourism industry (Ohnuma 2008; Pierce 2004), as a marker of non-haole status, and as a means of stratification within non-haole (and specifically Asian Pacific) populations (Okamura 1990; Labrador 2009).

This literature posits that "local" identity occupies a central position in the experiences of and discourse on race/ethnicity and class stratification. Arguing that colonization and racialization are complementary processes, Rohrer suggests that there are three dominant racial categories in Hawai'i: Kanaka Maoli, locals, and haoles (2008, 1111). "Local" identity emerged from the cultural and political economic experiences of plantation laborers in opposition to plantation owners, and as an amalgam of the Native Hawaiian, Asian Pacific, and European cultures of these workers. Hawaiian Pidgin English developed as the "local" lingua franca of plantation life in the late nineteenth century. It has evolved into what linguists characterize as Hawaiian Creole English, in effect the "local" language of twenty-first century Hawai'i (Romaine 1994, 527–31; see also Warner 2001, 134). Thus "local" works as a mediating category, obscuring either end of the identity spectrum. One on hand, a racial structure built around the "local" naturalizes haole folk as "simply 'one of the tribe' of people living in the islands," and at the same time effaces the violence of colonialism, the (continuing) dispossession of Native Hawaiians, and the political-economic details of white supremacy[7] (Rohrer 2008, 1112–13). As Labrador (2009) noted,

> The elevation of the Local as the mainstream disguises differential access to wealth and power and frames multiculturalism not merely as a political symbol or ideal, but also as the ideological underpinning of everyday social, cultural, political, and economic realities. (289)

The mediating "local" of the Islands' racial structure lends itself to a garrulous public discourse intent on promoting notions of harmonious race relations that thinly disguise Hawai'i's race, ethnic, and class tension. This discourse served the needs of haole advocates of statehood—"to reassure a race-anxious continent that 'the natives' were . . . docile and happy" (Rohrer 2008, 1112). The "aloha"[8] brand, as an iteration of the racial harmony discourse, continues to be useful in the quest for tourists' dollars (Ohnuma 2008, 366, 370; Pierce 2004, 145).

Keiko Ohnuma (2008, 366) argues that the thin veneer of the "aloha" brand further ignores traumatic colonial and labor histories and attempts to "bind a cultural and political entity whose membership is contested." The multiculturalism implied in the fantasy of "aloha" has diverted attention from the glaring racial and ethnic disparities in health and socioeconomic status that mark the reality of Hawai'i, particularly for Native Hawaiians (see chapter 3). According to Ohnuma:

> [A]loha spirit as a state ideology effectively serves to contain or dissipate political resistance . . . [and] inhibits calling attention to the way that certain ethnic groups . . . have fared much better than others. Indeed, melting-pot aloha was the dominant ideology for so many years that is was not until the 1980s that Native Hawaiian activists, political analysts, and sociologists started to quantify the huge gaps becoming apparent between the status of the early Asian immigrants—some subgroups of which now have higher average incomes than whites—and Native Hawaiians, Filipinos and Pacific Islanders. (2008, 374)

Ohnuma's essay explores the difference between the brand "aloha," defined as an empty commodity, which soothes "injury with the layers of hope and myth that constitute the product itself" (Ohnuma 2008, 388), and the Hawaiian term *aloha 'āina*, which "expresses a duty to care for the earth from which the people originate, to reciprocate its support of the people" (379). Ohnuma's work traces the complications of "local" as an identity that forcefully (re)emerges in the years after statehood as a means of resistance by the Japanese and Chinese to the growing influence and control by outsider, mainland whites (375). At the same time, "local" became an assertion of *national* belonging by Asian Pacific ethnic groups in the face of the burgeoning Native Hawaiian sovereignty movement—a movement that highlighted the complicity of Japanese and Chinese immigrants and their descendants in the ongoing oppression of indigenous Hawaiians. Haunani-Kay Trask put it this way:

> Ideologically, the appearance of this "local nation" is a response to a twenty-year-old sovereignty movement among Hawaiians. Organized Natives . . . are quickly perceived as a threat by many Asians uneasy about their obvious benefit from the dispossession and marginalization of Natives. . . . Any complicity in the subjugation of Hawaiians is denied by the assertion that Asians, too, comprise a "nation." In truth, "local" ideology tells a familiar, and false, tale of success: Asians came as poor plantation workers and triumphed decades later as the new, democratically-elected ruling class. . . . [T]he responsibility for continued

Hawaiian dispossession falls to imperialist haole and incapacitated Natives, that is, not to Asians. Thus do these settlers deny their ascendancy was made possible by the continued national oppression of Hawaiians, particularly the theft of our lands and the crushing of our independence. (Trask 2000, 4)

During my fieldwork in Wai'anae I encountered few piha, or "pure" Hawaiians. The vast majority of the people I worked with were comfortable with identities as Native Hawaiians *and* as people who were racially/ethnically mixed. There were no expressed contradictions, and although being piha was highly valued, being mixed did not in any way preclude identity as Native Hawaiian. "Local" was a common self-designation in Wai'anae and a common means of distinguishing outsiders (retirees, vacationers, and the influx of haoles seeking cheaper rents in Wai'anae). The complexities and tensions of "local" identity explored in the literature were not immediately apparent to me. Indeed, in Wai'anae, those who defined themselves as Kanaka Maoli, and many who defined themselves as "local," were engaged in efforts toward decolonization. Perhaps the distinctions were sharper in parts of Hawai'i where there were fewer Native Hawaiians. In Wai'anae, where nearly one third of the population was counted as Native Hawaiian in the 2000 Census, the lines between indigenousness and localness were considerably blurred.[9]

END OF THE ROAD

The status of Wai'anae as "really, really local" and the fears it evoked in Honolulu have grown out of earlier colonial descriptions that portrayed colonized men, particularly, as lazy, undisciplined, and hypersexual (see Tengan 2008, 35, 40). In 1932, racial tensions boiled over after the alleged rape of a white Navy lieutenant's wife by a Native Hawaiian man. The incident, known as the Massie Case, provoked a heated debate between haole leaders in Honolulu, military officials, and journalists writing for newspapers on the continent. Some scholars have argued that the Massie Case intensified "local" identity by forging a collective opposition to haole racism (Yamamoto 1979, 102, cited in Rohrer 2008, 1119). Wallace R. Farrington, former governor of Hawai'i and editor of the *Honolulu Star Bulletin* during the Massie Case, defended Honolulu's racial harmony.[10] Farrington's defense of Honolulu race relations decried the inflammatory and "half-cocked" responses of naval admirals, who apparently condoned the killing of the Native Hawaiian defendant before the trial (Farrington 1932, 4). However, the *New York American* published an editorial that portrayed Hawai'i as a place of great danger for white women:

The situation in Hawai'i is deplorable. It is an unsafe place for white
women outside the small cities and towns. The roads go through jun-
gles and in these remote places bands of degenerate natives lie in wait
for white women driving by. . . . At least 40 cases of these outrages have
occurred, and nobody has been punished. ("Martial Law Needed,"
New York American, January 12, 1932, cited in Wright 1966, 195)[11]

Notice that Farrington was defending the racial harmony of *Honolulu*, while the
New York American editorial attacked rural areas of Hawai'i as being unsafe for
white women. This distinction between the metropolitan and the "local" was
still evident in media accounts of Wai'anae late in the twentieth century.

A 1996 article "The End of the Road," which appeared in *Honolulu Weekly*,
described the environmental degradation of Ka'ena Point, a nature preserve
forming the northwestern border of the Wai'anae Coast. According to the article:

"This has been an area in limbo, so that's why it has been abused," [a
state official] said. Skeletons of rusted out cars, stripped and dumped,
dot the access road. On a recent visit, loose pages from a male nudie
magazine blew along the trail. . . . In the past, people used Ka'ena as a
shooting range, a late-night party spot and a dump for dead bodies. All
of which contributed to Ka'ena's image as O'ahu's Wild West. Ka'ena
was a "lawless wilderness, a no-man's land," says [a longtime resident of
the North Shore, an adjacent area more attractive to tourists on the
eastern side of Ka'ena Point]. (Emerson 1996, 5)

The *Honolulu Weekly* article invoked images of illicit sexuality, criminal "lawless-
ness," and a sense of uncivilized "wilderness." The notion that Wai'anae was "an
area in limbo" implicitly marked it as a space resistant to the civilizing influences
of the modern West. The North Shore critic who described the area as "lawless"
was making an implicit point that Wai'anae was largely outside of the civilized
tourist circuit. The article reiterated and recodified outsider views of Wai'anae as
being savage and dangerous.

Maps of O'ahu in the 1990s show a dotted line along the coast around
Ka'ena, the northwesterly point of the Wai'anae Coast, and the spot mentioned
in the *Honolulu Weekly* article. The dotted line signified a dirt path that most
automobiles could not pass, making it impossible for tourist traffic to circum-
navigate the island. Georgia Rodriguez, a "local" resident of Wai'anae, told me
that during the 1960s an influx of federal dollars through the Model Cities Program encouraged some developers to imagine Wai'anae as a haven for tourists.
The community, which opposed the development, fought to keep the road
unpaved. A road circumnavigating O'ahu would have encouraged an influx of
tourists and other haole outsiders. It would have bypassed the local people, she
said, and further marginalized local identity. Most tourists avoided Wai'anae in

the 1990s, although some came for surfing events at Mākaha Beach, and as part of packaged tours to see the dolphins swim at Mākua.

I did not experience Wai'anae as wild, or dangerous, although like Central Harlem, Wai'anae in the mid-1990s was a poor, working-class community in which the struggle to survive was paramount for many. In a local economy where decent wages were hard to come by, adults often had to work more than one job to pay the rent on time. There was a flourishing trade in illicit drugs, a growing problem of homelessness, and widespread perception that the crime rate was much higher than in other areas of the state. The array of factors taxing the people of Wai'anae also included physical and mental disease, such as substance abuse, diabetes, bipolar disorder, and family violence.

The U.S. military in Wai'anae was a huge presence. Lualualei and Mākua Valleys both contained sprawling military installations that traversed the Wai'anae mountain range. At Ka'ena Point, a naval satellite tracking station and a mysterious, balloon-like structure high in the mountains were oddly juxtaposed with the natural beauty of the nature preserve. In Mākaha Valley the boom of bomb detonations and the rattle of artillery charges were common sounds, echoing off the walls of the mountains. The single bar licensed to sell liquor in the community was known as "Rest Camp," and although open to the public, it was run by the U.S. military.

What I encountered in Wai'anae was a strong sense of local pride and opposition to outside "development" forces. Indeed, the term *local* there was one of honor that signified belonging, fortitude, and self-sufficiency. It evoked roots and pride in the culture and history of Native Hawaiians, and the Chinese, Japanese, Portuguese, Puerto Rican, and Filipino immigrant groups that had come to Wai'anae as plantation labor. "Local" meant easy and relaxed in contrast to the attitude and tempo of nonlocals in Honolulu. "Local" meant a focus on the family, pride in Pidgin-speaking, and in a non-haole identity, elaborately expressed in accountings of intermixed ethnicity down to the level of one sixteenth (as in "I am one half Hawaiian-Chinese, a quarter Portuguese, and one sixteenth Scotch, one sixteenth German, one sixteenth English and one sixteenth Armenian").

This sense of "local" pride and resistance was characteristic of a vibrant cadre of Native Hawaiian leaders dedicated to improving the well-being of the community. They defined their work as "decolonization" and drew on the history of Wai'anae as a geo-political space with a contentious history and culture of resistance to the introduction of foreign ways.

A HISTORY OF RESISTANCE

Contemporary outsider perceptions of Wai'anae as wild and untamable echo depictions of the coast and its inhabitants in history and myth. In the mid-nineteenth century, the people of Wai'anae, under the leadership of Chief Boki, were resistant to the subversion of the traditional Hawaiian religion (see chapter 1), and the insertion of Christianity. Boki was a kahuna lā'au lapa'au (medical practitioner), trained in the art of diagnosis. He was a sandalwood trader, the owner of a sugar plantation, the keeper of a Honolulu brothel, and a political opponent of the Hawaiian elite that increasingly tolerated the intrusion of foreigners. Although he was appointed governor of O'ahu by the Hawaiian king in the early nineteenth century, Boki and his "wife,"[12] Chiefess Liliha, did not support the adoption of the Christian Ten Commandments as the basis of Hawaiian law[13] and refused to privilege Protestant missionaries, preferring instead the Roman Catholic variety of Christians (Kuykendall 1965[1938], vol. 1, 123–25, 141–42; Davenport 1969, 15). Boki and Liliha were reviled by the Protestants and their allies among the Hawaiian elite because they opposed the prohibition on liquor, the ban on gambling, and the law to punish desecrators of the Sabbath. In direct opposition to the law prohibiting the selling of liquor licenses, Boki and Liliha sold such licenses and encouraged "the traffic in rum" (Kuykendall 1965[1938] 1938, 130).

In search of sandalwood, Boki embarked for the South Pacific and died at sea. However, his impact on the people of Wai'anae continued after his death. The association between Boki and resistance to foreign ways, and the threat he posed to the Hawaiian elite of Honolulu, is demonstrated in a story told by Kamakau, one of the earliest Hawaiian historians. According to Kamakau, after Boki had been lost at sea in 1832,

> . . . great excitement was caused by a man from Wai'anae coming into [Honolulu] shouting, "Boki is at Wai'anae . . . with a warship!" The people were in an uproar, some frightened, some pleased. People ran from place to place in their joy. The red dust rose in clouds . . . as natives and foreigners started out on horseback for Wai'anae. The church party who had declared Boki a stinking spirit became like a blunted needle. When messengers and horsemen returned reporting all false, the man was given a hundred strokes with a rope's end . . . for his lying tale. (Kamakau 1992, 301)

Boki's wife, Liliha, staged a failed insurrection against Ka'ahumanu, the ruling chief who instigated the subversion of the 'aikapu. As the daughter of a high-ranking counselor to the ruling family, Liliha had influence, and she used it to indict foreigners meddling in Hawaiian affairs. Ka'ahumanu despised Liliha and spared no effort to discredit her; she charged Liliha with drunkenness and licentiousness and barred her presence from the court of the king. Gathering her allies, Liliha plotted an insurrection against Ka'ahumanu. According to

Kamakau, Liliha spoke to a gathering of insurrectionists, arguing that her name had been slandered:

> Chiefs and people of my Chief, hear me. The stink of my name and that of my husband Boki has spread from Hawai'i to Kaua'i. It is said that we do evil and have led the young king to do evil, and so he has been taken away from me. But we are not guilty; it is the white people and the naval officers who are guilty; it is they who tempted the king; and the blame has been put on me. (Kamakau 1992, 300)

Liliha's rebellion was thwarted, but the people of Wai'anae, according to Kamakau, continued to adore her. When she died in 1839, the common people publicly mourned her passing. "Few of the chiefs were so beloved by the common people as Liliha," Kamakau wrote:

> It is said that never before has there been such lamentation for the death of a chief as on the night she died. . . . Common people loved the name of Liliha, . . . and when she died they tattooed their skins with . . . [her name] as an everlasting memorial of their affection. (Kamakau 1992, 351–52)

Despite the overthrow of the traditional religious system, many Hawaiians, especially in areas remote from centers such as Honolulu and Lāhainā, which were dominated by Euro/American business and missionary interests, continued to worship ancestral deities and the gods and goddesses of the Hawaiian pantheon. And they continued to seek cures from practitioners of Hawaiian medicine. Although Protestant and Roman Catholic churches (along with Buddhist temples that followed Japanese plantation laborers) were established on the Wai'anae Coast, it remained a place remote from the haole influences of Honolulu. It became a harbor of Kanaka Maoli tradition, and a space of "local" resistance.

The people of Wai'anae wept when in 1893 news of the overthrow of Queen Lili'uokalani reached them. A haole plantation owner who had adopted Hawaiian ways plotted a counter-revolution and stored guns and ammunition in Mākaha Valley. McGrath, Brewer, and Krauss (1973), in *Historic Wai'anae*, recorded oral histories of the area, including the words to a mele lāhui (protest song) sung by plantation laborers:

> Famous are the children of Hawai'i
> Standing firmly behind the land
> When the evil hearted messenger comes
> With his document of extortion.

No one will fix a signature
To the paper of the enemy
With its sin of annexation
And the sale of native civil rights.
We do not value the sums
Of dollars of the government.
We are satisfied with stones,
The mystic food of the land.
We back Liluokalani.
She will be crowned again.
Tell the story of the people
Who have loved the land.
                    (McGrath, Brewer, and Krauss 1973, 52)

Noenoe Silva (2004) described the central place of haku mele (composers of music) in the times of ka poʻe kahiko. Haku mele required education, skill, and artistry to produce multivalent works reflecting the "interwoven nature of politics, religion," and poetry in Hawaiian life (183). Haku mele were "responsible for remembering." They transmitted genealogical knowledge that traced the aliʻi "to the birth of the land itself and to the gods" (182). Other mele glorified the divine, celebrated sexuality, and praised the geo-theological or historical significance of certain places. Foreign missionaries (and their descendants) detested the chanting and singing of Hawaiians, especially mele, which celebrated Hawaiian origin stories. According to Silva, "[M]any cosmogonical chants were lost, and the composition of new ones ceased to be part of the nineteenth-century haku mele's profession" (183).

Mele became "a genre of resistance to cultural imperialism" and a popular literary form in the pages of Hawaiian newspapers beginning in 1834 (Silva 2004, 184). Indicative of historical, cultural, and poetic erudition, the compositions conveyed both messages of opposition and signals of cultural and national pride. But the multiple meanings of mele lāhui, which resisted American incursion and celebrated the Hawaiian nation, were obscure to unenlightened haole. Silva suggested that "the understanding by poets and audiences that mele should contain these several levels of meaning made the genre particularly well suited to communicating thoughts and feelings undetected but yet in plain sight of hostile forces. The shared understanding also bound the lāhui (nation, people) together" (2004, 184–85).

After the American coup that removed Liliʻuokalani from power, the queen composed mele as a means of communicating her love and commitment to her people. In the years between the coup and the establishment of the American-controlled territory of Hawaiʻi, "approximately 250 mele lāhui [were] published in the Hawaiian papers" (Silva 2004, 186). While the queen was imprisoned, songs expressing her love for her people were smuggled out to be printed in the newspaper *Ka Maka'āinana*. The mele lāhui of Wai'anae plantation laborers documented by McGrath, Brewer, and Krauss (1973, 52) was one of many composed in response to the queen, as a message of loyalty, solidarity, and the performance of rage (Silva 2004, 187, 190; Stillman 1999, 95). The last line of the Wai'anae mele ("Tell the story of the people/Who have loved the land") was a common theme echoed in the many mele lāhui, communicating love and loyalty between the people and the queen (Silva 2004, 190–91; Stillman 1989, 11, 12, 20).

Despite resistance, "progress" steadily bore down on Wai'anae. A railroad extending out to Ka'ena Point put Wai'anae within the reach of land speculators and other economic developers. On horseback, the forty-mile journey from Honolulu was often interrupted by impassable trails. The steamship that plied the waters between Honolulu and Wai'anae ran only once a week. With the new railroad extension, Wai'anae was an hour and a half from the center of the city. According to McGrath, Brewer, and Krauss, "[D]uring the first week after the rail line opened, the Wai'anae Coast had more visitors than the whole year previously" (1973, 61). But the encroachment of haole business interests, the confiscation of acres of land by the territory of Hawai'i's military, and the diversion of water from subsistence taro farmers to large plantations did not succeed in crushing Hawaiian beliefs and practices. Based on oral histories collected by McGrath, Brewer, and Krauss, Wai'anae Hawaiians persisted in their beliefs.

> Old timer Moses Soares says that "between 1910 and 1912 there lived in the Wai'anae area about 25 kahunas known (only) to the Hawaiians. There was one kahuna above all others. He wore a red malo and a red rag around his head. Once to show the people his power he went to . . . Pōka'ī Bay. Here on the beach with 25 to 50 people watching he built a sand pile around which he wrapped a kowale vine. Upon completion of this, he went into the water and began tapping the water with his hand. He also began chanting at this time. Soon a great number of fish came to him including the great shark of Ka'ena Cave. Women kahunas of the area would go to the beach at night where they would call the shark by name and upon his arrival would feed him with their breasts. As late as 1909– 1914 these women kahunas were still feeding the [shark] this way." (1973, 84)

A REFUGE FOR TRADITION

At the end of the twentieth century, Wai'anae Hawaiians still found meaning in the beliefs and practices of ka po'e kahiko and continued to view the Wai'anae Coast as a refuge of Hawaiian knowledge, traditions, values, and spirituality. The clutter of fast-food restaurants and the traffic on Farrington Highway, the only road in and out of Waiʻanae, made it sometimes difficult to see the persistence of Hawaiian ways. Pōkā Laenui, who was born and raised in Waiʻanae, and was an attorney and a sovereignty movement leader, wrote that "if one observes carefully . . . the continuing spirit of the indigenous people of Hawaiʻi" is evident. Laenui wrote about a celebration and blessing on the occasion of the completion of an ʻōpelu fishnet:

> A group of about 30, age stretching from great-grandparents to toddlers, gathered for the dedication of the fishnet. Kupuna (elder) Kaʻananā stood at the front, leading the ceremony, recalling from as long ago as his childhood, how his *kūpuna* (elders, ancestors) would give thanks to our ancestors' Gods, in the same way we would this day. He . . . recall[s] that we must take this time to remember that we are part of the same creation as everything about us, that as we must respect and treat one another with *aloha*, that the gods within everyone of us are also in all creation. In his prayer of dedication, he calls upon the fishnet to bring good fortune upon its fishing folks, and calls upon us to always keep intact . . . *aloha* for the waters and all of our relations found in and about them. (Laenui 1993b, 14–15)

I heard many stories about the spirituality of Waiʻanae in the present and in the past. A Hawaiian elder, Walter Kaleopono, described Mt. Kaʻala, the highest mountain in Waiʻanae and all of Oʻahu, as a sacred place where the god Kāne draped his golden cloak across the undulating pleats of the Waiʻanae range. Kaʻala is the path of the sun, he said, guardian of the road to the West, a resting place where the souls of the dead prepare to move among the living.

Kaleopono, it should be noted, was a self-professed Christian and a member of one of the coast's largest Protestant churches. His belief in Jesus and in the power of Hawaiian gods and ancestors sat easily side by side and were not for him contradictory. He was deeply critical of "the familiar story of whites invited into Hawaiian churches" who then "take over, kicking out all the Hawaiians." He believed that an intense Hawaiian spirituality had protected the people of the Waiʻanae Coast from the influence of foreigners: "Whenever defenders of the island of Oʻahu were defeated, they gathered in Waiʻanae to sort of regroup and then reclaim the island," he told me. "The gods here are very strong, they protect and care for the Hawaiian people here, they leave a very strong spirit with the people of this area."

With regard to both the mundane and the sacred, from everyday ways of knowing and being to a deep understanding of the potency of mana in the late twentieth century, Waiʻanae Hawaiians in the mid-1990s demonstrated that American colonialism was unsuccessful in stamping out a specifically Hawaiian worldview. But decolonization was not simply a matter of the spiritual. Wai'anae Hawaiians called on their ancestors while they were sharpening their sociocultural and political-economic critiques of neocolonialism. The project of decolonization depended on an ability to challenge present neocolonial realities such as poverty and disease. The challenge meant transcending the limits of Hawaiian culture expressed through a colonial frame. Decolonization consciously, reflectively, and fluidly embraced the practices and epistemologies of the past in order to imagine and construct a future that transcended the limits of colonialism.

TRANSCENDING NEOCOLONIAL LIMITS

But if Wai'anae Hawaiians were looking to the past as a source of wisdom and insight, they did not reject those aspects of Western modernity that facilitated decolonization and enabled the resurgence of a vibrant late-twentieth-century Hawaiian-ness. Laenui and Kaleopono demonstrated the ease with which Hawaiians practiced a fluid hermeneutic so that science, technology, spirituality, and tradition were all possible means for challenging Western power. This fluid epistemology was based upon a dialogic refraction between that which is traditional and that which is modern (Conklin 1997, 712).

There were (and are) a multitude of forces arrayed against the sovereignty movement. One anti-sovereignty strategy involved the notion that the culture of Hawaiians had ceased to exist. An "Anti-Hawaiian Sovereignty [Web] Page" initiated in 1997 argued that the "Hawaiian culture of today is kitsch and fragmented":

> The Hawaiians of today have become . . . totally dissociated from their culture. They are predominantly Christian and therefore have abandoned the culture and values that were intrinsic to the religion of pre-missionary Hawai'i. In addition, they use U.S. currency and vote in U.S. sponsored elections, yet they claim to be a distinct culture deserving a special political/racial status.
>
> In the culture of the State of Hawai'i people who are of interracial descent are very common. People who are 100% Hawaiian have become virtually nonexistent because almost all people living today who are of Hawaiian descent are of interracial backgrounds. (The Anti-Hawaiian Sovereignty Page, accessed at http://www.geocities.com/capitolhill/lobby/4478, March 4, 2008)

The notion that Hawaiian use of U.S. currency or participation in U.S. elections was an indication of the abandonment of culture reiterated a dangerous Western stereotype about "native" changelessness and authenticity. In this stereotype

Western technology was seen as a corrupting force that undermined and erased tradition (Conklin 1997, 711). There are more sophisticated variants on this theme, including works by anthropologists.

A large literature in anthropology explores the "dialectical invention" of culture, and the process of cultural revitalization as cultural creation (see Wagner 1975; Radin 2008[1926]; Linton and Hallowell 1943; Wallace 1957; Linnekin 1991, 1983a; Handler and Linnekin 1984). An essay by Handler and Linnekin (1984) offered the important insight that all tradition, Western and otherwise, is "defined in the present" and never exists outside of contemporary interpretations (288). But the anthropological literature on invention was sometimes turned against indigenous cultural revitalization movements (see Keesing 1991). In an earlier essay, Linnekin (1983b) distinguished between the traditions of rural and urban Native Hawaiians. Her discussion of the rural community of Ke'anae on Maui conveyed the image of a people engaged in organic and dialectical creation of culture according to a fluid conception of tradition. "Tradition," she wrote, "is both lived and invented, as rural Hawaiians conform to their own and others' expectations of what that tradition comprises. The people on the land have a model of Hawaiianness—but it is a changing model" (Linnekin 1983b, 244).

In contrast, however, Linnekin portrayed urban Native Hawaiians under the influence of a "nationalist" intelligentsia staging a cultural revival in which "isolated facts have been transformed into symbols of Hawaiianness and accorded . . . significance without precedent in aboriginal Hawaiian society" (1983b, 244–45). As opposed to the fluid creation of rural Hawaiian culture,

> . . . Hawaiian nationalists look to the rural lifestyle, use it, and idealize it to create a new version. . . . But in their self-conscious adherence to a model of Hawaiianness, the nationalists tend to circumscribe and delimit the range of behavior that conforms to that model. The definition of "acting Hawaiian" takes on a new rigidity; it becomes obligatory, rather than customary. . . . The Hawaiian identity is thus objectified, made into an emblematic icon to be sculpted and consciously emulated. (1983b, 244–45)

But in Wai'anae in the 1990s, the process of decolonization—and not the ideology of nationalism—was the goal. The efforts of Wai'anae Hawaiians to translate tradition into meaningful contemporary practices that moved the process of decolonization forward did not lead to circumscribed and delimited behaviors based on abstract and rigid models of tradition. Instead, Wai'anae Hawaiians understood tradition as a means of expanding the limits of neocolonialism.

The work of Brazilian philosopher and educator Paolo Freire (1989) was influential among key decolonization leaders in Wai'anae. Freire was committed to developing education as a libratory tool for the oppressed. His philosophy of social change and his conceptions of oppression, liberation, and transformation have had an enormous impact around the world, particularly in Latin America and Africa. As a theory of cultural action for liberation, Freire's work has inspired and influenced anti-colonial activists and organizers around the world, and this was true in Wai'anae in the 1990s.

Freire believed that humans are uncompleted beings for whom both humanization and dehumanization were equally possible alternatives. In Freire's view, humanization was the specific "ontological vocation" of men and women (1989, 61). It must be underscored that, for Freire, humanization was neither soteriological nor teleological, but, rather, a continuous process that sought the transformation of social life through critical engagement with the world. As opposed to the notion that the goal of revolutionary struggle was the attainment of a new, less oppressive historical stage, Freire understood the goal to be the continuous transformative process of oppressed humans toward greater human-ity (Blackburn 2000, 6). Colonialism, as well as other forms of oppression, was to be understood as a dehumanizing process that thwarted the yearning for full humanity (Freire 1989, 28). Freire emphasized the vast capacity of humans for creative, critical thinking and the unique ability to transform—and not simply adapt to—reality. He wrote about the struggles of the oppressed with great love and hope, and his work validated the culture of the oppressed, "while at the same time challenging their common sense" in order to transform oppression into a process of liberation (O'Cadiz and Torres 1994, 221).

Perhaps the central concept around which Freire's philosophy is based is the notion of *conscientization*, which refers to the growing ability of the colonized to recognize both their oppression, and the possibilities for making social change—a process that enables "the peoples' transformation into the subject of their own history" (Municipal Secretariat of Education, São Paulo, Brazil, 1992 cited in O'Cadiz and Torres 1994, 210–11).

> [The people] *emerge* from their *submersion* and acquire the ability to *intervene* in reality as it is unveiled. *Intervention* in reality—historical awareness itself—thus represents a step forward from *emergence*, and results from the *conscientização* of the situation. *Conscientização* is the deepening of the attitude of awareness characteristic of all emergence. (Freire 1989, 100, emphasis in original)

Freire conceived of culture as a "thematic universe." Themes were the ways in which the colonized envisioned and embodied their reality. They were educa-tional tools for training the oppressed to think, to rethink, and ultimately to act on reality. They were generative when they "unfolded" into other themes, when they pointed to other problems to be solved. In Freire's view, generative themes were located in "concentric circles" that moved from the general to the particular. "I consider the fundamental theme of our epoch," Freire wrote, "to be that of domination—which implies its opposite, the theme of liberation" (1989, 93). It is this Freirian view of culture[14] that most closely theorizes the use of tradition in decolonization efforts in Wai'anae.

DEBATING TRADITION

During an intermission at the hula show at the Bishop Museum, a Hawaiian woman playing 'ukulele spoke to the audience about "traditional Hawai'i." She was careful to alert the crowd of mainly Japanese and American tourists that she was not a "radical" sovereignty movement activist. "Don't get me wrong," she said, "I'm not one who wants to go back. I like being part of America. Why should we go back to dirt paths, grass shacks and no toilets?"

In *Wretched of the Earth*, Fanon wrote that in the colonial era the colonizer spared no effort to ensure that domination

> convinces the natives that colonialism came to lighten their darkness. The effect consciously sought by colonialism was to drive into the natives' heads the idea that if the settlers were to leave, they would at once fall back into barbarism, degradation, and bestiality. (Fanon 1963, 210–11; see also Rodney 2005[15])

In Wai'anae, the topic of "ancient Hawaiian" versus "modern Hawaiian" culture and lifestyle was a frequent subject of conversation and debate, which indicated how ubiquitous the issue of cultural revitalization had become. As people reconstructed and interpreted their history, both of the past of Hawai'i and of their own lives, questions about the impact and appropriateness of Western technology on Hawaiian culture frequently arose. Some expressed the view that it would be a good thing to live without Western clothes, time, and technology. Indeed, part of the performance of "being Hawaiian" involved an emphasis on traditional techniques such as cooking in an imu (earth oven), wearing malo (loincloths), and practicing low-technology farming, which emphasized the irrigation techniques of pre-European Hawai'i. However, others argued that practicing traditional values did not preclude the uses of modern technology, and that Hawaiian culture was neither static nor moribund. In this view, practicing traditional forms of aquaculture, worshipping Hawaiian goddesses and gods, or using lā'au lapa'au (Hawaiian medicine) did not preclude the use of appropriate Western technologies.

Indeed, middle-class Native Hawaiians with a sense of cultural pride were the target of an advertising campaign by a cell phone company. A television commercial advertising wireless phone service featured a Hawaiian man, in Western dress, driving in a convertible sports car up the Kaiwi Coast of O'ahu. The man grabbed his cell phone and dialed. The scene switched to a Hawaiian man, wearing malo, aboard the Hōkūle'a, a traditional Hawaiian sailing vessel. Standing on the bow, the man held a ringing cell phone in his hand and answered ("Aloha") the call of the man in the convertible. Designed to attract the business of middle-class Hawaiians, many of whom are involved in the "Hawaiian cultural renaissance," the advertisement reassured potential mobile phone consumers that there was no conflict between satellite technology and Hawaiian tradition. While the advertisement may be understood as representing Hawaiian culture for commercial purposes, it also reflects the view of many Hawaiians who do not view the blending of modernity and tradition as problematic. Indeed, in the mid-1990s, the activists and professionals with whom I worked in Wai'anae were wired. E-mail and faxing were essential tools for communicating across town, across the islands, and across the Pacific to the continent. Many of the people I worked with owned pagers, cellular phones, and portable and hand-held computers.

DEFINING DECOLONIZATION

In much of the public conversation about "being Hawaiian," there was a persistent lament for the cultural expressions of "ancient Hawai'i." The lament, which can be heard in Hawaiian music, poses a disjuncture between Western and Hawaiian culture, and can also be understood as a passive form of subversive commentary on the West (Scott 1990, ch. 6). But the impulse to understand Hawaiian cultural revitalization as movement "back" to "ancient" times was viewed as problematic by community leaders in Wai'anae. Pōkā Laenui, the leading Wai'anae theorist of decolonization in the 1990s, posited the stages of decolonization necessary in order for Hawaiians to achieve sovereignty. Laenui argued that colonization requires that indigenous people go through a process in which the colonizer's denial of the validity of indigenous culture is accompanied by indigenous people denying and withdrawing from their culture. Although the process of colonization, according to Laenui, proceeded through stages of eradication and denigration, the final stages involved a co-optation of indigenous culture into the epistemological framework of the dominant society, and an exploitation of indigenous cultural practice for "commercial, artistic or political value" (Laenui 1993a, 1–2).

In Laenui's schema, there are five stages of decolonization: (1) rediscovery and recovery; (2) mourning; (3) dreaming; (4) commitment; and (5) action (1993a, 2). The final stages of colonization blend easily with the initial stages of decolonization, creating the possibility that the recuperation of Native culture is subverted by foreign frameworks.

One of the dangers in this phase is the elevation of form over substance, of dealing with a traditional culture from the perspective of a foreign culture. . . . This danger may include those who have taken on the trappings of their "traditional" culture, wearing forests of leaves and flowers on their heads, speaking the indigenous language which they learned at colonial colleges, and otherwise playing the foreigner's concept of the indigenous person, especially those able to speak in evening news sound bites and who may present pleasing images to still and movie cameras. Theatrics which make good media clips could eventually substitute for substance. (1993a, 3)

Laenui echoes Fanon, who argued that Native intellectuals who drape themselves in "culture" are in fact behaving like foreigners. The culture of the intellectual, in Fanon's view, was nothing more than a "stock of particularisms," or the "outer garments" of culture that diminished the substance of the people, "teeming and perpetually in motion" (Fanon 1963, 223–24). The intellectual, in Fanon's view, is dazzled by "mummified fragments,"

which because they are static are in fact symbols of negation and outworn contrivances. Culture has never the translucidity of custom; it abhors all simplification. In its essence it is opposed to custom, for custom is always the deterioration of culture. . . . When a people undertakes an armed struggle or even a political struggle against a relentless colonialism, the significance of tradition changes. (Fanon 1963, 224, emphasis added)[16]

Laenui told me that it was wrong for Hawaiians to act as though the culture had ceased to develop after the arrival of Captain Cook, and that the idea that Hawaiians should unreflexively adopt the ways of "ancient times" was a colonial fabrication lending credence to the notion that Hawaiians and Hawaiian culture were extinct. The substance of Hawaiian culture had continued to evolve, Laenui argued, albeit often in response to colonial oppression.

Fanon argued that "the people who take destiny into their own hands assimilate the most modern forms of technology at an extraordinary rate" (1963, 9). Laenui's pragmatic approach to the revitalization of Hawaiian culture included the use of appropriate Western technologies. Indeed, to quote Nandy, Laenui supported the notion that the "tradition of the reinterpretation of traditions [can] create new traditions" (Nandy 1983, xvii). Laenui argued that Hawaiian culture continued to develop along with the introduction of reading and writing, electricity, telephones, and so on.

In a series of public lectures on Hawaiian history open to the public and held in the Wai'anae Mall, Laenui turned the "gift of civilization" theme on its head by asserting that foreign technologies should be seen as culturally specific enhancements to Hawaiian life. Foreign missionaries were the ones who transliterated the Hawaiian language into the English alphabet and built the first printing press. But if, on one hand, books can be viewed as a foreign technology, Laenui argued that when appropriated by Hawaiians, books and the love of learning became a central feature of Hawaiian culture.

CROSSROADS AND KĪPUKA

Waiʻanae contained the largest concentration of indigenous people in the Hawaiian archipelago, and Native Hawaiians were the numerically dominant racial/ethnic group on the coast.[17] In some respects, Waiʻanae was a center for Hawaiians from other islands and other parts of Oʻahu. A longtime Waiʻanae resident, who was born on Molokaʻi, remarked that "Waiʻanae is like the Honolulu to the other islands." People came to Waiʻanae to search for employment and affordable housing, and because of the ties of kinship and culture.

During the mid-twentieth century, when Hawaiʻi was transformed from a third-world colony into the fiftieth state, Native Hawaiians and other "locals" who were displaced by development pressures often migrated to Waiʻanae. In the years before statehood, clusters of neighborhoods characterized as slums encircled Honolulu. Theon Wright described the conditions in the parts of Honolulu where "tourists were seldom taken," as "slums . . . filled with strange smells and muddy streets and small frame houses that were little more than shacks. . . . This part of Honolulu had become a conglomeration of poverty, vice and disease" (Wright 1966, 17–18). Urban renewal (or slum removal) was a precondition for the transformation of Honolulu into a modern, cosmopolitan center, as it was for cities in the continental United States (see Fullilove 2005; Saunders and Shackelford 1998). I often heard stories of the forced removal of Hawaiians and other working-class people from the areas around Aloha Tower Marketplace, Tripler Hospital, Honolulu International Airport, and the Kakaʻako Industrial Area.

Hokuokalani Sussex, a poet, teacher, and sovereignty movement leader in Waiʻanae, remembered the circumstances of her family's move to Waiʻanae in the late 1950s:

> . . . *[M]y family was very nomadic, typical of urban Hawaiians who move from place to place. And, how we got to Waiʻanae, was that Waiʻanae was one of the places where people moved to who were not welcomed in or could not find housing anyplace else. There was a place called Damon Track, it was Hawaiian Homelands . . . and it was a ghetto. . . . It was where the Honolulu International Airport is right now. . . . There were a huge group*

of Hawaiians who lived there . . . and then . . . they evicted everyone to
build the airport. A lot of us from Damon Track moved to Waiʻanae. . . .
Part of the reason why we moved to Waiʻanae is that my grandmother had
owned those Quonset huts and was renting them and so we became one of
the renters along with my mother's sisters, who had also moved to the area.
(Interview with Hokuokalani Sussex, January 7, 1997, Waiʻanae,
Hawaiʻi)[18]

In rural places on the "outer" islands, subsistence livelihoods played a crucial role
in the survival of Hawaiian culture. But Waiʻanae was a semi-suburban, semi-
rural space on the immediate periphery of Honolulu. Farrington Highway was
the only public road in Waiʻanae that connected with Honolulu and the rest of
the Oʻahu. The highway hugged the coastline and was punctuated by Burger
Kings, McDonalds, Taco Bells, and convenience stores. Near the highway, several suburban-style tract housing settlements, built on lands specifically set aside
for Native Hawaiians, contrasted with the rural scene in the upland valleys. In
the valleys of Waiʻanae, where families still lived in Quonset huts (sold by the
military as surplus after World War II), the land was zoned for agriculture, and
the fragrance of basil and plumeria competed with the odor from cow barns and
piggeries.

While some of the Hawaiʻi literature has focused on the survival of traditional indigenous culture in rural Hawaiian communities, less has been written
about the tactical use of tradition in less rural places, and about the creation of
traditionally informed modern practices. In my use of the term *tactic* I am following De Certeau (1988[1984]), who argued that while *strategies* are produced
by subjects with will and power in the interests of mastery, *tactics* were the
weapons of the weak. Colonizing Hawaiʻi, in a Certeauian sense, required "the
power of knowledge . . . , [the] ability of the [colonizers] to transform the uncer-
tainties of history into readable spaces." Tactics, on the other hand, were calcu-
lated actions "determined by the absence of a proper locus" (36, 37).

> The space of the tactic is the space of the other. Thus it must play on
> and with a terrain imposed on it and organized by the law of a foreign
> power. It does not have the means to keep to itself, at a distance, in a
> position of withdrawal, foresight, and self-collection; it is a maneuver
> "within the enemy's field of vision," . . . and within enemy territory. . . .
>   It must vigilantly make use of the cracks that particular conjunc-
> tions open in the surveillance of the proprietary powers. It poaches in
> them. It creates surprises in them. It can be where it is least expected. It
> is a guileful ruse. (1988[1984], 30–37)

The question of survival was a key issue for Hawaiians as a group, whose health
and well-being were tenuous. Native Hawaiians in the 1990s had higher inci-

dences of heart disease, cancer, and diabetes than any other of the Islands' ethnic groups. Hawaiian young and elderly males had higher suicide rates than others, and rates of child abuse and neglect, substance abuse, crime, and other social and psychological disorders were high. Some Native Hawaiian health and social welfare professionals in Wai'anae believed that chronic depression, alcoholism, drug addiction, and family dysfunction were expressions of despair. In this view, the loss of culture and the disenfranchisement of Native Hawaiians on a structural level ramified into disease and despair on the level of the individual and of the family.

Luciano Minerbi, a professor of urban planning at the University of Hawai'i-Mānoa, has argued that the "[i]ndividual self-esteem of Native Hawaiians is linked to personal identity, sense of place, and an ability" to recognize nature and spirit in the landscape (Minerbi 1994, 27). This "strong sense of place" is a legacy of modern Hawaiians, which Minerbi argues, can form the basis of therapeutic and healing processes that will perpetuate the culture, inculcate a positive worldview, and prepare Hawaiians for the continuous assault of "the alien, Western world." Similarly, Davianna McGregor, professor of ethnic studies at the University of Hawai'i, Mānoa, posits that "[r]ural communities where Hawaiians have maintained a close relationship to the land through their subsistence livelihoods have played a crucial role in the survival of Hawaiian culture" (McGregor 1996, 12). Minerbi and McGregor argue that "[p]ristine conditions of the natural environments allow Hawaiians to experience place therapy," and that without the careful preservation of the natural world, there can be no Hawaiian culture (Minerbi, McGregor, and Matsuoka 1993, 5).

McGregor uses the metaphor of kīpuka to describe those spaces within neo-colonial society in which Native Hawaiian culture has survived, and as an analogy for how such traditional culture can be revitalized elsewhere. Kīpuka describes a natural phenomenon in the volcanic rainforest.

> Botanists who study the volcanic rainforest have observed that eruptions [of lava], leave oases of native trees and plants called *kipuka*. From these natural *kipuka* come the seeds and spores for the eventual regeneration of the native flora upon fresh lava. Rural Hawaiian communities are cultural *kipuka* from which Native Hawaiian culture can be regenerated and revitalized in the contemporary setting. Protection of the natural resources and the integrity of the lifestyle and livelihoods of the Hawaiians in these rural districts is essential to the perpetuation of Hawaiian culture. (McGregor 1996, 14)

The few Hawaiian communities that have "survived the onslaught of post statehood (1959) development," include (according to McGregor 1996, 15) the islands of Moloka'i and Ni'ihau, the districts of Hāna and Kahakuloa on Maui, the districts of Ka'ū, Puna, and other small communities in Kona on the island of Hawai'i, Kekaha and Anahola on Kaua'i, and Hau'ula, Lā'ie, and "sections of the Wai'anae Coast" on O'ahu. McGregor argues that these cultural kīpuka were traditional centers of spiritual power that were geographically isolated and did not suffer the presence of permanent missionary stations until much later than more accessible locales. Thus "Hawaiian spiritual beliefs and practices persisted . . . without competition, for a longer period of time. As Christian influences entered these areas, they coexisted with traditional beliefs and practices" (1996, 15).

But the theory that the pristine natural conditions preserve Native Hawaiian culture rests upon a notion that elides the dynamism of Native Hawaiian cultural expression in less than perfect natural surroundings. Military installations, housing developments, and general suburban sprawl circumscribed indigenous people's access to the land and the ocean and to the sacred spaces and places of healing and refuge. For many in Wai'anae, connection to the earth was a privilege and a struggle. Affected by both the dangers and opportunities of the Westernized, urbanized center of Honolulu, Wai'anae was also perceived as a sacred place of refuge where the creation and recreation of Hawaiian values and visions were actively taking place. The role played by a committed group of leaders was crucial. The mass resurgence in Hawaiian cultural and political awareness depended upon the ability of leaders committed to decolonization to marshal a variety of resources (traditional and otherwise) to make being Hawaiian meaningful in a neocolonial context.

It was precisely this sense of Wai'anae as a crossroad between "local" and Western culture and values, between the job opportunities and the cosmopolitan nature of Honolulu and the emphasis on Hawaiian tradition in Wai'anae, that created a strong dynamic for cultural revitalization and decolonization. In contrast to rural Hawaiian communities on other islands, Wai'anae could be described as a border zone or crossroads, in Renato Rosaldo's sense, because it was "a zone of difference within and between cultures" (1993, 20). Hawaiian culture thrived there not only because the area was remote for the first 100 years of colonization, but because proximity to the metropolis generated new opportunities and required new skills for survival. Wai'anae was both a crossroads and a kīpuka.

Mahealani Kamau'u, a Native Hawaiian activist and poet, argued that she was

> . . . a product of Hawai'i that is completely mixed. My mother is Hawaiian, and my dad is full-blooded Spanish. I have friends from all ethnic groups. . . . [W]e Hawaiians are not stuck in a time warp where only the past is authentic. . . . Look, my mother rode the backs of sea turtles in Hilo where she was born. She lived this way as a girl. But when she moved to Honolulu, she evolved. She loved the music of the

Dorsey Brothers, danced the boogie woogie, got a city edge. Why should she have stuck to someone's idea of an ancient Hawaiian? (in Caraway 1996)

Leaders in Wai'anae who were committed to decolonization transposed and mediated categories of tradition and represented them to a marginal population of Native Hawaiians in a framework that included appropriate Western technologies. Organizations like Ho'o Mōhala, the Native Hawaiian substance abuse treatment center, renewed the meaning of traditional healing practices by deploying them as therapeutic modalities in a framework of clinical practice. According to de Certeau, the colonized

> insinuates [herself] into the system imposed on [her]. . . . [She] superimposes them and, by that combination, creates for [herself] a space in which [she] can find *ways of using* the constraining order of place. . . . Without leaving the place where [she] has no choice but to live and which lays down its law for [her], [she] establishes within it a degree of *plurality* and creativity. By an art of being in between, [she] draws unexpected results from [her] situation. (de Certeau 1988[1984], 30, emphasis in original)

In the imaginariness of some outsiders and in media representations, and by data-driven socioeconomic and health reports, Wai'anae was a zone of "local" culture, and a scene of poverty, disease, addiction, crime, and dysfunction. But there was an alternative reading and writing of Wai'anae, one linked to dreams of decolonization and the recreation of a viable Native Hawaiian nation. In these alternative readings, Wai'anae was a refuge, a space outside of "America," a mecca for Hawaiians in recovery from disease and colonialism, a place where the maintenance of sobriety is closely linked to the recovery of Hawaiian culture. In opposition to the narratives of crime and poverty, Wai'anae intelligentsia, community activists, and a cohort of behavioral health professionals engaged in creating the means for healing and decolonization.

3

MANA

What the Data Hide

. . . [R]esistance to the strangulation of our people and culture is interwoven with a celebration of the magnificence of our nation: the lavish
beauty of our delicate islands; the intricate relationship between our
emotional ties to each other and our ties to the land; the centuries-old
ways of caring for the ʻāina, the kai, and, of course, the mana that is
generated by human beings in love with and dependent upon the natural world. (Trask 2000, 52; see also Trask 1993, 117–18)

In a world dominated by myths of empiricism, fact, of course, is synonymous with truth. (Obeyesekere 1992, 98)

This chapter explores the health status of Native Hawaiians in the late twentieth century, the conditions that produced the diseases affecting them, and
the reinterpretations of the facts of Native Hawaiian morbidity and mortality
from an epistemology of decolonization. The beliefs and practices of Native
Hawaiians were not extinguished by American history, Western science, politics,
religion, or capitalist economics. The descendants of ka poʻe kahiko endured.
They survived the deadly epidemics that occurred in the midst of American colonization. They persisted through lethal narratives that portrayed their history,
culture, language, and society as diseased and degenerate and that belied their
strengths and ability to overcome. In the late twentieth century, a burgeoning
sovereignty movement and an intense focus on cultural revitalization and decolonization demonstrated the potent mana of a people determined to thrive.

THE EXIGENCY OF MANA

In 1677, in *The Primitive Origination of Mankind*, Sir Matthew Hale, a seven-teenth-century English legal scholar, illuminated the Christian principle of dominion over nature derived from Genesis 1:28 in the Hebrew Bible.[1]

> In relation to this inferior World of Brutes and Vegetables, the End of Man's Creation was, that he should be VICE-ROY [*sic*] of the great God of Heaven and Earth in this inferior World; his Steward . . . of this goodly Farm of the lower World, and reserved to himself the supreme Domination, and the Tribute of Fidelity, Obedience, and Gratitude, as the greatest Recognition of Rent for the same, making his Usufructuary of this inferior World to husband and order it, and enjoy the Fruits thereof with sobriety, moderation, and thankfulness. (cited in Black 2006, 94–95)

While theories about the meaning of nature injunctions in the Judeo-Christian-Islamic tradition have been contested (see Kay 1989; Faber 2004), it is clear that *in practice* the meaning of dominion was well expressed by Hale. The god of the Hebrew Bible's injunction for dominion resulted in exploitation, plunder, and death of the natural world. David Abulafia's (2008) *The Discovery of Mankind* makes clear that Hale's definition of "this inferior World of Brutes and Vegeta-bles" included the humans that Europeans discovered beginning in the fifteenth century. According to Abulafia, there were "great scholastic debates" in Christen-dom about the "right to dominion of non-Christian peoples" (308). The debate was settled by the Spanish, who decreed that "it was right [for Christian Euro-peans] to claim dominion in lands inhabited solely by primitive people's."[2] In the Pacific, the British demoted "the Aborigine's territorial sense" and claimed it as a "*terra nullis*, a vast no-man's-land." They "treated the Aborigines as wild beasts, extirpating completely the native population of Tasmania" (312). For the most part, Abulafia noted that "greed for material resources . . . pushed aside any sense" that the people inhabiting the land that Europeans desired were "rational, sentient human beings with rights" (312).[3]

The practice of dominion and its results can also be understood through the lens of biology. Marxist scientists Richard Lewontin and Richard Levins (2007) described the relationship between dominion, conquest, capitalism and health. "Waves of European conquest," they argued, spread infectious disease. The destruction of forest lands fueled by the profit motive "exposes us to mosquito-borne, tick-borne, or rodent-carried diseases." The agro-capitalist imperative for monocultures of grain feed rodent populations, "and if the owls and jaguars and snakes that eat the mice are exterminated, the mouse populations erupt with their own reservoirs of diseases." Development projects mortgage lives and health in the Global South. The building of enormous hydroelectric dams and canals for irrigation, for example, "spread snails that carry liver flukes and allow mosquitoes to breed" (Lewontin and Levins 2007, 19).

This Western concept of dominion, and its political-economic and biological effects, is in stark contrast to the Polynesian concept of mana. As I discussed in the Introduction, mana is an indigenous ontology based upon notions of reciprocity, kinship, and love between gods, human beings, and the land (Kameʻeleihiwa 1992, 31; Shore 1989, 142; Valeri 1985, 99). Mana is more than a theory; it is an exigent cosmological practice that in the times of ka poʻe kahiko was the source of health, vitality, and abundance for humans and the land. For ka poʻe kahiko, a thriving world was the co-creation of divinity, humanity, and nature understood as indivisible and inalienable, as "mystically one and the same" (Kameʻeleihiwa 1992, 31).

Scholars of mana have recognized the centrality of the concept of ʻai (usually translated into English as to eat, to feed, to consume), and of its elaboration in the term *ʻāina* (land, sea, earth) in Hawaiian cosmology. In translation, the English words "food," "eat," and "land," however, do not begin to approach the multivalent depth of the cluster of Hawaiian concepts centered on ʻai. Valeri (1985, 104) used the term *commensal* as way to translate the meaning of ʻai. Commensal is defined as an adjective, with three meanings: "eating together at the same table"; "(of an animal, plant, fungus, etc.) living with, on, or in another, without injury to either"; and as a sociological term that connotes a person or group "not competing while residing in or occupying the same area as another individual or group having independent or different values or customs."[4] "Eat," in contrast, means to "take into the mouth and swallow for nourishment," and to "consume by or as if by to devour gradually."[5] There is a vast conceptual distance between ʻai and "eat," and between concepts of commensality and consumption, that clearly marks differences in ontology and practice. These distinctions reflect the "incompossibility" (Dimakopoulou 2006; Deleuze 1998, 60–66) of "dominion" and mana.[6]

In order to understand mana and its relevance to Hawaiian healing and health in the late twentieth century, it is imperative to focus on commensality as the most appropriate English translation of the Hawaiian root word ʻai. Shore's (1989) analysis also recognized the dearth of meaning in the English concept of "eat," and he argued that such notions as ripening and reproduction were inextricably bound to the concept of mana. I reiterate two of Shore's key points here: mana "bears a special relationship to the . . . sources of human life: food and sex" (Shore 1989, 139, 165; see also Firth 1940, 505; Firth 2004[1936]); the society of ka poʻe kahiko was an "economy of *mana* in which generative powers were appropriated, channeled, transformed and bound" (Shore 1989, 140–41, 143; see also Perrett and Patterson 1991, 193). Thus for ka poʻe kahiko the source of vitality, abundance, and health depended upon the ubiquity of mana.

Despite centuries of Western demotion of indigenous knowledge (see Rappaport and Overing 2000, 279), mana remained an ontological exchange between ka poʻe kahiko and their late-twentieth-century descendants. This sustaining knowledge, this recognition of the "reciprocal codetermination" (Lewontin and Levins 2007, 12) of all living things, is an exigency of the health of Native Hawaiians and is a foundational goal of decolonization. Colonialism in Hawaiʻi was (is) an injustice that occurred in the political-economic and sociocultural realms. But the injustices—the trauma of land dispossession, political disenfranchisement, and changes in agricultural production and diet, as well as the community-wide disorientation that ensued from the enforcement of foreign practices and ideologies—were not experienced only as formal, abstract, and structural. The effects of these processes were etched deeply onto the bodies and souls of the colonized. The long-term effects of colonialism and neocolonialism on the health and well-being of Native Hawaiʻi in the late twentieth century meant that reclaiming mana was urgent.

MANA MISCONSTRUED

At the turn of the twentieth century, the effects of 200 years of colonialism and neocolonialism in Hawaiʻi were evident in the health status of Native Hawaiians. Native Hawaiians had higher rates of morbidity and mortality from chronic and infectious disease when compared to other ethnic groups in the Islands and in the United States as a whole. This maldistribution of disease and disparity in health was a visible, bodily manifestation of centuries of colonial rule and of the ongoing neocolonial oppression of Native Hawaiians.

There is a stark contrast between the lyric descriptions[7] of Hawaiʻi that flow from the mouths and pens of Native Hawaiians and the portrait painted by foreign academics in history and anthropology. Puanani Burgess, a Waiʻanae decolonization leader in the 1990s, and a poet and professor of urban and rural planning, described this gap in a poem called *Face to Face*.

> Face to Face
> That's how you learn about what makes us weep.
> Face to Face
> That's how you learn about what makes us bleed.
> Face to Face
> That's how you learn about what makes us feel.
> what makes us work.
> what makes us sing.
> what makes us bitter.

what makes us fight.
what makes us laugh.
what makes us stand against the wind.
what makes up sit in the flow of power.
what makes us, us.
Not from a distance.
Not from miles away
Not from a book
Not from an article you read
Not from the Newspaper
Not from what somebody told you
Not from a "reliable source"
Not from a cliff
Not from a cave
Not from your reality
Not from your darkness
But,
Face to Face
Or,
else,
Shut tight, your mouth
The top of the cliff isn't the place to look at us; come down here
    and learn of the big and little current face to face.
And come and help us dig, the loʻi,[8] deep.
    (Burgess 1993, xi–xii)

Burgess's poem underscores the foreignness of Western (mis)understandings of Hawaiian ways of being and knowing. Similarly, in her essay "From a Native Daughter" (1993, 147–59), Haunani-Kay Trask wrote of patterns in Western writing about Hawaiʻi in which "[o]ur ways were inferior to those of the West, to those of the historian's own culture" (152).

> Suddenly the entire sweep of our written history was clear to me. I was reading the West's view of itself through the degradation of my own past. When historians wrote . . . that we were superstitious, believing in the mana of nature and people, they meant that the West has long since lost a deep spiritual and cultural relationship to the earth. . . .
>
> For so long I had misunderstood this written record, thinking it described my own people. But my history was no where present. For we had not written. We had chanted and sailed and fished and built and prayed. And we told stories through the great blood lines of memory: genealogy. (Trask 1993, 153–54)

But it is not only interpretive disciplines such as history and anthropology that misconstrue Hawaiian life. Other disparaging narratives about Native Hawaiians are generated by the collection, analysis, and dissemination of health and social statistical data by governmental and academic centers. Although seemingly straightforward and noncontroversial in describing the true conditions of Native Hawaiian lives, the discourse of the statistically real results is a bleak representation of Native Hawaiian life. Whose truth is told by the statistically real? And for what purpose?[9]

A STATISTICAL PORTRAIT OF NATIVE HAWAIIANS

In his essay "Poetry and Knowledge," Aimé Cesairé (1990, xlii) argued that while science produced a certain impression of the world, it was "summary and superficial."

> Physics classifies and explains, but the essence of things eludes it. . . . As for mathematics, what eludes its abstract and logical activity is reality itself. In short, scientific knowledge enumerates, measures, classifies, and kills. But it is not sufficient to state that scientific knowledge is summary. It is necessary to add that it is *poor and half-starved*. To acquire it mankind has sacrificed everything: desires, fears, feelings. . . . An impoverished knowledge, I submit, for at its inception—whatever other wealth it may have—there stands an impoverished humanity. (Cesairé 1990, xlii)

Cesairé insisted that poetry was "born in the great silence of scientific knowledge." While science allowed humans "to utilize the world," it was knowledge "[g]nawed by hunger, the hunger of feeling, the hunger of life" (1990, xliii). Cesairé's work in "Poetry and Knowledge" warns us that statistical portraits, counting, and classification are limited means of understanding humanity.

A destructive narrative emerges from the marshaling of socioeconomic and health data about Native Hawaiians. In this discourse the Hawaiian "race" is held in comparison to other "races" and ethnicities in an abstract, ahistorical and depoliticized field based on the logic of quantity. The people inhabiting the Islands of Hawai'i are viewed as a "population," an aggregate of decontextualized individuals, detached portions of a whole. The dynamic social relations of colonialism, indeed, of Western modernity, are reduced to that which can be expressed by a ratio of integers. The physiological and sociological condition of Hawaiians is compared statewide with Chinese, Filipino, Japanese, and white groups. The statewide data also are compared to whites, blacks, American Indians, and Alaskan Natives, and Asian or Pacific Islanders on the continent. The meaning of socioeconomic and health data is also obscured by comparative practices and criteria of inclusion through which racial and ethnic groups are bounded. In regard to Native Hawaiians, some statistical data distinguish between "pure" and "part" Hawaiian on the basis of ancestry, while some data are based on respondent self-report. Some federal data are based on the category "Pacific Islanders" that does not distinguish the groups that form this category,[10] although Native Hawaiians, at 38.3 percent, form the largest group among Pacific Islanders. Before the 2000 U.S. Census, Native Hawaiians and other Pacific Islanders were grouped with Asian Americans for data-collecting purposes.

According to the Office of Hawaiian Affairs, in 1992 Native Hawaiians comprised 19.3 percent of the state's total population and numbered 220,747 out of a total population of 1,140,859. On many indicators measuring health and socioeconomic condition, Native Hawaiians were clearly disadvantaged. Levels of food insecurity, illiteracy, the prevalence of tobacco use, and rates of incarceration were high among Native Hawaiians based on data collected in the mid-1990s to 2000. Areas such as Waimānalo and Waiʻanae—communities with significant Native Hawaiian populations—had the highest percentage of individuals in the state of Hawaiʻi living in food insecure households, at 36.2 and 33.2 percent, respectively (Kent 2003, 1). Native Hawaiian men (at 42 percent) and women (at 34 percent) had the highest smoking rates in the state (Lew and Tanjasiri 2003, 765; Glanz et al. 2003, 296). Thirty percent of Native Hawaiian adults were counted among those described as functionally illiterate (Murphy 2002). Native Hawaiians were the largest ethnic group behind bars: at 39 percent, Native Hawaiians comprised the majority of inmates in Hawaiʻi adult correctional facilities, and Native Hawaiian youth had arrest rates (at 38 percent) higher than all the other ethnic groups in the state (Office of Native Hawaiian Affairs [OHA] 2002, 27–29).

The data also were grim in regard to income, financial capabilities, and other economic factors affecting Native Hawaiians. Native Hawaiian families with minor children had the lowest mean family income (at $55,865) than all other ethnic groups in the state, and nearly 16 percent lower than the statewide average of $66,413. For Native Hawaiian families headed by single mothers with minor children, median family income (at $19,530) was $700 lower than the national average of $20,284 (Kanaʻiaupuni et al. 2005, 2). Native Hawaiian families tended to be larger than the state averages (3.4 individuals per household compared to 2.9 in the statewide average), thus comparatively low incomes supported relatively greater numbers of individuals within Native Hawaiian families. Per capita income, a measure of individual income, gives a clearer picture of the economic condition of Native Hawaiians. In 2000, Native Hawaiian per capita income was $14,199—the lowest among all state ethnic groups, less than half of the per capita income for non-Hispanic whites (at $30,199) and nearly

35 percent lower than statewide per capita income (at $21,525) (4). Furthermore, when figures are adjusted to reflect Hawai'i's cost of living, which is among the highest in the United States, the adjusted per capita income of Native Hawaiians was $13,386—substantially lower than per capita income for the United States as a whole and for other groups in the state (Kana'iaupuni et al. 2005, 6).

Based on 2000 U.S. Census data for the state of Hawai'i (which are not adjusted for the high cost of living), the largest percentage of individuals living below the poverty line were Native Hawaiian. More than 16 percent of Native Hawaiians had income below the poverty line in 1999, compared to 10.7 percent of the statewide population (Kana'iaupuni et al. 2005, 6–7). Furthermore, Native Hawaiian poverty rates have increased at an annual rate of 4.3 percent since 1979 (Naya 2007, table 1).

Evidence from the mortgage industry has indicated that even Native Hawaiians who have achieved a middle income have more difficulty securing loans for home purchases, and when they do, they have less equity than whites. Middle-income Native Hawaiians were twice as likely to receive subprime mortgages as middle-income whites. Thus the ability of Native Hawaiians "to build wealth through homeownership" was negatively impacted by the prevalence of high-interest lending that diminished homeowner equity (National Community Reinvestment Coalition [NCRI] 2006, 1, 29). Data from the 2004 U.S. Census indicated that about half of Pacific Islander households lived in owner-occupied homes, compared to nearly three quarters of non-Hispanic white households. For the half of the Pacific Islanders who lived in rental housing, median rental payments, at $805 a month, were substantially higher than for non-Hispanic whites, at $694 a month (U.S. Census Bureau [UCB] 2007, figs. 14, 15).

Given the inequities in wealth generated through homeownership and the high median rents of Native Hawaiians and other Pacific Islanders, it is not surprising that homelessness was a growing problem. In 2000, Native Hawaiians accounted for 29.8 percent of the homeless, second only to whites, who comprised almost 41 percent of the homeless (OHA 2002, 35). Based on utilization data from state-run homeless programs providing temporary shelter in 2006, Native Hawaiians were disproportionately represented among the homeless. "Caucasians" were the most frequent users of the programs, at 29 percent, followed by Native Hawaiians, at 26 percent. However, when the Native Hawaiian group is coupled with the "Other Pacific Islander" group, Pacific Islander people comprised nearly half (49 percent) of those receiving state services. Native Hawaiians were the single largest group receiving state-funded outreach services for the homeless, at 44 percent[11] (Center on the Family 2007, 4, 9).

In terms of education, Native Hawaiians earned 11.7 percent of degrees and certificates awarded by the state's university and community college system.

However, nearly half of the degrees earned by Native Hawaiians were at the certificate of achievement and associate degree levels (OHA 2002, 23). Only 15.2 percent of Native Hawaiians had completed at least four years of college, compared to 42.5 percent of non-Hispanic whites (OHA 2002, 24).

Based on data from 2000, the morbidity and mortality rates of Native Hawaiians were shockingly high compared to the rest of state and to the United States as a whole. Native Hawaiians had the highest morbidity and mortality and the highest age-adjusted mortality rates of all of the groups in the Islands. Native Hawaiians had the shortest life expectancy, the highest rate of infant mortality, and a rising incidence of low-birth-weight babies. Native Hawaiians had the highest age-adjusted mortality rate from heart disease, diabetes, asthma, and cancer (Anderson et al. 2006, 1779; OHA 2002, 16). According to the U.S. Office of Minority Health Disparities, Native Hawaiians were 2.5 times more likely to be diagnosed with diabetes than non-Hispanic whites, and they were more than 5.7 times more likely to die from diabetes than whites. Native Hawaiians had an asthma rate that was twice the rate for all races in Hawai'i.

The Native Hawaiian infant mortality rate was 60 percent higher than for whites in the state. Native Hawaiian women were twice as likely as whites to begin prenatal care in their third trimester or to receive no prenatal care at all (OMH 2007). After African American and Alaska Native women, Native Hawaiian women have the highest total cancer incident rates in the United States, and the cancer rate among Native Hawaiians of both genders is among the highest in the world (Glanz et al. 2003, 9).

What does this tragic litany of data tell us about Kanaka Maoli? What is obscured by this portrait of the statistically real? Beyond the structures of hierarchy that define the condition of Native Hawaiian lives, and beyond the effects of clear and persistent disadvantage, what do all of these data convey? James Scott's work in *Seeing Like a State* (1999) helps explicate the cultural work of socioeconomic and health data. Statistical realism is a form of macro-analysis ultimately imbricated with the Western nation-building project of high modernism. It is a muscular form of apprehending and mapping reality that abjures the primacy of social relations, local ways of knowing, and the specific textures of situated lives. It creates society as a rational object that can be manipulated toward perfectibility through interventions in "every nook and cranny." And in place of what is perceived as the inferior knowledge of the primitive, science is posited as the route to a superior social order (Scott 1999, 92). Statistically, realist visions are about fixing organic bodies. They are not meant to challenge the structures that create disparity or heal the wounds of colonialism. Health, understood simply as the absence of disease, is a marker of success in the United States. Being diseased is a sign of the inability to practice the quintessential American values of "self-control, independence and productivity" (McMullin 2005, 810). The conspicuous focus on Kanaka Maoli morbidity

and mortality statistics shifts attention away from neocolonial social relationships toward "'unhealthy' [personal] behaviors . . . lack of self-control and failure to progress" (811).

In the logic of Western science and medicine, Hawaiian disease rates are
viewed as unquestioned indicators of physical, emotional, sociocultural, and
racial pathology. But as sociologist Tukufu Zuberi (2001) has argued, it is the
interpretation of statistical results—the underlying causal theory—that renders
statistical models useful analytic tools. The problem with social statistics as they
are commonly deployed is that statistical methods are upheld as the strength of
the analysis, although it is causal theory that makes statistical data meaningful
in the first place. Arguing about the use of health statistics on African Americans, but equally applicable to Native Hawaiians, Zuberi asserted that statistical
data collected on racial groups confound race as a process of social and political
classification, with race as a biological or demographic reality (2001, 105). And
it is not just race as a process of hierarchical classification that is obscured in the
common usage of biostatistics but also the social relations of colonialism and
differential access to basic resources that produce and exacerbate Native Hawaiian disease.

AWAKENING THE KNOWING BODY

Native Hawaiians have developed other theories about what makes them sick.
Their explanatory models of health and disease are epistemologically distinct
from causal models in biomedicine and even in social epidemiology. Beyond a
focus on pathology originating in the organic body, and beyond the analytics of
race, class, and gender in social epidemiology, Native Hawaiians offer a particularly indigenous critique of health and disease in Western societies. From this perspective, the etiology of disease can be located within Western modernity itself.

Native Hawaiian understandings of health and disease index aspirations for
cultural integrity, sovereignty, and decolonization. But this epistemology is also
fundamentally rooted in Native Hawaiian ways of knowing and being, in the
mana cosmology, and traditions of ka po'e kahiko, and in the subsequent history
and memory of a colonized people. Although it was demoted by the West, the
epistemology of Native Hawaiians is both prior to and parallel with Euro/Amer-
ican knowing. The fierce resurgence of this epistemology through the cultural
and political work of the sovereignty movement at the turn of the twentieth century demonstrated the visceral and spiritual connection between ka po'e kahiko
and their late-twentieth-century descendants.

In an interview with Kalama Liu, a Native Hawaiian social worker, I asked
for an explanation of Native Hawaiian health and disease.

From my father's side . . . we can document [our genealogy] back only to a point, and then from there . . . I see as parallel or equal to the written documents are the stories that are told. We are a people who are very proud of our ability to remember history through the spoken language . . . [On] my father's side [we go] back to Maui. . . .

I think it's a combination of things. We have adopted unhealthy foreign ways, [like] smoking and eating the wrong foods. . . . [W]e have moved away from the foods that our bodies for seventeen centuries lived off of, that we have become very accustomed to, that our bodies know—ma'a [accustomed] to certain types of food, and our body is able to digest that. We have moved away from that, and have taken up high salt, high sugar, high fat diets. I really believe that, because I feel better when I eat like more Hawaiian, traditional Hawaiian foods. I'm not only feeding my body, I'm feeding my soul. I'm nourishing all those parts of me, and for me that feels pono [good, upright, moral], feels good. And that is pono. (Interview with Kalama Liu, March 11, 1997, Wai'anae, Hawai'i; see also McMullin 2005, 814)

In this view an imaginary Hawaiian body/spirit flows across seventeen centuries, a body that spent eons growing accustomed to taro, sweet potato, breadfruit, lū'au leaf, fresh fish, and limu, a body with a soul that must also be fed. I use the word "imaginary" here to evoke a sense of illusory, immaterial, and dreamlike bodies, and not to imply that Liu's understanding is fabricated, fantastic, or unreal. From the first people in Hawai'i nei (this beloved Hawai'i) down to current generations, this imaginary Hawaiian body encompasses Western time. Although the colonization of Hawai'i severely impacted Hawaiian bodies, Liu's notion implies that Hawaiian bodies remember history and custom, that Hawaiian bodies "know." Indeed, Liu's notion implies that even colonial subjugation could not erase the memory of the knowing body. The short, 200-year span of imposed Westernization, in this narrative, is poised against the eternity of seventeen centuries, a time of cultural imperialism against an infinitude of custom, practice, and memory. In some sense, then, the Hawaiian cultural revitalization movement is about awakening and nourishing the knowing Hawaiian body/soul.[12]

As noted earlier, the Hawaiian sense of deep familial interrelation with the environment is foreign to dominant Judeo-Christian-Islamic religious tradition in the West, and it is this sense that explains aloha 'āina (love of the land), ea o ka 'āina (the life force of the land), and the sense of spiritual awe that the 'āina evoked in Hawaiians at the turn of the twentieth century. Minerbi (1994) wrote that "Native Hawaiians . . . perceive nature, plants, animals and rocks as sentient, divine and ancestral forms. . . . Nature is not only conscious, much of it is divine" (103). To understand the Native Hawaiian critique of Western models of health and disease it is useful to begin with the issue of food and its connection to life and the land. The kalo (taro) plant plays a central role in Native Hawaiian life, both as a means of nourishment and as a metaphor for kinship, origins, and belonging. In the cosmology of Hawai'i, the origins of kalo are the origins of humanity. In the late twentieth century, Wai'anae Hawaiians expressed their reverence for kalo in a cookbook written for those who were engaged in returning to more traditional diets. The cookbook tells the mo'olelo (story) of Hāloa:

> . . . [W]hen there were only the heavens and the earth, Wākea (sky father) kept watch over the heavens and Papa (earth mother) ruled the earth. Through the mating of Wākea and Papa, a keiki [child] was conceived. This keiki was stillborn and put to the earth in the eastern corner where the sun shone first on each new day.
>
> Soon a strange plant sprouted from the spot where the keiki had been buried. Its broad green leaves grew on long stalks that swayed in the breeze. They named this first born keiki kāne [man child] "Hāloanaka" because of its naka (quivering) leaves and hāloa (long) stems. The kalo continued to grow, producing many offshoots . . . until the kalo was bountiful in Hawai'i.
>
> Another child was later born and he was named "Hāloa" after his older brother. He has many . . . children and his descendants are the kānaka maoli [Hawaiian people, or indigenous people].
>
> A strong bond holds the kānaka maoli to the kalo. Ka po'e kahiko say that it was the will of God that Hāloanaka was born first, for he provided the necessary food for all those who came later. (Wai'anae Coast Comprehensive Health Center 1995, 10; see also Handy and Pukui 1972[1958], 80)

As Pukui (Handy and Pukui 1972[1958]) described in *The Polynesian Family System*, the centrality of kalo was evident in the terms 'āina and 'ohana (family). 'Ai, as discussed earlier, signifies commensality, eating, and food (as well as "rule"; see p. xx). 'Ai also refers to the paste made from the starchy root of the kalo, known as poi, which was the staple food in Hawai'i before the arrival of the Europeans.[13] Embedded within the Hawaiian word for "land" ('āina) is the source of sustenance, a concept that was foreign to Westerners who viewed land as the source of profit. Kalo is propagated by means of 'ohā (or sprouts) that form along the root of the plant. According to Pukui:

> The planter breaks off and transplants the 'oha. As the 'oha or sprouts form the parent taro . . . serve to propagate the taro and produce the

staple of life, or *'ai*, on the land (*'ai-na*) cultivated through generations by a given family, so the family or the *'oha-na* is identified physically and psychically with the homeland (*'ai-na*) whose soil has produced the staple of life (*'ai*, food made from taro). (Handy and Pukui 1972[1958], 3–4)

In this Hawaiian view, the natural, spiritual, and human worlds are irrevocably enmeshed in a relationship of mutuality and reciprocity. The gods and ancestral spirits are evoked and incarnated in and through the 'ai and the 'āina. Nature, too, is alive, conscious and divine. Identity, kinship, and place are then thoroughly interconnected. The vitality of each individual is transmitted genealogically, but kinship is also established through substances that dwell in the land. Kinship is about blood, but it is also about land. According to McGregor (1996, 16), who conducted research on the persistence of traditional customs and practices in late-twentieth-century Hawai'i, "[T]he land is not a commodity to [Hawaiians]. . . . The land is a part of their *'ohana* and they care for it as they do the other living members of their families."

In the late twentieth century, poi was served in Native Hawaiian homes and at community, political, and cultural events. Poi was sometimes eaten in ritual silence as a sign of respect for an elder brother, and it was very much perceived as an expression of cultural pride. But poi had become a commodity, manufactured in factories and sold in grocery stores. I spent two hours in a Wai'anae grocery store one day waiting for the distributor to restock the empty poi shelves. By the time the distributor arrived, a crowd of fifteen or so shoppers had gathered, waiting for the delivery. Because the demand for poi exceeded the supply, prices were high compared to other staples such as rice and potatoes, and restrictions were often placed on the number of bags of poi that each customer was allowed to purchase. "You see," one woman remarked, "we got plen'y rice, plen'y potatoes, but even though poi is the traditional food of Hawaiian people, here in Hawai'i we got to wait in line for poi."

The wait for poi in the grocery store contrasts with the plethora of local and transnational fast-food outlets that line the main road in and out of Wai'anae. Like many low-wealth people in the continental United States, poor and working-class people in Wai'anae eat a lot of junk food. McDonalds, Burger King, Kentucky Fried Chicken, and Taco Bell line the main road in and out of town. Some locally owned, independent food shops compete with the corporate stores by serving a "plate lunch"—two scoops of white rice, macaroni salad in mayonnaise, and (often fried) meat or fish. Although poi was scarce, and although community-run farming projects grew kalo and tilapia, they were not in a position to meet community-wide demand. As in the continental United States, Wai'anae was caught in the tentacles of the transnational food industry that, as Eric Schlosser (2001) noted in *Fast Food Nation*, provided tasty but nutritionally and environmentally suspect sustenance, produced by an underpaid and overexploited workforce.[14] According to Schlosser:

> Hundreds of millions of people buy fast food every day without giving it much thought, unaware of the subtle and not so subtle ramifications of their purchases. They rarely consider where this food came from, how it was made, what it is doing to the community around them. They just grab their tray off the counter, find a table, take a seat, unwrap the paper and dig in. The whole experience is transitory and soon forgotten. I've written this book out of a belief that people should know what lies behind the shiny, happy surface of every fast food transaction. They should know what really lurks between those sesame seed buns. (2001, 10)

In his discussion of the lack of a uniquely American cuisine, Mintz (1996) noted that in the late twentieth century Americans frequently ate fast food, ordered takeout, and used prepared and packaged foods "which required intense heat or nothing at all to be 'cooked'" (117–18) when eating at home. And, despite the garrulousness of public discourse on healthy eating, the major sources of calories in the U.S. diet were "whole and low-fat milk; white bread, white flour, rolls, and buns; soft drinks, margarine, and sugar; and ground beef and American cheese" (118). In 1993, Americans spent 6 percent of per capita income buying food at restaurants and only 7.2 percent for food eaten at home (119).

Similarly, Schlosser (2001) noted that three hamburgers and four orders of french fries were consumed weekly in the typical turn of the twentieth-century American diet. Reflecting a glorification of technology and an uncritical faith in science, the fast-food industry had created fundamental changes in the way human beings eat. As Schlosser argued:

> A fast food kitchen is merely the final stage in a vast and highly complex system of mass production. Foods that may look familiar have in fact been completely reformulated. What we eat has changed more in the last forty years than in the previous forty thousand. (2001, 7)

In Hawaiian cosmology, both humans and nutritional food share the same origins, the same substance. Indeed, the primogeniture of kalo, illustrates mana, in Trask's (2000) exquisite definition, as the dependence and love between humanity, divinity, and sanctified land. What happens to genealogical lines when transnational corporations are the source of nutrients? What mana dwells in a Whopper™ with cheese? From the perspective of Hawaiian cosmology, one that informs an epistemological critique of Hawaiian health in the late twentieth century, the danger of ingesting fast food is not simply about sodium, fat, and fiber content and the risk of physical degradation, but about cultural and spiritual extinction, since being Hawaiian depends upon nurturing the body with food produced on ancestral lands, within the relationship defined by mana.

FOOD, HEALTH, AND HAWAIIAN BODIES

There is a substantial epidemiological literature in the West that examines the link between nutrition and the risk of disease. Studies have found an inverse relationship between diets high in vegetables, fruits, whole grains, fish and poultry and the onset of coronary heart disease (Hu et al. 2000, 912; Menotti et al. 1999, 507; Kromhout et al. 1985, 1205); between diets high in calcium, magnesium, vitamin K, fiber, fruits and vegetables and lower blood pressure levels (Ascherio et al. 1996, 1065; Massey 2001, 1875; Appel et al. 1997, 637); and between the ingestion of foods high in fiber and dietary magnesium and low in fat and lower risks of diabetes (Gittlesohn et al. 1996, 541; Franz et al. 2002, 148–98; Meyer et al. 2000, 921). Cancer risk also has been linked to food and nutrition. A landmark 1981 study estimated that 35 percent of U.S. cancer deaths were attributable to dietary factors (Doll and Peto 1981; see also Willett 1995, 165). High levels of fat consumption were associated with elevated risk of breast, colon, prostate, and other cancers (Willett 2005, 233). Epidemiological research also has linked the introduction of store-bought and processed foods and a decline in traditional indigenous diets to an increase in obesity and diabetes in indigenous populations in Canada (Gittlesohn et al. 1998, 542) and the United States (Ravussin et al. 1994, 1067).

Native Hawaiians were the focus of a study in 1991 linking nutrition and improved health, and specifically linking a traditional Hawaiian diet to reduced risk. "The Wai'anae Diet Program" was a community-based intervention that measured the impact of a diet based on traditional Hawaiian foods that were low in fat, high in complex carbohydrates, and moderate in protein on blood pressure, blood glucose, cholesterol level, and weight. The program menu consisted of foods

> available in Hawai'i before Western contact, such as taro (a starchy root-like potatoes), sweet potato, yams, breadfruit, greens (fern shoots and leaves of taro, sweet potato and yams), fruit, seaweed, fish and chicken. All foods were served either raw or steamed in a manner that approximated ancient styles of cooking. (Shintani et al. 1991, 1648)

Twenty Native Hawaiians ages 25–64[15] were enrolled in the study for a period of twenty-one days. Study participants were required to eat breakfast and dinner at the study center kitchen and dining room that had been set up at a local clinic. The evening meal was accompanied by health and cultural education sessions. Lunches were prepared and premeasured in containers to be taken away. Participants were scored on a daily basis on a hunger-satiety scale and were told to take as much as they liked. They were encouraged to "eat more and take enough snacks so that they would be fully satisfied" (Shintani et al. 1991, 1648). An integral part of the program was the incorporation of cultural concepts that "emphasized spirituality, group outreach, and informal interactional styles (Hughes et al. 1996, 1562).

The results of the study included lowered serum cholesterol levels, significant declines in both systolic and diastolic blood pressure, "a striking decrease" in serum glucose levels, and weight loss (Shintani et al. 1991, 1648–49). The study report concluded that a traditional Hawaiian diet administered *ad libitum* (at the discretion of the participant) was an "effective approach in the treatment of obesity and associated cardiovascular disease risk factors in the population of Native Hawaiians" (Shintani et al. 1991, 1650).

The Wai'anae diet study confirmed what Native Hawaiians already knew: Native Hawaiian food was critical for Native Hawaiian culture, health, and well-being. The results, which were published in an academic medical journal, gave scientific authority to indigenous knowledge. Joined with indigenous ontologies, science earned the potential to become an allied epistemology that opened doors to government resources for further research and programmatic interventions. The data from the Wai'anae diet study were driven by a causal hypothesis that questioned the health efficacy of a modern, Western diet. In this case, the data supported anti-colonial critiques that rooted the disease of Hawaiians in the conditions of colonialism and neocolonialism. Thus data derived from scientific methods supported Native Hawaiian understandings of health and disease and healing methods based on Hawaiian spirituality and connection to the land. Indeed, studies of Native Hawaiian health,[16] which emphasized traditional foods and culturally appropriate healing methods, influenced efforts to promote "community-based participatory research" and "cultural competency" in leading U.S. government and private health research agencies, including the U.S. Department of Health and Human Services and the Kaiser Foundation (see Oxendine 2000; "Compendium of Cultural Competence" 2003).

The science of studies, like the Wai'anae diet, had clear political implications that supported the notion that Native Hawaiian health depended upon Native Hawaiian political power (see Blaisdell 1995; Casken 2001). In an interview, Rachelle Kino, a Native Hawaiian health researcher, explained to me the importance of the Wai'anae diet:

> *Well it is interesting; the evolution of a race as far as their dietary evolution. . . . So, European races apparently metabolized white potatoes just*

fine, whereas Hawaiians get fat on 'em. We can't do that [eat white pota-
toes]. We need other starches in order not to raise our glucose levels, or
whatever the science of it is. . . . *There was that whole thing on the Pima*
Indians . . . where they put them back on their traditional diet and people
lost hundreds of pounds and diabetes went away. . . . They mobilized,
they stabilized and their health improved, *and this was just eating basi-*
cally roots and things that their ancestors ate. That is what their bodies had
evolved to metabolize, it just doesn't do it on pinto beans and fry bread and
the other stuff that the government gives out. (Interview with Rachelle
Kino, December 18, 1996, emphasis added)

In Kino's explanation of why the Wai'anae diet works for Hawaiians, what
emerges as key is not "the science of it" but the ways in which "dietary evolution" traces back to ancestors. When Kino cites the Pima Indians as an example
of a certain kind of dietary evolution, what is important is that "they mobilized
[and] stabilized and their health improved." Indeed, political mobilization is key
to Native Hawaiian health, and a focus on health was clearly articulated as a critical arena of struggle within the sovereignty movement.

Native Hawaiian health activism has resulted in a number of laws and programs specifically designed to improve health and increase Native Hawaiian representation in the health care and social work professions. Beginning in 1973,
the University of Hawai'i-Mānoa School of Social Work's Health Careers
Opportunity Program provided financial assistance to Pacific Islander students.
Between 1973 and 1988, one tenth of each class was comprised of Native
Hawaiians. In 1988, the U.S. Congress passed the Native Hawaiian Health Profession Scholarship Program to increase the number of Hawaiian health professionals in federally designated Health Professional Shortage Areas.

In 1986, the few Native Hawaiian faculty and graduates of the University of
Hawai'i's Schools of Medicine and Public Health formed an association of
Native health workers called E Ola Mau (in English, "Live On"). E Ola Mau
members were active in providing the U.S. Congress with some of the final language for the Native Hawaiian Health Care Acts of 1988 and 1992. Among
other significant features of the 1988 and 1992 Acts was language providing for
"maximum participation by Native Hawaiians" in programs to raise the health
status of indigenous Hawaiians "to the highest possible level"; the establishment
of Native Hawaiian health centers to receive federal funding for health promotion, disease prevention, and primary care; and the provision of services by "traditional Native Hawaiian healers, cultural educators and outreach workers as
well as Western-trained health practitioners" (Blaisdell 1992, 140–41). While
the licensure system for kāhuna lapa'au (traditional medical practitioners) was
terminated in 1965, E Ola Mau was determined to assist traditional healers to
reemerge and to organize themselves in a professional association that would

ensure the involvement of traditional medicine in the healing of Native Hawaiians (Blaisdell 1993, 141).[17]

As a result of the acts, Papa Ola Lōkahi was formed as a ten-member board comprised of representatives from several organizations concerned with Native Hawaiian health[18] and representatives of community-based health centers. Under the direction of Papa Ola Lōkahi, an island-wide system of community-based health was established with centers on each of the islands, with funding from the U.S. Public Health Service. While the Native Hawaiian Health Care Acts established that it was U.S. policy to provide "all resources necessary," only $2.3 million was appropriated annually. In practice, this meant that the Papa Ola Lōkahi systems have been unable to achieve coverage in every Native Hawaiian community. Furthermore, the congressional staff report accompanying the act "blamed Hawaiian health problems on Hawaiians, claiming that they did not control their own obesity, smoking and drinking. . . . [The report] faulted Hawaiians for avoiding doctors until it was too late—a behavior typical, the report said, of Americans with low incomes" (Hartwell 1996, 159).

Dr. Kekuni Blaisdell, a respected physician, became an activist after working on the 1983 Federal Native Hawaiian Study Commission. Born in 1925, Blaisdell is a graduate of the Kamehameha Schools and the University of Chicago Medical College. He spent many years in the United States as a professor of pathology at both Duke and Chicago universities, and he was the founding chair of the Department of Medicine at the University of Hawai'i's School of Medicine. In 1961, he was appointed chief hematologist with the Atomic Bomb Casualty Commission in Hiroshima and Nagasaki, Japan (Blaisdell, in Dougherty 1992, 184).

Blaisdell, who advocated Hawai'i's total independence from the United States, argued that Hawaiian morbidity and mortality were an "embarrassing irony . . . (1993, 117) after a century of United States rule in a land that was touted in 1990 to be the healthiest state in the nation and a model in cost-effective health care delivery." He argued that Native Hawaiians were "being suffocated by more than 860,000 non-kānaka, with whites from the U.S. burgeoning" (117). Analyzing the grim data about the health status of Native Hawaiians moved Blaisdell to search for the ontology of the epidemic of chronic diseases affecting Hawaiians. He concluded that Hawaiians were more diseased because they are "victims of depopulation . . . [and] . . . continuing exploitation" (118). In Blaisdell's view, the clash between enforced Western culture and traditional Kanaka Maoli ways resulted in despair and self-destructive behavior for Hawaiians. The relentless and coercive cultural assimilation of Native Hawaiians was evident in the commercialization of Kanaka Maoli culture.

> While the native culture requires spiritual and physical interaction with the environment, the aboriginal people are currently without a single,

wholly functional ahupua'a.[19] Freeways have destroyed and desecrated heiau (sacred space). Other sacred sites have been bombed by the U.S. military. Water for taro gardens has been diverted to hotels and golf courses. Military installations, commercial enterprises and resort marinas have replaced shoreline fishing grounds. (Blaisdell 1993, 146)

The disturbing trends in Hawaiian morbidity and mortality in the 200 years since contact with the West convinced Blaisdell to reject the notion of ethnopluralism. His views were unequivocal:

There are Hawaiians who support the concept of Hawai'i as an ethnopluralistic society. That is a setting in which each ethnic group is respected and had equal opportunity in socioeconomic mobility. The fault there is that the system and its rules are not the result of equal input by each ethnic group, but are instead the imposed input of the controlling Western society. That means there is "equality" only for those who play the haole (white, foreign) game. Unfortunately, the haole game is one of money making materialism, individual exploitation of others and the destruction of the environment.

Such slanted games not only do not respect us as the indigenous people of Hawai'i, living in our homeland, but they degrade us as a people. Moreover, they perpetuate our oppression in our daily thinking and behavior as individual native Hawaiians. Many kānaka maoli are so de-Hawaiianized and Westernized that they are afraid and ashamed to be kānaka maoli. (Blaisdell 1982)

The link between Native Hawaiian political powerlessness, poverty, and disease and the relationship between shame and colonialism are central lessons informing processes of decolonization. At the end of the twentieth century, Native Hawaiians struggled with hunger, homelessness, and joblessness, along with diabetes, heart disease, and cancer. In Wai'anae, a cohort of leaders sought to mobilize the community by involving them in projects that addressed both their immediate needs as well as the larger issues of power, decolonization, and sovereignty. Hokuokalani Sussex was in 1997 the executive director of the 'Ōpelu Project, a community economic development organization focused on backyard aquaculture. I asked her to explain to me the connection between health and decolonization. She said that what drew people into larger political processes were not political theories about oppression. In poor communities like Wai'anae, she said, projects and programs based on the question "Why can't we feed ourselves, why can't we heal ourselves, why can't we?" encouraged involvement.[20] She said that political activism and the language of "issues" often obscured what was most important. Issue words such as racism, injustice, and oppression "masked" the simple reality of "My babies only have the worst food." For Sussex, a focus on health and food held the potential of bringing even the most marginal, especially Native Hawaiian, women into the political process, because, she said, "Food . . . [and] health . . . so touch the lives of everyone."

The data purporting to describe Native Hawaiian life efface the mana of a people determined to survive and to reclaim the traditions and worldviews of their ancestors. In reinterpreting the data from an epistemology of decolonization that privileged Native Hawaiian cosmology and meaning, Hawaiians of Waiʻanae were deeply engaged in processes that demonstrated how Hawaiian ways of being and knowing—Hawaiian culture, language, and self-determination—were imperative for Hawaiian life (perhaps all life) in the twenty-first century.

4

THE STENCH OF MAUNA ALA,
COLONIALISM, AND MENTAL HEALTH

In the mid-twentieth century, a woman named Mauna Ala "became crazed with the pain of being unable to be Hawaiian in her Hawaiian land" (interview with Mauna Ala's daughter 1997). She was institutionalized in the Territorial Hospital for the Insane and eventually died there. The establishment of a modern, rationalized mental health system followed annexation by the United States in the early twentieth century. It was guided by European theories of heredity, notions about the superiority of Western civilization, and the *inherent* imperfectability of non-Europeans. Colonial psychologists treated Mauna Ala as if she were socially deviant and mentally inferior. Her story illustrates how the mental health care system in much of the twentieth century served colonial interests to the extreme detriment of Hawaiians. It was not until 1976, when the U.S. government found the state of Hawai'i to be in violation of the Civil Rights Act, that a space opened to allow for the possibility of treating Hawaiians in culturally specific and appropriate ways.

ORIGINS

According to Western sources, the origins of Hawaiian history lie in the drama that culminates in the "unification" of ka pae 'āina and the founding of a nation-state (see Anderson 1865, 37; Ellis 1979[1825], 11; Kuykendall 1965[1938], 47). In these narrations, Kamehameha's army lands at Waikīkī, and with little resistance from the forces of the O'ahu Chief Kalanikūpule, advances up through Nu'uanu Valley. Kalanikūpule's army is forced to retreat (the army is said to have "fought stubbornly") up over the mountain cliffs known as the Pali. Some of Kalanikūpule's men escape by climbing down the mountains, and "some were simply tumbled over the *pali* . . . and dashed to destruction on the rocks below" (Kuykendall 1965[1938], vol. 1, 47). In this mythic battle, the possibility for the existence of ka pae 'āina is disposed, enabling history to proceed toward the telos of a modern nation-state called Hawai'i.

The foundation upon which the nation-state would rest was complete following Kamehameha's victory at Nu'uanu. The influence of foreigners who arrived with regularity beginning in the late eighteenth century was a signal factor in these battles. Indeed, in the battle at Nu'uanu, European weapons played a decisive part. Kamehameha's army had small cannons taken from an American ship, along with small-caliber guns. Kalanikūpule had only muskets. With the advantage of superior Western weapons and British war council, Kamehameha succeeded in winning the war and uniting ka pae 'āina under his lineage (Davenport 1969, 14, 17, 18; Seaton 1974, 195). Thus Europeans and Americans who sought trade relations had the foundations of what they comprehended as a state, an entity with which they could conduct commercial and other forms of intercourse.

As an official history, the *one* that circulates as *the* certain truth, and that valorizes the West, the story of Kamehameha implies an inevitable progress toward Western civilization. But as scholar Linda Tuhiwai Smith has argued, such official narratives are "mostly about power . . . [about] the powerful and how they became powerful, and then how they use their power to keep them in a position . . . to dominate others." They are, Smith argues, denigrating displacements of Polynesian origin stories that represent them as descendants of "sky and earth parents" and examples of the systematic exclusion of Natives from the writing of legitimate history (Smith 1999, 33–34).

The story of Mauna Ala, which follows, is an example of an alternative rendering of the history of mental health care in colonial Hawai'i. It is important that stories like these be told, because they demonstrate that, although there are few written histories that challenge colonial narratives, under the radar of official discourse, anti-colonial and oppositional stories are circulated. Kaomea (2006, 335) has argued that Hawaiian women in particular have "engaged in veiled communications" that expressed their anti-colonial views through "hidden references and double meanings." Native Hawaiian women, she wrote, "became the secret keepers of missionary-outlawed [knowledge]."

THE STENCH OF MAUNA ALA

My mother was a brown-skinned Hawaiian woman: big nose, big hips, big feet. My mother's name was Mauna Ala. She was named after the pu'u [hill] where Kamehameha waged a battle against the warriors of O'ahu. After the battle of Mauna 'Ala, the defeated warriors retreated up the Pali and died by hurling themselves over the cliff. As a result of the battle, Mauna 'Ala was saturated with blood and carnage. The stench of Mauna 'Ala was powerful.

My mother did not fit the mold. . . . She was one of the few Hawaiians that went to [an elite school for newly rich Japanese and Chinese]. . . . She was a scholarship student and she did well, won awards. And my mother was the one who really encouraged the intellectual in me. And life was always chaotic in my household because of who she was. . . . My father always appeared to be so passive, he's the Japanese person, really passive, and my mother led the way in everything. She led the way in stability and she led the way in instability. . . . And it was the most intense way of growing up with someone who is sick and well intermittently, and experiences those conditions intensely. When my mother was sick, when she was mentally unstable, she was really unstable, and when she was well, she was really well and really there.

My mother, Mauna Ala, when she died she was 45. She was a woman who became crazed with the pain of being unable to be Hawaiian in her Hawaiian land. She died in the state mental hospital. (Interview with Mauna Ala's daughter, 1997)

The daughter of Mauna Ala, the teller of this tale, was a poet, a writer, and a sovereignty movement leader, and one deeply engaged in the creation of possibilities for decolonization. She employed the English language with poetic precision and craft and was well versed in Hawaiian language and history. These things are important to consider, because Mauna Ala is not the name of a hill upon which the battle at Nu'uanu was waged. Rather, Mauna'ala is a mausoleum located in the highlands of Nu'uanu Valley, where all of the Hawaiian monarchs from the colonial era, except for Kamehameha, are interred. The mausoleum's name—"Mauna'ala"—means fragrant mountain (Pukui et al. 1974, 148), and it is not a reference to a stinking, blood-soaked battlefield. The meaning of the historical site and the recollection about a woman named Mauna Ala who was rendered insane are discordant, but it is in these inconsistencies that the suggestion of a heterodox interpretation that challenges the official, colonialist history of Hawai'i lies. In the storyteller's memory of Mauna Ala as a Hawaiian woman, who was both intelligent and insane, traces of the daughter's struggle can be found, "the way the handprints of the potter cling to the clay" (Benjamin 1968, 92).

It is impossible to imagine that the storyteller was not aware of the mausoleum, and the meaning of its name. It is likely that in telling the story she chose to transpose the meaning of the entombment of nineteenth-century Hawaiian monarchs into the site where the first battle of modern Hawai'i was waged. And, it is likely that she deliberately reversed the notion of a fragrant mountain into that of a stinking, blood-soaked hill.

Mauna Ala's daughter told this story to me in an unstructured interview. Given the context of a non-Hawaiian anthropologist attempting to "collect data" about Hawaiian health in colonial and neocolonial times, the transposition of "facts" and the reversals of meaning take on a certain relevance. It did not at first occur to me that the story of Mauna Ala was not based on historical fact. I assumed that it was, and that the story expressed an oppositional view of the historical transformation of ka pae 'āina into the Hawaiian nation. My discovery that there was no *historical* hill named Mauna Ala intrigued me, and I came to understand that the story's transpositions were deliberate. Jennifer Noelani Goodyear-Ka'ōpua (2005, 321) posited that the "production of genealogical knowledge" cannot be understood within the modernist Western dichotomy of fact or fiction. She argued that "Kanaka Maoli have consciously used genealogical narratives in struggles for power, both between Kanaka Maoli and against foreign imperial encroachment." I came to understand the story of Mauna Ala as a form of genealogical knowledge that led me to a more profound understanding of the impact of colonialism on Hawaiian history and Hawaiian health (see also Smith 1999, 145, 146; Spivak 1988, 103–104).

Walter Benjamin described storytelling as a process through which the experiences of the storyteller are transferred to the listener, because "[i]n every case the storyteller is a [wo]man who has counsel for" her audience (Benjamin 1968, 86, 87). The story of Mauna Ala weaves Hawaiian history and familial remembrance into a tale that conjures a conjunction between the insanity of a mid-twentieth-century Hawaiian woman and the late-eighteenth-century beginnings of the Hawaiian nation under the influence of the West. The arc of the story rises from a bloody battle to the death of Mauna Ala in the state mental hospital. It alerts us to the impossibility of Hawaiian well-being in the American colony. The story is framed by an institutional tangle: violent Western-style combat that lays the groundwork for a nation, an elite school that trains the colonized middle class, a state-run mental hospital. The battle becomes an illegitimate birth, one that, as we shall see, vitiates Hawaiian origin stories. It also becomes an insane asylum, as we shall also see, and a tomb suffocating life. In the middle, Mauna Ala struggles to live up to the exigencies of being colonized. And it is this institutional tangle that makes Mauna Ala crazy.

Haunani-Kay Trask, writing on the question of Hawaiian storytelling, argued that the tradition of orature was a critical platform for the emergence of Hawaiian voices against the grain of hegemonic colonialist and non-Native writing. Trask wrote that the banning of the Hawaiian language in the late nineteenth century was clearly intended to extinguish any resistance speech or critical literary voices, and to "obliterate . . . a unique Native understanding of who and where and how we are" (Trask 1999, 167, 168). The memory of Mauna Ala can be understood as "resistance speech," but also something more. Feminist literary critics might analyze the story as an example of poetic memory and the magically real akin to the work of Toni Morrison (1987), Isabel Allende (1986), and Gloria Naylor (1989). These genres animate the voices of those who have been trivialized, hospitalized, and otherwise silenced. And, as feminist writing strategy, poetic memory and the magically real resist the boundaries of the purely literary and demand recognition that politics is crucial, because in the writing of history the stakes are so high (Ebron 1998, 162–63; Foreman 1992, 369–71).

The story of Mauna Ala, its transposition of history and meaning, challenges the epistemological certainty of academic histories by affirming the priority and centrality of a Hawaiian woman's life. As Trouillot noted in his discussion of the Haitian Revolution, the past is entirely dependent upon the present (1995, 15), and the story of Mauna Ala is not simply individual memory but is connected to a collective political and historical project meant to uncover the violence of Americanization and the disease of being colonized.

The tale of Kamehameha's victory at Nuʻuanu is history for the purpose of validating Western intrusion. It is a triumphalist narrative that seeks to legitimate the Americanization of Hawaiʻi in the twentieth century, to celebrate conquerors and their schemes for modernization while denying the suffering, silencing, and subjugating of Hawaiian people. By invoking Western representations of Kamehameha, and alluding to the ways in which his kingdom was coproduced by Western intrusions, the narrative elides the possibility for the sociopolitical integrity of ka pae ʻāina in the eons before collision with the West. In casting Kamehameha as a "great man," and producing his conquest of the Islands as the Hawaiian origin story, the entanglement of Western myth and history becomes the means of sabotaging Mauna Ala's sanity.

Colonialist historians of Hawaiʻi have made a fetish of Kamehameha. Kuykendall wrote that "Kamehameha is universally recognized as the most outstanding of all the Hawaiian chiefs of his own and of all other epochs. We can, perhaps, go even farther and say that he was one of the great men of the world" (1965[1938], 29). By fetish, I invoke Taussig's (1991, 9) notion that the state as fetish serves to mask the violence of political practice. Kamehameha's apotheosis by Euro/Americans to the status of "great man" elides the violent disjuncture between a chain of islands under decentralized leadership and without European weapons, and a unified, militarized Hawaiʻi now seen as capable of intercourse with the West. Histories of Hawaiʻi such as Kuykendall's are master narratives that employ the trajectory of modernity as historiography. History begins when Kamehameha unifies the islands of Hawaiʻi into a single "nation."

GENEALOGICAL SEQUENCE

But as Kameʻeleihiwa pointed out in *Native Land and Foreign Desires* (1992), "history in Hawaiian terms" begins with "that distant, dark beginning of the earth." Against modernist narratives that mark the origins of Hawaiian history in the ascendance of a king, partially produced by Europe, Kameʻeleihiwa casts history back to the primordial moment of creation, as told in the Kumulipo, the Hawaiian myth of origin.[1]

In a late-twentieth-century interpretation of the meaning of the Kumulipo, Kameʻeleihiwa (1992) posits that the chant symbolizes the source of all Hawaiian identity. From the first moment of creation, according to Kameʻeleihiwa, "the world and everything in it . . . [unfolds] . . . in genealogical sequence." In this view, the "essential lesson" of the Kumulipo is "that every aspect of the Hawaiian world" exists as "one indivisible lineage" (1992, 1–3).

For the late-twentieth-century Hawaiian physician and scholar Kekuni Blaisdell, the Kumulipo is the origin story that matters. The vast and vital web of relations described in its passages is perceived as the source of Hawaiian well-being, strength, and mana.

> "O ke au i kahuli wela ka honua. O ke au i kahuli lole ka lani." Now those are probably the most powerful words in our corpus of unwritten literature. They're the opening line to Kumulipo, which is the oldest chant we know of. . . . It refers to the mating of Sky-Father, Wakea, with Papa, our Earth-Mother. Out of that mating came, and continues to come, everything in our cosmos. To us everything is living: the rocks, the wind, the water, the clouds, the sky, as well as the birds and the trees and the fish. Everything is also conscious and everything communicates. . . . Since all things in our cosmos are products of conception of the same parents, we are all siblings, we are all related. Everything is sacred; everything is to be respected, not to be exploited, destroyed, contaminated, or polluted. (Blaisdell 1996, 170)

The notion of the world as a sacred web of earth and sky and sea that emerged from the "deep darkness darkening" stands in sharp contrast to a version of the origins of Hawaiian history in a bloody massacre. But the power of the Kumulipo to serve as a model and metaphor for the world of ka pae ʻāina was sundered by Euro/American intrusions and by a hermeneutic of conquest in which history unfolds in developmental stages. Successful European colonial ventures around the globe made the view of a linear unfolding of human life particularly persuasive, while the worldview contained within the Kumulipo was demoted to the level of folklore and perceived as superseded ancient wisdom.

But even though American economic and cultural forms were forced upon the Islands, Hawaiians persevered in an epistemology of decolonization based on a relational notion of mana and a worldview in which all beings are connected, and the land is source, sibling, and sustenance. Hawaiians in the late twentieth century said that they were struggling to live according to the principles of pono and lōkahi, an interlocking harmony and balance between humans, the ʻāina, and the divine. Kameʻeleihiwa described pono as perhaps the most significant basis on which to understand the history of colonialism in Hawaiʻi. She has argued that pono defined the unity between Hawaiian commoners and Hawaiian rulers in the time before the collision with the West. Pono expressed the "perfect" state of equilibrium that was the model for Hawaiian society, and the standard by which the relationship between the rulers and the ruled was judged. When the ʻaikapu, the religion that Hawaiians had practiced before 1819, was overthrown by a combination of factors that were both internal and external to Hawaiian society, the means of achieving pono were disrupted. The arrival of Calvinist missionaries, the devastation and depopulation of epidemic diseases, and the spread of capitalism and its concomitant, the neglect of agriculture in the countryside, all worked to disarrange Hawaiian society and create a rupture that produced pono's opposite. The culture of Hawaiians under conditions of colonialism can be understood as a lack of pono, in Kameʻeleihiwa's full sense of the term.

Similarly, in *From a Native Daughter: Colonialism and Sovereignty in Hawaiʻi*, Haunani-Kay Trask (1999, 58–64) discussed the clashing of indigenous and modern worldviews and argued that the Hawaiian worldview was suffocated by the imposition of Western modernity. She points out that according to the genealogy of the Kumulipo, Hawaiians on the cusp of the twenty-first century *still* were derived from Papahānaumoku—earth mother, and her union with Wākea—sky father. For Kameʻeleihiwa, Trask, and other scholars committed to the process of decolonization, the relationship between living Hawaiians and the cosmos is familial, and based upon "the wisdom . . . [of] reciprocal obligation" (Trask 1993, 80–81). Trask identifies this reciprocity as mālama ʻāina, defined as a relationship between the land and the people in which "an ancient, umbilical wisdom" serves as a model and a metaphor for stewardship of the land, and the preservation of a natural world. But, Trask points out, both the land and the people of Hawaiʻi are under siege. "The history of the modern period," she argues, "is the history of increasing conformity, paid for in genocide and ecocide." The Hawaiian people are forced to conform to Western, capitalist, standards, a modern mode of life that precludes the possibility of reciprocity with the land, and renders the practice of mālama ʻāina impossible. "As the people are transformed," Trask argues, "or more likely, exterminated, their environment is progressively degraded, parts of it destroyed forever. *Physi-*

cal despoliation is reflected in cultural degradation. A dead land is preceded by a dying people" (Trask 1993, 80–81, emphasis added).

Trask believes that the well-being of Hawaiian people was undermined by colonial penetration and Westernization, a notion that reverberates through the story of Mauna Ala. In this formulation, diseases of the body/mind are reflections of the imbalance of Western living, the lack of pono, lōkahi, and a familial connection between humans and the 'āina. But if the collision between Hawaiian and Western culture is at the root of Hawaiian illness—if Westernization equals death—then the struggle to redeem and reclaim Hawaiian cosmology signifies a struggle for Hawaiian life, and in this struggle Hawaiian culture is the source.

THE HOSPITAL WHERE MAUNA ALA DIED

In the years after the American coup d'etat and the formal assumption of American rule, Hawaiians conspired to restore the Hawaiian nation (Andrade 1996, 149–67; "The Uprising in Hawai'i" 1895). But insurgencies were up against a formidable foe, since the territorial militia was backed by the armed forces of the United States, symbolized by the presence of American warships sailing in and out of Honolulu Harbor. American justifications for the coup that ended the Hawaiian monarchy were reiterated versions of the narratives of extinction that characterized the Euro/American discourse on Natives in the earlier years of the colonial collision. In 1894, a leading haole newspaper editor and missionary descendant wrote that Lili'uokalani was the "debauched Queen of a heathenish monarchy" and a member of a "lewd and drunken . . . native race" (cited in Dougherty 1992, 166). Euro-Americans found it impossible to recognize the ties between Native Hawaiians and the 'āina; indeed, Hawaiian beliefs and practices concerning the land were in direct contradiction to the American notion of land as an alienable commodity.

From the queen to commoners, rebellious or not, Hawaiians were then construed by the Americans in power as a problem population in need of fixing. Daws (1968) and Fuchs (1961), two historians of modern Hawai'i, briefly describe the condition of Kanaka Maoli in the years after annexation.[2] They note that Hawaiians found it difficult to adjust to the morality of private property and wage labor, and that the haole rulers of the territory viewed indigenous Hawaiians as a problem population in need of rehabilitation. Daws wrote, "[T]he Hawaiian had all but ceased to be a person; he was defined as a problem. Other people talked about him in abstract terms, and one of the most frequently used was 'rehabilitation'" (Daws 1968, 97; Fuchs 1961, 71–72). The attempt to "rehabilitate" Native Hawaiians occurred on many levels,[3] but it was through the Board of Health, and later the Department of Institutions,[4] that techniques of rehabilitation that reached deep into the body became public policy.

It is, perhaps, in the realm of science that racism finds its most coherent amplification. The science that justified and reflected colonial racism, beginning in the late nineteenth century, posited that the etiology of psychiatric and psychological symptoms was rooted in the temporal, organic bodies of the disturbed, or in their culture—the collective expression of these biologically rooted pathologies (McCulloch 1995, 5, 9). Disease and deviance in the theories of some late-nineteenth and early-twentieth-century European and American scholars[5] were perceived as functions of civilizational grades articulated through racial categories that mimicked perceptions of class divisions in Europe (Zuberi 2001, 18). Exemplified in the work of Francis Galton, theories guiding colonial psychology in the early decades of the twentieth century were based on comparisons between grades of civilization across a scale in which Europeans were the near nadir[6] (Galton 1892, 340). Galton argued that Europeans had the potential to be improved upon, and that this process could be facilitated by "the science of eugenics," through laws and policies that encouraged "the inborn qualities of a race" (Galton 1909, 1). These views about the perfectibility of Europeans were essentially inseparable from notions of manifest destiny, and Galton was convinced that the practice of eugenics would raise the level of "civic worth" and produce adult male Europeans "better fitted to fulfill . . . vast imperial opportunities" (1909, 3). Within this Galtonian framework, the colonized people of the world were viewed as flawed and imperfectable. Charles Darwin, who was Galton's first cousin, supported these notions of heritability in *Descent of Man and Selection in Relations to Sex*.

> The variability or diversity of the mental facilities in men of the same race, not to mention the greater difference between men of distinct races, is so notorious that not a word need be said. . . . [A]nd we now know, through the admirable labours of Mr. Galton, that genius which implies a wonderfully complex combination of high facilities, tend to be inherited; and on the other hand, it is too certain that insanity and deteriorated mental powers likewise run in families. (Darwin 1995, 414, cited in Zuberi 2001, 41)

Indeed, such views became justifications for the social relations of colonialism (Zuberi 2001; Smedley and Smedley 2005; Jackson 2004).

These Western views about the heritability of deviance and the superiority of whites were reflected in the mental health system that developed in colonial Hawai'i. Although the O'ahu Insane Asylum, the first institution to address insanity, was constructed in 1866 during the reign of Hawaiian King Kamehameha V (Kimmich 1956, 345), it was not until the Islands were annexed as a territory of the United States that a professional, rationalized mental health *system* was developed. The Waimanalo Home for the Feebleminded and the Psychological Clinic at the University of Hawai'i were funded by the territorial legislature in the early 1920s. At the same time, Australian psychologist Stanley Porteus was appointed to oversee the clinic at the university and to provide consultation and oversight to the Insane Asylum, which was renamed the Territorial Hospital, and eventually became the State Hospital, where Mauna Ala died.

Porteus was an advocate of Galtonian theories of hereditability, the developer of an intelligence test to measure "ethnic" differences, and a believer in the efficacy of frontal lobotomy as treatment for the mentally ill (Porteus 1965, 6–7, 56–57, 156–57). Under Porteus's leadership in the first half of the century, psychology in Hawai'i was preoccupied with the imperfectability of indigenous Hawaiians, and it expressed these concerns in highly medicalized terms that offered biological explanations for behavior deemed socially deviant. Porteus posited that Hawai'i was "a proving ground for the hypothesis of racial difference," based upon "organic . . . traits" that were "part of man's original endowment" (Porteus, cited in Stannard 1999, 96, 99). He argued that Hawaiians were "racially immature" and afflicted with "reasoning deficits" that placed them just above "the absolute inferiority of the negro" (99). These views were backed by the collection of data indicating that among those unable to function according to the demands of this higher grade of civilization, Native Hawaiians figured disproportionately.

Colonial psychology in Hawai'i located the source of the problem of mental illness and social deviance in the racialized bodies of the socially misfit. Legislation that would have permitted eugenics, or the forced sterilization of those deemed "unfit," was introduced in the Hawai'i territorial legislature during the 1920s and 1930s but was defeated. However, brain surgery, also called "prefrontal lobotomy," was not illegal, and this technique was hailed by the Territorial Board of Health as a "spectacular advance" in the treatment of mental illness and social deviance. "When the operation is completely successful (about 30 percent of the time), results are most impressive. The anxious and oppressed become cheerful and optimistic, and the violently excited calm down" (Porteus 1948, 83–84). Indeed, under Porteus, the University of Hawai'i was considered to be at the forefront of research into the efficacy of brain surgery.

There were other less medicalized and less invasive procedures for rehabilitating the problem population (Leong 1933; Territory of Hawai'i 1930; Honolulu Chamber of Commerce 1941; Department of Institutions 1943), and these included prisons, reform schools (Governor's Advisory Committee 1935; Miller 1938), industrial training schools (Thompson 1953), and homes for the "feebleminded." But to follow the story of Mauna Ala's life and death, we focus here on the mental health system.

As Irving Zola argued, the practice of biomedicine was "a major institution of social control," which had come to exist alongside such traditional mechanisms as religion and law. Specifically, psychiatry was a medical specialty that first used techniques clearly meant to control unruly and deviant populations (Zola 1978, 80). The psychiatrist (and critic of psychiatry) Thomas Szasz (1958a, 509) viewed sanity "as the ability to play whatever the game of social living might consist of and to play it well. Conversely," he wrote, "to refuse to play, or to play badly, means that the person is mentally ill." Concerned with (un)ethical premises of mid-twentieth-century psychiatry in a secular, democratic society (Szasz 1958b, 184), he argued that the difference expressed by the statements " 'He is wrong' and 'He is mentally ill' " reflected the status of social relations between the subject and the one who diagnosed.

> If we take him seriously, consider him to have human rights and dignities, and look upon him as more or less our equal—we then speak of disagreements, deviations, fights, crimes, perhaps even of treason. Should we feel, however, that we cannot communicate with him, that he is somehow "basically" different from us, we shall then be inclined to consider him no longer as an equal but rather as an inferior . . . person; and we then speak of him as being crazy, mentally ill, insane, psychotic, [and] immature. (Szasz 1958a, 509)

According to the 1930 federal census of the population, the 50,860 Native Hawaiians were just under 14 percent of the total population, although they comprised 41 percent of the territory's institutionalized population that year. The mental hospital was a medicalized space, in which Euro/American views of inherent indigenous pathology guided clinical practice and the development of treatments and cures. Goffman (1973, 352) noted that "the official mandate of the public mental hospital is to protect the community from danger and nuisance of certain kinds of misconduct." He argued that the asylum was not based upon a medical-service model, although it was assumed to fit within such a model. For Goffman, the basis of the mental hospital was the "self-alienating moral servitude" of the patient (386).

> The limited applicability of the medical model brings together a doctor who cannot easily afford to construe his activity in other than medical terms and a patient who may well feel he must fight and hate his keepers if any sense is to be made of the hardship he is undergoing. Mental hospitals institutionalize a kind of grotesque of the service relationship. (Goffman 1973, 369)

Utilizing a professionalized sector of healers, it existed outside of the kind of kin-based communal structures that defined healing in the sociocultural logics of Hawaiians. For Kanaka Maoli, the mental hospital was a place of punishment that was cloaked in the language of medicine and healing. Its purpose to transform—or at least silence—the oppositional culture of the colonized was political.

In 1941, a "Survey of the Feebleminded in the Territory of Hawai'i" was published by the Mental Hygiene Committee of the Honolulu Chamber of Commerce (1941). The survey was conducted on the islands of O'ahu, Hawai'i, Maui, and Kaua'i. The study did not attempt to survey all of the population deemed "feebleminded." Rather, it concentrated on individual cases that were considered "acute problems" and in immediate need of institutional care. Of the 230 cases studied in detail, 100 were from the Psychological Clinic at the University of Hawai'i, run by Stanley Porteus himself, and 130 were referred from other public and private agencies, including the Territorial Hospital. The purpose of the study was to gauge the extent of the "feebleminded" population in order to project the need for their care.

According to the results of the survey, determining the number of "feebleminded" by race, Native Hawaiians (counted separately as "Hawaiian" and "Part-Hawaiian") accounted for 31 percent of all cases, 39 percent of all cases at Porteus's clinic, and 25.3 percent of all other agency cases. The 1940 federal census of the population counted 64,310 Hawaiians and Part-Hawaiians, approximately 15 percent of the population. In numbers and proportion, then, Native Hawaiians comprised the largest racial group among the "feebleminded" surveyed.

COLONIAL ELEGIAC

In 1948, Porteus, then the former head of University of Hawai'i's Psychology Clinic, reminisced about "simpler times" in a report to Governor Ingram Stainbeck on the status of the territory's institutions and the provision of care for delinquents, criminals, and the feebleminded.

> These were the days before unions and mechanical harvesters and large welfare funds. Our population was small and rather stable, our city of convenient size without a single industrial building between the *Advertiser* [a daily newspaper] building and Waikiki. When we went away for weekends we left our houses unlocked, domestic help was cheap and faithful, yard boys earned two dollars a day, and you tore up your . . . parking tickets if the police officer was presumptuous enough to give you one. If he did it too often you spoke to your friend the sheriff. (Porteus 1948, 5)

Porteus's memory of an earlier time demonstrates both stereotypical colonial arrogance as well as colonial dependence on the non-haole majority—the "faithful" and underpaid house servants, yard "boys," and non-unionized plantation labor. And, although colonial power was always contested, Porteus's elegiac reflects a colonial desire for uncontested hegemony, for power above the law.

The Porteus report attempted to explain the rise of crime, social deviance, and social dependency in Hawai'i in the 1940s. The problem for the territory was the increased expenditure in tax dollars needed to support the institutions designed to care for the problem population. The origin of the problem, according to Porteus, was that the industrial development of Hawai'i had fostered a "higher grade of civilization," leaving some percentage of the population unable to keep up. "I am afraid," he wrote,

> [t]hat this increased expenditure is one of the penalties of growth and development. While our centers of population were small and our economy a rather simple one of agriculture on a mule-team and cane-knife level, the problems of social adjustment were not great. But immediately [when] we changed to mechanical operations by means of tractors, cane-loaders and truck haulage, there was much less work for the man with the hoe. A large number of workers were able to function at a higher industrial level but there is always a proportion of those who cannot do so and fall behind.
>
> A more complex and variegated industrial development, a higher grade of civilization, means a larger number of individuals who cannot keep up with the pace of progress. (Porteus 1948, 1)

Notice that in Porteus's narrative it is not the structural conditions of capitalism—mechanization meant less work for the "man with the hoe"—or the economics of colonialism—"domestic help was cheap and faithful, yard boys earned two dollars a day"—or the forces removing indigenous people from the land that were at the root of the problem. Rather, it was the social and mental "deficiencies" of a population unable to keep up with civilization. In the scholarly assessment of Stanley Porteus—an assessment that had the power to shape public policy—a higher grade of civilization produced a population of misfits aware of their plight.

> To the degree that people are conscious of deprivation, of inferior social standing or their other inequalities of attainment the more rebellious, delinquent, or criminal they will be. The greater the load of anxiety that failure engenders, the more people take refuge in alcoholism, suicide, or mental breakdown. (Porteus 1948, 3)

The modern mental health apparatus represented Native Hawaiians and other non-haole people as self-consciously mentally inferior, unable to cope with a higher grade of civilization, and seeking refuge in self-destruction. Contained in this representation are elements of blame based on both sin and disease.

Eugenics, or forced sterilization of the "unfit," was an idea that Porteus enthusiastically supported (Stannard 1999, 106–17), especially since it seemed to him to be the most cost effective. Sterilization measures had been proposed before the Territorial legislature in the 1930s, but they were defeated.[7] Porteus argued that since the public was not yet ready for "eugenical measures such as the sterilization of the unfit. . . . Since [the public] will not tolerate methods for diminishing social incompetence at its source we must proceed with more humane but more expensive policies" (Porteus 1948, 3–4). Given the expense of rehabilitation efforts ("The population of this small group of Pacific Islands is paying generously for its unfit. If it could all be counted up it would be a staggering sum"), Porteus wondered how effective programs were "in recovering any portion of this huge amount of human wastage." Cure, he argued, was too much to expect, but at the very least the efforts of the territory should "offset the stream of new cases, so that the army of social incompetents does not grow progressively until society staggers under the load" (Porteus 1948, 4, 6).

The Porteus report discussed the prison system, reform schools for juvenile offenders, and the Territorial Hospital for the mentally ill, the hospital that after statehood became known as the State Mental Hospital—where Mauna Ala died. In his discussion of the hospital, Porteus noted that the most serious problems facing the institution were the "difficulties involved in getting adequate and properly trained staff," and the inadequate "allotment of 17 cents per patient per meal for raw food" (Porteus 1948, 68–69). However, Porteus praised advances in medical science that, he argued, aided in the rehabilitation of the mentally ill at the Territorial Hospital. "Only ten years ago," he wrote, "the Territorial Hospital was to all intents and purposes a mere custodial institution, giving only shelter and supervision to the mentally ill entrusted to its care" (Porteus 1948, 75). But with the advent of brain surgery, or prefrontal lobotomy, a new day had dawned in the treatment of mental disease. According to the Porteus report,

> In about one third of the lobotomy cases, the patient recovers his mental balance, improves his social readjustment, reestablishes initiative in every day affairs and is able to return to the community to earn his living as before. He retains his former mental capacity but his high level planning is much reduced. In another third of the cases, a considerable improvement is noticeable so that excitability and impulsiveness are considerably diminished. But the psychotic symptoms remain to such an extent that the patient cannot be returned to ordinary community life. His adjustment in the hospital is however made much easier.

In still another third of the cases the operation makes no significant change in the patient's behavior except that occasionally he becomes more vegetative in his reactions. *When the operation is completely successful results are most impressive. The anxious and the oppressed become cheerful and optimistic, the violently excited calm down.* (Porteus 1948, 83–84, emphasis added)[8]

Prefrontal lobotomy was, perhaps, the most physically violent measure in the spectrum of techniques meant to facilitate mental health cures. Although relatively few patients were subjected to lobotomy, the fact that brain surgery was an option at all helps define both the colonizers' perception of the colonized and the extent to which the mental health system in Territorial Hawai'i was willing to go to obscure the injustices of colonialism, and the possibility of resistance and rebellion.

Although psychosurgery represents a particularly radically invasive medical technique for the "rehabilitation" of the mentally ill, there were other, less medicalized methods for the training and treatment of the "delinquent" population. The territorial government defined delinquency as a hazard resulting from the large number of people in the Islands failing to adjust to the "new culture." A report from the territory's Bureau of the Budget, attempting to make a case for increased funding for the Department of Institutions in 1930, argued that the problem population, which included Japanese, Chinese, Filipino, and other immigrants imported as plantation labor as well as Native Hawaiians, was having difficulty adjusting to "American ideals, standards and practices." According to the report, the problem was that "in moral and spiritual matters" there were "many" who were unable to meet the new demands which are being made upon them by the "changing complex life" and were therefore becoming wards of the territory (Territory of Hawai'i 1930, 28). The territorial government's argument was that the problem of delinquency was created by a moral and an ethical gap between parents and children, and the blame was put on Hawaiian and immigrant parents, since they were seen as being unable to lead children in the new standards of society. In the absence of proper standards in the home, it was the duty of the territory to take on the parental role of authority and discipline (Territory of Hawai'i 1930, 28).

It was clearly in the interests of the colonial state to locate "the problem" in the biology and morality of the colonized. The business of the territorial government was to protect American economic and geopolitical interests in the Islands. State institutions responsible for mental health were created to support the exigencies of colonial rule and capitalist hegemony. The successful functioning of U.S. military bases and sugar plantations depended, in part, on coercive mechanisms designed to keep "problem populations" in line. Defining the problem as rooted in the bodies and souls of the colonized shifted the blame away from undemocratic and oppressive systems of colonial rule. Blame was assigned to Native Hawaiians, who were the central target of the institutional gaze, forming the single largest "racial" group among the institutionalized population.

But the story of Mauna Ala resists this blaming and turns the gaze the other way around. In the years following the absorption of Hawai'i as the fiftieth state, Native Hawaiians began to publicly resist and organize against the health system. And, they began to assert the need to define the meaning of health and the means to achieve it in ways that reflected the specific culture and worldviews of their ancestors.

"SHUTTING THEM DOWN"

[T]he Hawai'i Department of Health . . . was run almost as if it were located in a white-middle class, English-dominant community on the mainland. (Haas 1981, 52)

In 1974, the Hawai'i Association of Asian and Pacific Peoples (HAAP) was formed to advocate for health care services appropriate to the needs of their constituencies. Statehood had not transformed the mental health system, which continued to operate on the basis of racialized notions that pathologized Hawaiians and some immigrant groups who had come to Hawai'i as low-wage plantation labor. In exploring its options, the group was informed by the federal Department of Health, Education, and Welfare (HEW) that it could file a formal complaint against the Hawai'i Department of Health, but the organization demurred. A representative of HAAP told a HEW investigator that they "feared" reprisals if such a complaint were made. The HAAP spokesperson said that those who complained were "guaranteed not to survive very well on the island . . . ," and that "silence is the rule unless you are in a position of power" (cited in Haas 1981, 3).

However, federal laws and policies designed to protect racial "minorities" on the mainland gave advocates seeking to reform the system a crucial tool. In 1976, formal charges of discrimination were filed against Hawai'i's Department of Health by a University of Hawai'i professor. The U.S. Department of Health, Education, and Welfare found the state of Hawai'i in violation of the Civil Rights Act of 1964 for "inadequate methods of administration for servicing non-whites" (Haas 1981, 1). Indeed, the entire system of health care in the state was geared toward the needs of the haoles and Japanese, and particularly Hawaiians and Filipinos consistently "underutilized" the Department of Health's mental health services. Under threats that the federal government would suspend funding to Hawai'i, the wheels of change appeared to slowly turn.

In 1979, a Native Hawaiian social service organization gathered data on the mental health status of the Native Hawaiian population. The report cited alarming statistics on the Native Hawaiian suicide rates: Native Hawaiian young men between the ages of fifteen and twenty-four comprised 31.3 percent of all suicides in that age group, and Native Hawaiians in general had the highest suicide rate of all ethnic groups in the Islands. They found that the high rates of unemployment, poverty, single parenthood, and poor physical health among Native Hawaiians were factors associated with high stress and subsequent mental disorders, including substance abuse (Alu Like 1979, 7). The data also showed that less than 7 percent of the professional positions in state-run mental health services were filled by Native Hawaiians, and that "very little usage was found of any specific cultural practices in the treatment of mentally disturbed Native Hawaiian clients" (7). The report stressed the need for culturally appropriate services that were strongly family-centered and that would provide disturbed individuals without viable families with "substitute family situations" in accordance with Hawaiian cultural values (7, 9, 19).

In the years following the discrimination suit against the Department of Health and the report on the status of indigenous mental health, Native Hawaiians began a process leading to self-administered health organizations. In Wai'anae, a community-based organization known as Hale Ola Ho'opākōlea[9] was formed in 1981 in order to meet the demand for Native Hawaiian mental health services that were culturally sensitive. The agency was funded initially by the federal Administration for Native American Programs and the National Institute of Mental Health. In the mission statement, the founders of Hale Ola Ho'opākōlea linked Hawaiian culture and Hawaiian health:

> To promote holistic healing through Hawaiian cultural practices, using the positive lifestyles, spiritual values, communication skills and beliefs of Native Hawaiians. Particular emphasis is to be on people of Hawaiian ancestry and people in need whose cultural patterns are vital to their well-being. (Ke Kino, Ka Mana'o, and A Me Ka 'Uhane 1989, 1)

But this first attempt at a Native Hawaiian-run agency providing mental health services was beset with both internal difficulties and a lack of support from its principal contracting organization, the Wai'anae Coast Community Mental Health Center (WCCMHC). In 1989, the WCCMHC charged Hale Ola Ho'opākōlea with noncompliance of contract specifications. The report generated by the board of Hale Ola Ho'opākōlea, in response to the charges of noncompliance, provides a glimpse into the challenges facing this pioneering attempt to provide culturally sensitive mental health care for Native Hawaiians.

According to the response, the agency had insufficient funding to be fully staffed. Between 1986 and 1989, staff composition was reduced by 40 percent. By 1989, one full-time project director, one full-time clerk typist, one part-time custodian, and one full-time and two part-time neighborhood counselors remained to carry out the agency's agenda. The staff reduction from five full-time neighborhood counselors to two counselors meant that the agency was unable to fulfill its commitments to clients and other Wai'anae Coast agencies. The report cites low level of service to clients, low staff morale, and increased counselor caseload as the three major problems resulting from lack of funding.

While Hale Ola accepted the criticism from the WCCMHC that there was "room for improvement [by staff] in areas of written and oral communication skills," the major thrust of the report was the stance that "[i]nterpretation of contract policies, rules and regulations set by [the WCCMHC] may be in conflict with the overall mission of Hale Ola and its cultural based and cultural specific health service delivery system" (Ke Kino, Ka Mana'o, and A Me Ka 'Uhane 1989, 10). Hale Ola argued that communication barriers based on cultural insensitivity marked the clinical supervision sessions, the required weekly consultations between Hale Ola staff and WCCMHC psychiatrists.

Turning on its head the criticism of Hale Ola by the WCCMHC, the report argued that the problem was that policies and regulations governing Western health care delivery did not reflect Hawaiian cultural healing practices. The report posited that

> practices such as lomilomi (a form of massage) and ho'oponopono were under review and scrutinization by [the WCCMHC] because there was no comprehensive plan of action illustrating and demonstrating the linkages between the use of Hawaiian cultural healing practices (non-traditional mental health delivery system) in accordance [with] compliancy procedures, rules and regulations. . . . Hale Ola . . . failed to provide the clinical documentation . . . which bridges both traditional and non-traditional approaches to mental health services. (Ke Kino, Ka Mana'o, and A Me Ka 'Uhane 1989, 14)

The staff and board of Hale Ola admitted in the report that they failed to be accountable to procedures, rules, and regulations associated with state-funded Western health care delivery systems. But the problem, as framed by Hale Ola, was an inability to translate Hawaiian healing practices in ways that were intelligible to the state health bureaucracy.

Furthermore, the Hale Ola report challenged the efficacy of Western mental health care provision, stating that "the community" needed to carefully reassess the "philosophy, founding principles, and mission objectives" of the WCCMHC. The report also challenged the relationship between Hale Ola and the WCCMHC, noting that although Hale Ola was a subcontractor of the WCCMHC, the organizations were competing for state and federal funds, and that the WCCMHC had become an "enforcement agent rather than a facilitator . . . of services to the Wai'anae Coast communities" (Ke Kino, Ka Mana'o, and A Me Ka 'Uhane 1989, 34).

The bulk of the Hale Ola report was an analysis of survey results conducted by the Hale Ola staff. Those surveyed included twenty clients, current and former board members, and fifteen former and current staff members. "The majority of clients," according to the report, "found [the] services of Hale Ola to be much better than the western style care." Ninety percent of clients surveyed reported that Hale Ola had helped them in "spirit," 95 percent reported being helped in "mind," and 90 percent reported being helped in "body." Over 65 percent of current and former board members surveyed said that Hale Ola had room for improvement in management, service delivery, and staff supervision. Forty percent of those surveyed answered that the board had room for improvement in areas such as participation, knowledge of agency objectives, and guidance in meeting agency objectives. Like the clients surveyed, 86 percent of board members surveyed said that Hale Ola had a "significant impact on clients' spiritual [and mental health] needs," while 71 percent said that the agency had a positive impact on the body. Of the current and former staff surveyed, half said there was room for improvement in areas such as managerial function, program administration, and supervision and evaluation of staff. Nearly half said there was need for improvement in "areas of cultural training and staff skills building."

The report's recommendations included the need for further research into cultural healing practices, the development of culturally sensitive standards of performance and evaluation, the need for board training and development, a reassessment of the relationship between Hale Ola and the WCCMHC, and a "careful review" of WCCMHC services to the community.

Hale Ola's report succeeded in generating renewed community interest in the role of the WCCMHC. Spurred by the report and the findings supporting client preference for Native healing techniques, community activists waged a battle to shut down the WCCMHC and to win funding for an agency independent of the Department of Health. Meipala Silva, a longtime Wai'anae resident and community activist, remembered the struggle:

> *Here in Wai'anae we have a great need for mental health services. But the mental health center was not providing good care for our Hawaiian people. The Western services were not recognizing the importance of family to the treatment of Hawaiians, and they did not respect Hawaiian spirituality. And so we had to shut them down.* (Field notes)

The struggle led by Wai'anae community leaders to shut down the WCCMHC was eventually successful, and a new independent agency formed in its place. Hale Ola continued to exist but focused on providing substance abuse and mental health care services to Native Hawaiian veterans.

Hale Ola challenged the efficacy of Western mental health care, argued for specifically Native Hawaiian healing methods as fundamental to indigenous well-being, and charged that state of Hawai'i policies and regulations were potentially in conflict with culturally specific health service delivery. The Hawaiians involved with Hale Ola identified "cultural insensitivity" on the part of haole clinical supervisors as a barrier to their success as healers of troubled Hawaiians. The founding of the clinic and the response to the charges of noncompliance represent an important move to shift the blame from the bodies and souls of Hawaiians. Reinterpreting the meaning of Hawaiian disease, the agency relocated the root of the problem in the colonialist policies and practices of the state-run mental health care system.

THE SOURCE

When Lili'uokalani, the last queen of Hawai'i, died in 1917, she bequeathed her wealth to "the benefit of orphan and other destitute children in the Hawaiian Islands, the preference to be given to Hawaiian children of pure or part aboriginal blood."[10] Her wealth became the basis for the Queen Lili'uokalani Children's Center (QLCC), and eventually for a formal process of research and remembering to develop remedies for the mental health problems of Hawaiian families (Pukui et al. 1972). It was apparent to QLCC social workers that American solutions to the mental health problems of mid-twentieth-century Hawaiians had failed to achieve results. The QLCC convened a "Culture Committee" to explore the meaning of Hawaiian illness in a specifically Hawaiian framework. At the center of this process was a woman named Mary Kawena Pukui.

Born in 1895, on the cusp of the American coup that overthrew Queen Lili'uokalani, Pukui was raised in Ka'ū on the island of Hawai'i. Her mother, Paahana Wiggin, was piha, or pure Hawaiian, and her father was haole from New England. Pukui was a pioneer in the field of Hawaiian studies. With her collaborator, haole anthropologist E. S. Craighill Handy, Pukui set out in the 1930s to challenge the prevailing view that "all knowledge the Hawaiians might have had was lost forever" (Handy and Pukui 1972[1958], xi). Although in the early 1920s anthropologist Alfred Kroeber (1921, 131–32) described Hawaiians as nearly bereft of culture, Pukui knew that these views did not reflect her life and experience.

Pukui was employed at the Bishop Museum as a translator and an informant for E. S. Handy. In colonial Hawai'i, Pukui would have needed to be legitimized by a haole scholar such as Handy in order for her ideas about Hawaiian cultural integrity to circulate at the level of scholarly discourse. It was not simply that she was a non-credentialed Hawaiian woman (although in 1960 she was awarded an honorary doctorate of letters from the University of Hawai'i)—it was also that she thought and wrote against the grain of researchers whose anthropological models were based on what they perceived as the dead past of Hawaiian culture and history.

In 1935, Pukui, in collaboration with E. S. Craighill Handy and Handy's wife, Elizabeth Green Handy, began an ethnographic project that gave "living Hawaiians . . . a central role" (Handy and Pukui 1972[1958], xi). In Ka'ū, Pukui's natal community, they collected ethnographic data from the members of Pukui's extensive clan. As a result of this work, Pukui and Handy were the first ethnographers to conduct fieldwork in a Hawaiian community (Burrows 1970[1947], 16).

Pukui's subordinate position as Handy's assistant belies her centrality to the collaborative research—the work would have been impossible without her. *The Polynesian Family System in Ka'ū, Hawai'i* was published with Handy as lead author, although Pukui was responsible for most of the writing. When *Native Planters* was first published in 1972, Pukui was demoted to "collaborator," although most of the essays in the book were based on earlier writing that listed Pukui as the author (Howard 1996, cited in White and Tengan 2001, 390).

Some anthropologists have critiqued Pukui's scholarship. Linnekin (1983a) argued that Pukui's elderly Hawaiian informants, who were born in the mid-nineteenth century, were basing their accounts of traditional life on inaccurate memories, since they were influenced by their "own interpretation of past life-ways" and developments in the late nineteenth and early twentieth centuries. White and Tengan (2001, 390), although more respectful of Pukui's contribution to Hawaiian studies, criticize Pukui's descriptions of Hawaiian life as "timeless, static, and occurring in the past," and for complicity with the tactic of spatial distancing, which renders people from remote, rural areas as the only authentic objects of study.

However, it is clear that Pukui made a significant contribution to the literature on Hawaiian culture and to an understanding of Hawaiian resistance and resilience. There is no clearer example of this than Pukui's contribution in two volumes of *Nānā I Ke Kumu* (*Look to the Source*) (1972).

When the QLCC convened the Culture Committee in the late 1960s, Mary Kawena Pukui was a widely respected scholar and kupuna. She was at the center of the QLCC Culture Committee process that involved analyzing the case files of troubled families from her perspective as a Hawaiian culture expert. Pukui's role was to listen to the presentation of cases and to research and remember Hawaiian practices and beliefs that might be reflected in troubled family members' perception of the problem or that might point to specifically Hawaiian solutions.

The view of *Nānā I Ke Kumu* was that before contact with the West, a viable Hawaiian culture met the needs of a "thriving, industrious and religious people." Powerful foreign perceptions of Hawaiians as "pagan and inferior" led to a process of internalized oppression and a gradual adoption of Western ways. Key to the understanding of Hawaiian mental health presented in *Nānā I Ke Kumu* is that the power of foreigners drove Hawaiian culture underground, so that what was once "explicit became implicit." The Culture Committee,

however, found that Hawaiians had secretly harbored Hawaiian beliefs and practices, and that Hawaiian culture often was expressed unconsciously. Existing in
the gap between the hegemony of the colonizer and the secret, underground culture of the colonized, Hawaiians were torn and confused about their identities
(Pukui et al. 1972, vol. 1, vii).

The secret culture of Hawaiians often emerged in sessions between QLCC
social workers and troubled family members. However, the Hawaiian and non-
Hawaiian staff of the QLCC "felt uncomfortable" when confronted with these
"deeply felt beliefs," and as a result they avoided discussing and exploring them,
even though such avoidance hindered the resolution of family conflicts. It is
important to note that the impetus for the creation of the Culture Committee
came from both the expression of Hawaiian beliefs and practices by QLCC
clients, as well as from discomfort with these beliefs and practices by the organization's Western-trained social work staff. This contradiction "pointed to . . .
[the] need to learn and understand the authentic Hawaiian culture in order" for
QLCC social workers "to increase . . . [their] effectiveness in helping those . . .
[they] serve[d]" (Pukui et al. 1972, vol. 2, vii).

Hawaiian families and their social workers, the Culture Committee posited,
needed to engage in a process of remembering and "recapturing" positive Hawaiian beliefs and practices. Among the most important beliefs and practices identified by the Culture Committee were: the importance of ʻohana; respect for
kūpuna; and ensuring harmonious interdependence within the ʻohana through
hoʻoponopono, or family therapy (Pukui et al. 1972, vol. 2, vii). The "physical
and mystical linking of the [Hawaiian] body with the forebears of old and
descendants yet to come" was also central to the view of the Hawaiian psyche
presented in *Nānā I Ke Kumu* (Pukui et al. 1972, vol. 2, 293–94).

In the 1920s and 1930s, when Pukui and the Handys were engaged with
ethnographic research in Kaʻū and were collecting the stories of Hawaiians born
in the mid-nineteenth century, Mauna Ala was struggling with the insanity of
being colonized. In the same era, Stanley Porteus, the chair of the University of
Hawaiʻi's psychology department, was writing about Native Hawaiians'
entrenched dysfunction. Criticisms of her work notwithstanding, Pukui's
research and writing (particularly in *Nānā I Ke Kumu*) demonstrated that the
specific wisdom of Hawaiian culture was a necessary source for healing Hawaiians. In the logic of colonialism, it was essential for the life and spirit of both the
people and the land to be usurped. Colonial efforts to convert the ʻāina from
living entity to lifeless commodity were the basis of Mauna Ala's insanity. But in
the late twentieth century, the resilience of Hawaiians, their ability to resist and
remember, produced a burgeoning movement whose critique of the insanity of
colonialism would provide a context for Mauna Ala's life and death.

5

KA LEO

Remembering Hawaiian

THE MANA OF ʻĀINA

The colonizers' notion that Western ways were superior and the enforcement of these Western ways rendered Hawaiian ways of knowing and being illegitimate. This was particularly true of the enforcement of the English language in Hawaiian schools, the hegemony of Christianity, and the demotion of Hawaiian cosmology. But Hawaiian ways did not disappear. In the 1990s, ideas and practices that had been harbored underground were reinterpreted and began emerging in public and academic conversations.

Fundamental to the colonizing project was the transformation of the ʻāina from a familial entity into a lifeless commodity. Hawaiians were dispossessed of the land by the middle of the nineteenth century, but Hawaiian conceptions of the ʻāina were not so easily displaced. In the 1990s a widespread Hawaiian understanding of the land as agent was evident. This sensibility derived from kino lau, the Hawaiian concept that was the basis for a world infused with life and sacred meaning, in which all things were endowed with creaturely sensibilities. Kino lau was the expression of a universe of reciprocity and communication among Kanaka, akua, ʻaumākua, and the ʻāina. Kino lau refers to the many forms that akua and ʻaumākua might take, and their ability to change back and forth at will. Shape-shifting gods might take the form of plants, minerals, animals, or rocks (Pukui et al. 1972, vol., 1, 35, 125).

While I was in Hawaiʻi, I listened to many stories in which the land, the ʻāina, became the agent of revenge against foreigners who mistook it for a commodity. Herbert Hunokeli,[1] an energetic kupuna in his eighties who was an active member of his Protestant Church and a director on the board of Hoʻo Mōhala, a Native Hawaiian substance abuse clinic, told me the story of Sacrifice

Rock. In the 1930s, he said, when the army was building a road in the Wai'anae Range near Kolekole Pass,[2] they came upon a boulder. This boulder was the marker of an ancient site where the enemies of a Hawaiian chief had been sacrificed. Although Hunokeli thought that the site should be treated with reverence as a marker of Hawaiian traditions equivalent to the "Statue of Liberty," the military did not recognize the site as sacred and proceeded to remove the boulder from the path. But on the following day, the rock was where it had been before the construction crew moved it. When they tried to move it again, one of the crew was badly injured.[3] The military, Hunokeli said, never managed to move the rock, and the road had to be rerouted (field notes).

I heard various iterations and elaborations on this theme. The mana of rocks taken by tourists from 'āina on the island of Hawai'i was said to cause visitors to fall ill once they returned to the mainland.[4] When the structural integrity of an apartment complex in Wai'anae was threatened by two unprecedented landslides, the Hawaiians I worked with said that the 'āina was taking its revenge. The Canadian-owned apartment complex—which Hawaiians and other anti-resort development groups protested when it was built in 1980 (Trumbull 1980)—housed mainly retired haoles who were not integrated into the Hawaiian community.

Kaona is a specifically Hawaiian analytic tool for the interpretation of a story's multiple meanings. In the times of ka po'e kahiko, "poetry and narrative were critically judged by the audience . . . depending on the levels of *kaona*" (Kame'eleihiwa Transcript 1996a, viii). In colonial times the technique was perfected as a tool for expressing both Hawaiian resistance to colonial politics and Hawaiian sexuality under the censorious gaze of Protestant missionaries and other foreigners. On one level, the stories of mana-filled rocks and their power to harm demonstrated a continuing belief in the 'āina as a living being. On another level, the stories encoded Hawaiian resistance to the commodification of land, inundation by tourism, and other manifestations of colonialism. In these stories, the 'āina becomes a threat to those who misperceive it as a resource for development rather than as a source and sacred being of creation.

A GIRDER COLLAPSE

The tourism industry is the most important source of economic activity in Hawai'i. One third of the state's people derive their income from tourism, and in the 1990s tourists outnumbered residents 6 to 1. Given the state's reliance on this single industry, it was deemed crucial that Hawai'i maintain the image of an "exotic yet safe destination" (Arakawa 2004). But the means of staging paradise depended upon a massive denial of the violence of a colonial past and a neocolonial present. In the summer of 1996, some of the political tensions between

Native Hawaiians and the haole and Japanese-American-dominated larger community that simmered below the formal aura of aloha erupted on the front page of a Honolulu newspaper. At issue was the power of the 'āina and a heterodox Native Hawaiian interpretation of a series of events.

In 1960, a year after statehood, Highway 3 (H3) was proposed in order to facilitate the movement of troops and equipment between the naval base at Pearl Harbor and the Kaneohe Bay Marine Corps Air Station. Eventually costing $80 million per mile (Yuen 1997), the construction of H3 was held up for thirty years by other construction priorities and opposition from environmentalist and Native Hawaiian rights groups (Plans for Hawaiian Highway 1985). The construction of the highway was also beset by accidents. Several workers were injured, some seriously, and two construction workers were killed (Ramires 1996, A1).

In August 1996, University of Hawai'i-Mānoa professor Lilikalā Kame'eleihiwa, then the director of the Center for Hawaiian Studies, was interviewed in a daily newspaper about the desecration of sacred Hawaiian land caused by the building of H3. She was quoted as saying, ". . . I get so angry when I see the desecration of our sacred grounds. So every time I hear about somebody dying in connection with [H3], I am happy. . . . So, for those people, people like [Senator Dan] Inouye, people like the guys who run the Department of Transportation, those guys who . . . insisted on putting through this freeway, for them I feel . . . the greatest joy when they drop dead" (Kame'eleihiwa Transcript 1996a). Weeks later, a large girder supporting the building of the highway collapsed, and four construction workers were injured. In retrospect, Kame'eleihiwa's earlier comments ignited a firestorm of controversy.

The *scientific* explanation for the collapse was a rare event known as thermal expansion (Murakawa 1996, A1). However, Kame'eleihiwa argued in an editorial response that the highway was "a sign of settler racism," and that the disasters befalling it had nothing to do with her power but reflected the anger of akua.

> The fact is, [she wrote] even if I had never existed, H3 would be plagued with disasters, because the freeway is destroying the *heiau*, ancient burials and lands sacred to Papahānaumoku, the earth mother. It is Hawaiian *Akua* (ancestral Gods) who in their anger have the power to make freeways fall apart; I have no power. (Kame'eleihiwa Transcript 1996a)

In the "Letters" section of the *Honolulu Star Bulletin*, some readers angrily reviled Kame'eleihiwa. One reader put her "on the same moral plane as terrorists who phone in bomb warnings" (Niles 1996), while others doubted her abilities as a scholar (Gardewin 1996; Niles 1996). However, many letters were from readers who agreed with Kame'eleihiwa's interpretation and disbelieved the scientific explanation. One reader argued:

If the land and yearning of its people for justice ultimately prevail over the fundamental evils of militarism, commercialism and colonialism, H3 may continue to be beset with problems. If H3's problem is fundamentally moral and spiritual, it will never be solved by scientific explanations. (Ikuta 1996)

Another reader asked the following:

How do you explain things that go against rational thinking? This sacred area has been trampled and desecrated, all for the construction of yet another freeway that we surely don't need.

As a Native Hawaiian, I appreciate and respect my kupunas (elders), who have instilled in me the sacredness and mana of an area such as Moanalua Valley. The true results of these investigation reports will not be made public because you cannot question "ghosts." (Akina 1996)

But it was not a just a matter of "ghosts," the girder collapse had economic implications as well. Walter Kupau, an official of the Hawaiian Carpenters Union, said that union members refused to work on the collapsed portion of H3 until the construction site was blessed by a Hawaiian priest.[5] "We'll picket if we have to," Kupau told the *Star Bulletin* (Christensen 1996, A5).

The controversy that erupted around Kameʻeleihiwa's commentary and the series of letters in support of her position offered a glimpse into the often concealed rage of colonized Hawaiians, a rage buried in the kaona of stories about the power of rocks. In the late twentieth century, just below the surface of aloha canned for the benefit of tourists and the rhetoric about Hawaiʻi's multiracial harmony, simmered a minefield of tensions that often had little space for public expression.[6] Sovereignty movement leaders, Kameʻeleihiwa in particular, made the rage public, but for Hawaiians not directly involved with the movement, the outrage was sometimes internalized or expressed indirectly. This was an effect of colonialism in Hawaiʻi, an effect of the hegemony of Western rational empiricism and its ability to render Hawaiian ways of knowing merely "superstitious." But if the stories of rocks as agent reflect a sense of Hawaiian anger, then the narratives also speak to the ways in which Hawaiians continue to understand the ʻāina as source and sustenance and not as the commodified means to profit.

CAN THE ANCESTORS SPEAK?

The supportive letters in response to Kameʻeleihiwa's understanding of the power of the ʻāina exemplified ways of knowing and perceiving the world that were distinct from Western conceptions of the rational and empirical. The disjuncture between scientific and spiritual epistemologies that was evident in the letters to the editor was also evident in the work of growing cohorts of Hawaiian university professors and other scholars who articulate ways of knowing history and culture outside of the rules of the traditions of Western rational empiricism.

Manu Aluli Meyer, a professor of education at the University of Hawaiʻi-Hilo, explored the "large and enduring" (Meyer 2001, 125) differences between Hawaiian and Western ways of knowing. Arguing that empiricism is culturally defined (145), Meyer posited that the Hawaiian structure of values, priorities, and spiritual beliefs shapes a uniquely Hawaiian epistemology. The "ontological premise" of Hawaiian empiricism is the conception of the world as "alive and filled with meaning . . . and metaphor" (Meyer 1998a, 39). The *relational* is a fundamental mode of Hawaiian knowing; it organizes experience, trains the senses, and establishes "social cannons of relevance" (Sahlins 1995, 155, cited in Meyer 1998b, 23). The ʻāina, ʻaumākua, the living family (ʻohana), and "the Christian God and the many Hawaiian gods" (akua) form a foundational web through which knowledge is drawn and made meaningful (Meyer 2001, 127). In Hawaiian cosmology, kalo is a fruit of the ʻāina, the historic food staple, and a synonym for the bonds of siblingship. Thus Meyer explores how a complex notion of "feeding" is a metaphor for knowing and understanding (1998b, 23) based on the imperative of interdependence and reciprocity among family, families, the ʻāina, and the gods. Hawaiian knowing also depends, as Meyer explains, upon differences in conceptions of the body. The gut, the naʻau, is the seat of Hawaiian wisdom. As opposed to the mind/body, heart/head dualism of (at least stereotypical conceptions of) Western knowing, the naʻau as the place where understanding begins merges emotional and analytical and intuitive and scientific knowing (Meyer 2001, 143).

Meyer is among the latest cohort of Native scholars[7] teaching in universities in Hawaiʻi and in the United States. Although these scholars were trained in a range of disciplines, their scholarly agendas are anti-colonial and driven by concerns for Hawaiian decolonization. They are as suspicious of haole claims about history and culture as they are about haole politics, in the colonial past and the neocolonial present. It would be incorrect to imagine this group of committed scholars as monolithic though. There are shades of difference between them, in style, in expression, and even in political leaning. As one Hawaiian scholar put it, these divisions often reflect differences in notions about how best to "protect and honor our integrity as a people" (Osorio 2002, 374). However, a critical characteristic of this group is a strong identification as colonized people, and an insistence that "identity (who we think we are)" (Osorio 2002, xx) is the basis for scholarship. Following a distinguished history of anti-colonial theorizing in Hawaiʻi, and in Africa, Asia, and other parts of Oceania and elsewhere, this group of scholars recognizes as primary the cultural, historical, and political degradation of Hawaiians that stemmed from contact with the West. In historian Jonathan Kay Kamakawiwoʻole Osorio's words, Hawaiians are

. . . still a beleaguered race, and our problems come not only from our poverty and homelessness, but from a lingering sense that our "failure" is the result of our own inadequacy as a people. That sense is the result not only of our political oppression, but an insidious discourse that portrays the Western conceptions of government, economics, education and ideals as the only proper and "realistic" models for contemporary societies. This discourse, this language was woven into the cloak of the colonizers in Hawai'i. To reject that colonization necessarily entails rejecting the discourse as well. (Osorio 2002, 259)

Being decolonized, then, depends on a refusal to submit to Western conceptions of the proper and the real and to overcome a shame-based sense of inadequacy. In this process Native Hawaiian scholars have explored the impossibility of knowing the history and culture of the colonized from a Western perspective and have repudiated the truth claims of Western writing about Hawai'i. In her intensely poetic way, Haunani-Kay Trask reads Western histories of Hawai'i in order to expose how they reveal much more about the culture and history of the colonizer.

When historians wrote that the king owned the land and the common people were bound to it, they were saying that ownership was the only way human beings in their world could relate to the land. . . . And when they said that our chiefs were despotic, they were telling of their own society, where hierarchy always results in domination. . . . And when they wrote that Hawaiians were lazy, they meant that work must be continuous and ever a burden. . . . And when they wrote that we were superstitious, believing in the *mana* of nature and people, they meant that the West has long since lost a deep spiritual and cultural relationship to the earth. (Trask 1993, 153)

Like Meyer, Trask posited that this connection with the land, the language, and the spirituality of the ancestors was a critical means of knowing Hawaiian history and culture. In *From a Native Daughter*, Trask described her process of learning Hawaiian history and language.

To know my history, I had to put away my books and return to the land. I had to plant taro in the earth before I could understand the inseparable bond between people and the *'āina*. I had to feel again the spirits of nature and take gifts of plants and fish to the ancient altars. I had to begin to speak my language with the elders and leave long silences for wisdom to grow. But before anything else, I needed to learn the language like a lover so that I could rock within her and lie at night in her dreaming arms. (1993, 154)

Defining distinct epistemologies, elucidating the expansive sense of Hawaiian empiricism, refusing to submit to Western conceptions of the real and rational, reading Western analysis as diagnostic of the West, and understanding that knowledge is a relationship with language, land and ancestors are joined by the powerful tools of retranslation and reinterpretation of nineteenth-century Hawaiian language texts. The scholar Noenoe K. Silva's (2004) fine book, *Aloha Betrayed: Native Hawaiian Resistance to American Colonialism*, meticulously documented the "consciously and continuously organized" struggle to preserve Hawaiian "lands and life ways" and to resist being colonized. Her groundbreaking work opens up the possibilities for a new understanding of the historical and cultural realities of being colonized and problematizes the troubling reality that the history, politics, and anthropology of Hawai'i have been conducted almost exclusively in English, ignoring the wealth of source material available in Hawaiian.

UBIQUITOUS DEBATE

As the letters to the editor in response to the demonizing of Kame'eleihiwa demonstrated, it was not just Native Hawaiian academics who were engaged in processes of (re)learning Hawaiian ways of being and knowing. In the mid-1990s the Hawaiian movement was heating up, and many cultural revitalization conversations and practices about what it meant to be Hawaiian were occurring across the Islands. These exchanges of thoughts and information about things Hawaiian occurred across educational levels, among Hawaiians of diverse class backgrounds and in a variety of public and private settings.

In Wai'anae (as elsewhere in the Islands) Hawaiians emphasized the project of *decolonization*. The overarching goal of the Native Hawaiian sovereignty movement in the 1990s was official, public recognition of a sovereign Hawaiian nation, but in Wai'anae, the emphasis was on the *internal* process that occurred in the bodies and souls of Hawaiians. In the lexicon of movement leaders in Wai'anae, decolonization was a process that involved dreaming, (re)membering, and (re)creating Hawaiian ways of understanding the body and soul and the means to heal it. In Wai'anae, decolonizing meant rejecting the shame and self-loathing that defines colonized people.

In the mid-1990s, Hawaiians in Wai'anae were actively debating the meaning of independence from the United States, and the crucial importance of cultural revitalization. One of the most important issues discussed in Wai'anae was the notion that colonialism was a deadly experience for Hawaiians, and that the damage and dispossession of colonialism continued to ramify as shame in the bodies and souls of Hawaiians in the late twentieth century. The ravages of Western living were perceived to include such manifestations as physical and mental disease, shame, and family dysfunction. High rates of heart disease, cancer, and diabetes were understood as the result of ingesting Western foods and living sedentary Western lifestyles, while drug and alcohol addiction were viewed as effects of Western modernity. Feelings of shame about being Hawaiian were thought to ramify in families and across generations and were supported by mainstream discourses that portrayed Hawaiian neighborhoods as crime-infested areas replete with single mothers on welfare. The cultural revitalization movement attempted to deal with these existential and discursive issues by treating shame as a source of ill-being, and by translating and reinterpreting traditions that had been driven underground and almost forgotten into a basis for contemporary healing and recovery.

Some argued that disease and dysfunction—the fact that Hawaiians were overrepresented among those incarcerated, those who dropped out of high school, those who were addicted to legal and illegal substances, and those who died and were debilitated by chronic and infectious disease—were a result of colonization and Americanization. Many Wai‘anae Hawaiians believed that colonization had diminished and degraded their ancestors, and that the effects of colonization had continuous and contemporary manifestations. The idea that shame was the most enduring colonial legacy was quite common, and some Wai‘anae Hawaiians argued that the intergenerational transmission of shame had a similar effect on families and communities as drug and alcohol addiction did.

It was common to hear Wai‘anae Hawaiians in the mid-1990s discussing a deep sense of grief for all that had been lost in the process of being colonized, and asserting the notion that a return to Hawaiian ways of being and knowing was the cure for the existential condition of Hawaiians under Western rule. Not everyone agreed on the meaning of Hawaiian culture, or the need for Hawaiian independence from the United States. These critical issues were constantly being debated, and it sometimes seemed as if the entire community was engaged in a cacophony of expression on what it meant to "be Hawaiian."

In jazz, a strong and flexible rhythmic repetition is the foundation for an overlay of sometimes discordant improvisational explorations. In Wai‘anae, an underlying theme was the struggle against shame and inadequacy, while the improvisational riffs were vast and tangled debates about the meaning of culture and nation in neocolonial, post-statehood Hawai‘i.

THEY CATCH YOUR SPIRIT AND MAKE YOU SICK

Herbert Hunokeli spoke with me about the shame he inherited from his parents. Hunokeli's father hid his ability to speak Hawaiian and made sure that his children were English-only speakers. His mother kept secrets about the ancestors.

Both parents made sure that Hunokeli and his siblings saw themselves as "different from the Hawaiians" (field notes).

Hunokeli's mother expressed a great deal of shame and embarrassment because her father was a kahuna. In the times of ka po'e kahiko, before inundation with Western ideas and practices attempted to strip nature of spiritual meaning, kāhuna were ritual experts whose training was rigorous and demanded superior intellect. There were kāhuna in several different fields: kāhuna pule, prayer experts who were temple priests belonging to hereditary castes; kāhuna 'anā'anā, experts in sorcery or wounding magic (Handy, Handy, and Pukui 1991, 322); and kāhuna lā'au lapa'au, or healing experts who used medicinal herbs and counter-sorcery to heal spiritual imbalance and loss of physical strength (Chun 1986, 23). Kāhuna 'anā'anā practiced "the dread arts of sorcery" by channeling their supernatural power toward the purposes of "death dealing prayers or spells." But 'anā'anā was only one form of expert knowledge among others. However, the Calvinist Christian emphasis on 'anā'anā, or negative sorcery, altered the meaning of the word kahuna. Under the influence of Christian dualistic notions of good and evil, kahuna came to mean "witch" or "sorcerer" rather than expert (Pukui et. al 1979, 147, 159–63, 311).

Christian notions of sin and danger influenced Hunokeli's mother, and when she married she refused to allow her father to visit her home. Hunokeli remembered his mother's descriptions of her father and stories about how his involvement in sorcery led to his illness:

> *Mom described him as a "no good slob." He was a kahuna and girls would come to ask him for love potion.[7] He prayed to his own gods. My Auntie remembers a glass of whiskey emptying on the table without anyone drinking it. There were two kinds of kahunas. Bad ones could hurt another person, paralyze or kill them, hex them—like they didn't have to be there to do it. They could get your underwear or a sock and use that to work against you. They could catch your spirit and make you sick. [My grandfather] sent out a spirit to do dirty work. But if you send a spirit out and it meets a stronger spirit it boomerangs back on you. . . . He got paralyzed and had his room painted black, and had the windows shuttered and nailed shut.*
> (Field notes)

Roland Barthes (1972, 142–43) argued that myth works to depoliticize speech, to rob it of historical contingency, to render it eternal. Myth, Barthes argued, brackets historical and social contexts, making stories about the past seem timeless and unattached to oppressive realities. Without taking into account critical colonial conditions—the hegemony of Christianity and the incessant denigration of Hawaiian culture by powerful foreigners—Hunokeli's memories of his mother's stories are not intelligible. In the story of the debasement of a kahuna, the imagery of a man trapped and paralyzed in a closed black space conjures up a sense of ignominy, and of odious and shameful acts that must be hidden away. In this way, Hawaiian cosmology and spirituality was demoted and mythologized, while Western religion was naturalized and made seamlessly unproblematic. Hunokeli's story, told from the perspective of his mother's shame about her father's Hawaiian gods, reinforced the claims of Christian righteousness. "If you send a spirit out and it meets a stronger spirit it boomerangs back on you," Hunokeli said. Implicitly marking Christianity as "the" powerful religion, the downfall of a kahuna can be attributed to the inability of Hawaiian sorcery to stand against the potent mana of Western religion.

The story of the kahuna is relevant for its description of the deep rift that occurred between generations as Americans attempted to inculcate the moral economy of capitalism into young Hawaiians. Hunokeli was educated in Territorial Hawai'i when schools were explicit about their work "in civilizational uplift" (Hyams 1985), and the goal of colonial education was the colonization of the mind and imagination (Hereniko 2001, 164). Barthes argued that the function of myth was to empty reality, to evaporate meaning, and to naturalize social productions in a colonized world. In Barthes's schema, to mythologize was to organize a "world . . . without contradictions" (1972, 143), a world in which voices of resistance and difference are silenced by the taken-for-granted quality of colonizer superiority.

In order for reality to be emptied, the colonized must be induced to forget. Being colonized by America meant that systematically and structurally in law, policy, and practice, and, in more subtle and implicit ways in mind and imagination, forgetting was enforced. The precolonial past was represented as shameful, and the debasement of Hawaiian culture and power was rendered inevitable.

I heard many stories of the derogation of Hawaiian bodies and beliefs and of the disruption of Hawaiian families in Wai'anae in the mid-1990s. What was extraordinary, however, were the ways in which shame and shameful memories were transformed by thoughtful processes of remembering that often occurred in community settings.

KŪPUNA SPEAK

In 1996, the "Year of the Hawaiian Language" was declared as a celebration of the fact that 'ōlelo Hawai'i (Hawaiian language) was alive and thriving. Schools where Hawaiian was the exclusive language of instruction (Celis 1994) were about to graduate a twelfth grade, and, for the first time in generations, children were *publicly* speaking Hawaiian. For those born during the years when Hawai'i was a territory of the United States, whose parents and grandparents spoke

Hawaiian, but who were forced to speak English in school, a new generation of children whose intellectual development occurred in the suppressed language of their ancestors was a momentous event and a motivation to remember.

The Hawaiian language was banned in public and private schools in 1893, after the coup overthrowing Queen Lili'uokalani. Banning the language was part of a larger American strategy for the education and assimilation of Natives in Hawai'i that was guided by American ideologies that justified colonialism. According to Benham and Heck (1998), American schools in Hawai'i were built upon three broad ideological assumptions. First, Protestant theology, which emphasized spiritual elevation and individual salvation and morality, attempted to instantiate Christianity as normative and hegemonic. Second, the schools taught a "savage-to-civilization paradigm of social evolution" (1998, 9) that rested on the notion that Native cultures and people would either be assimilated into the West, or would perish. Third, the concept of Anglo-American manifest destiny that provided the rationale for the taking of land and resources justified the colonization of Hawai'i. These ideological underpinnings shaped Hawaiian education from the mid-nineteenth century, and the enforcement of English is a clear example of these policies (1998, 9–10).

By the mid-twentieth century, English was the lingua franca and the official language of the Islands. Writing in 1942, anthropologist Martha Beckwith described the Hawaiian language as "lost to popular usage," and she claimed that less than 2 percent of Hawaiians could speak and read it. She noted, however, that Hawaiians in "out districts (rural places and places outside of the main cities)" spoke and understood the language "after a fashion" (Beckwith 1942, 255). In the 1920s, a recording of 300 Hawaiian chants was produced by the Bishop Museum from a group of Hawaiians who lived mainly in rural areas on Kaua'i and Hawai'i (Tatar 1981, 482). Thus although the Hawaiian language was degraded and diminished, it survived in the rural outskirts and sometimes in memory, and, in 1979, the Hawaiian State Legislature passed an amendment to the state's constitution, recognizing it as an official language of the state, along with English (Matsunaga 1994b). In the summer of 1996, Hawaiian language classes offered through local community associations were becoming more common as interest in (re)learning 'ōlelo Hawai'i spread beyond places of formal education and into the community.

A community-based Hawaiian language class that I attended in Wai'anae in the mid-1990s was free and open to all,[8] and most of the students were women in their fifties and sixties. Although the classes were ostensibly for beginners, many of the women in the class easily conversed at length in Hawaiian and appeared able to speak and comprehend the language at an advanced level. It was in such community-level language classes that women who had come of age in the mid-twentieth century were first able to confront their sense of shame around the language, one of the most enduring legacies of colonialism. One of the women in the class said that her grandchildren attended a Hawaiian language school and that she wanted to be able to speak with them in Hawaiian. "I hardly speak to them," she said. "They have a bigger [Hawaiian] vocabulary than I have. I wish I could speak to them though. But they understand that I have a hard time with my vocabulary, so they let me slide if I say something wrong" (field notes).

Albert Memi wrote that the colonized person "seems condemned to lose [her] memory" (1965, 103). Indeed, the women in the community language classes seemed to have forgotten that they could communicate in Hawaiian. Kalama Liu,[9] a Wai'anae social worker, shed light on why women who seemed to be fluent Hawaiian speakers would sign up for a beginner's class. Liu remembered his Auntie Leilani's stories about the effects of the colonial suppression of Hawaiian language. Although Leilani learned Hawaiian as her primary language, she learned to forget it as she made her way through a school system in which the English language was strictly enforced.

> When [Auntie Leilani] got to school, the first day . . . the teacher split the class in half and said all the Hawaiian kids get to that wall, and all the other kids get to that wall. And the teacher, she was part-Hawaiian. You know [this is an example of] . . . horizontal oppression.[10] She tells the Hawaiian kids: 'This is an English school. In English school you only speak English. I don't want to hear Hawaiian.' And that's part of that cultural cutting off the language. And my Auntie says she even remembers that first day, you know this is as a child, and Hawaiian is her first language, and she was on the play yard, and she calls on one of her friends, "Hūi Melia, huuuuuuui." And [the girl] told the teacher, "She called me Melia, I'm Mary." And so the teacher called my Auntie and she told her your name is not Leilani you are Lilly now. Renaming. . . . And then she said after school you stay here and you write "I will not speak Hawaiian." And my Auntie remembers as a child not even knowing the alphabet, she didn't know what she was writing, but the teacher wrote the first sentence and she had to copy it over and over again.[11]
>
> You get shame, it is very shame-based. And even when she went home she used to have arguments with her grandmother, because her grandmother used to tell her, "No, in this house you speak Hawaiian, you only speak Hawaiian." So she said that [at] about [age] 13 or 14 she stopped speaking Hawaiian altogether. (Interview with Kalama Liu, March 4, 1997, Wai'anae, Hawai'i)

Mailelani Campos,[12] a student in the community language class, was born in the 1930s and raised in a small fishing village on the island of Hawai'i. Mailelani told a similar story about "conversion" to English. Although Mailelani spoke fluent Hawaiian, and often helped me with my Hawaiian homework, she disparaged her own language abilities. Her Hawaiian was not that good, she said, because she didn't "know the rules" (field notes).

> *When we went to school in . . . Kona, the teacher . . . said just stop it. We could only speak English when we were in school. [At home] with all of my aunties and uncles we spoke Hawaiian. . . . [Now] I don't know the Hawaiian language, when I moved to Honolulu I lost it. Now I have to go to school [to relearn the language] . . . it's so hard.*
>
> *I remember at home one time with my tūtū [grandmother]. . . she wanted me to talk to her in Hawaiian . . . I could understand her but I couldn't remember what to say to her [in Hawaiian] . . . I couldn't remember how you say the [numbers] so I said "two loaf bread," and she said "two loaf bread?" I had lost the Hawaiian . . . but it wasn't our fault, when we went to school . . . all we used was English. [My tūtū was upset] because she couldn't speak English, so it was hard for her to understand us.* (Campos 1997)

Another language student, Hannah Dias,[13] remembered the trauma of school and the need to forget Hawaiian. She was, she said, very ashamed that she was a "full-blooded Hawaiian who cannot speak my language." Like Mailelani, Hannah mentioned her need to relearn the language in school and expressed regret that she had not learned it from her own mother. (field notes)

These stories demonstrate the way in which American colonial hegemony reached deep into Hawaiian families and disrupted intergenerational communication—the transmission of culture. The imposition of English on Hawaiian schoolchildren in the twentieth century created a language barrier that ruptured Hawaiian families and created the conditions of "forgetting." Between Hannah, Leilani, Mailelani, and their parents and grandparents, a gap opened up that signified the triumph of Americanization.

Memi argued that colonized schoolchildren are severed from their language, culture, and history and are assigned new memories and new histories as they are inculcated with the colonizer's language. Hawaiian was the mother tongue, the lingua franca of "feelings, emotions, and dreams," the means for the expression of "tenderness and wonder." But the language of the colonized becomes

> . . . precisely that one which is the least valued. It has no stature in the country or in the concert of peoples. If he wants to obtain a job, make a place for himself, exist in the community of the world, he must first bow to the language of his masters. In the linguistic conflict within the colonized, his mother tongue is that which is crushed. He himself sets

about discarding this infirm language hiding it from sight. (Memi 1965, 105, 107–108)

Similarly, in his discussion of Jewish self-hatred, Sander Gilman (1992) explored the effects of an imposed language. Since the marginal are forced to function within the discourse that labels them as "different," they are "forced to speak using the polluted language that designates them as Other." It is thus in questions of language, Gilman argues, that "tensions of Otherness and . . . of self-hatred can best be examined" (1992, 14–15; see also Ngugi Wa Thiong'o 1986).

At a Hawaiian language class I enrolled in at the University of Hawai'i, great emphasis was placed on the rules of grammar, on drilling and sentence structure, and on diacritical marks. Unlike classes held at community centers, the class at the university was meant to codify and unify a resurgent language. The community classes, however, were also social gatherings, with plenty of food and drink, singing, and joking (see Meyer 2001, 124–48). It seemed that one of the most important effects of the classes in the community was to authorize the process of remembering for a generation of submerged Hawaiian speakers, to give them permission to remember the language of their birth, to transcend their shame about being Hawaiian. The women in the community classes had been children in the territory of Hawai'i and had become adults as Hawai'i became a state. For some of them, Hawaiian was their first language. Their shame reflected school policy that prohibited speaking Hawaiian, discouraged the use of Hawaiian first names, and denigrated and infantilized discourse on nā mea Hawai'i (Hawaiian culture, language, spirituality). As Errington (2001, 21) noted, colonial linguistics was a "nexus of technology (literacy), reason, and faith and . . . a project of multiple conversion: of pagan to Christian, of speech to writing, and of the alien to the comprehensible." The value of missionary linguistic projects, he argued, was less in the collection of empirical data than "in the assertion of spiritual dominion through language." The language of the colonizer, he wrote, naturalized colonial categories of social difference and ethnocultural identity, which "concretize[d] and normalize[d] the territorial logic" of Euro/American power (2001, 23).

Fanon wrote in *Black Skins, White Masks* that "[t]he colonized is elevated above his jungle status in proportion to his adoption of the mother country's cultural standards. . . . To speak a language is to take on a world, a culture" (1967, 18, 38). The colonized gains privilege and access to the colonizer through subsuming her language, by forgetting it, in order to wield the cultural tool of the colonizer's language. For the generations that were born in the midst of this transition—Hawaiians born in the earlier twentieth century—being colonized meant an enduring sense of shame, an eroded sense of self-esteem, a lack of trust in Hawaiian language, culture, and spirituality, and the absolute imperative of adopting the language and cultural standards of America.

MOURNING "GENETIC" PAIN

The profound weight of this cultural shame was expressed eloquently in 1964 by John Dominis Holt, a (self-described) hapa-Hawaiian (half-Hawaiian) descended from royal Hawaiian lineage. Holt (1974) wrote in the essay *On Being Hawaiian*, which explored issues of Hawaiian identity and Hawaiian rage, about the "white power structure." Although it was written in the year following the publication of Fanon's *Wretched of the Earth* (1963), it was less an anti-colonial treatise than a plea for Hawaiian civil rights, ethnic pride, and dignity. It did not, for example, challenge the notion of statehood. Holt wrote that he was proud of being Hawaiian, as well as "proud to be linked to a heritage that gave the fiftieth state some of its blessed uniqueness of character." The question for Holt was how could Hawaiians become ". . . active, participating, productive, first-class citizens of the United States?" (1974, 17–18).

Holt laments the "devastatingly complete" losses that Hawaiians had suffered, including the loss of "ethnic consciousness," sovereignty, and the throne of Hawai'i. The self-respect of Hawaiians, he wrote, was constantly undermined by criticism of Hawaiian ways and stereotypes of lazy, laughing, loveable Natives. Hawaiians, he argued, shared a legacy of shame (7–8).

Holt wrote at the dawn of the modern Hawaiian cultural renaissance, at a moment when Hawaiians were beginning to remember the past. In a piece that echoes some of the concerns of Du Bois (1999) in the *Souls of Black Folk*,[14] Holt expressed the pain of Hawaiian shame.

> You cannot tell a people, whose very souls you have ensnared, that *everything* about their traditional way of life was bad, without breaking their spirit—especially when you offer no concrete social and economic solutions as a substitute for the old order. You cannot expect a people who must live with the reality of the total ruin of their centuries-old culture, and the loss by death of eighty percent of their numbers in one hundred years following the arrival of the first foreigners, to be suddenly bright-eyed and bushy tailed about the life around them. (Holt 1974, 17–18, emphasis in original)

The experience of transforming shame, of learning to be proud, was still a difficult journey for the grandchildren of those who had first been forced to speak English. But in the 1990s there were many more possibilities for the exercise of pride. Sherri Lynn Sussex, a Wai'anae resident, political activist, and granddaughter, was a high school student in the 1970s. She remembered that at Wai'anae High School in the mid-1970s that there was only one Hawaiian language class, and she had not yet understood that there "was anything wrong."

We had one teacher at Wai'anae High School who was teaching Hawaiian language, lucky ten of us signed up for it. . . . But mainly we learned how to play 'ukulele, I played the music, that's all I got today. You know now, my brother Palama [a sophomore in high school] is such a different character than I was. And he is so . . . you know he like talk the language. . . . That was not an option for me, the classes weren't offered. (Interview with Sherri Lynn Sussex, April 10, 1997, Wai'anae, Hawai'i)

What Sherri Lynn remembers as the catalyst for change was the release of Israel Kamakawiwo'ole's song "Hawai'i '78." When it was first released, the song created reverberations in the cultural consciousness of many Hawaiians. In the lead to "Hawai'i '78" on the album *Facing Future*, Kamakawiwo'ole's voice-over explains the subject of the song:

This song is entitled, Hawai'i 1978. To us . . . this song is a very touching song because it tells a story of our ancestors of yesterday. And of our society today. Specifically this song talks about our King and Queen. And if they had the chance to come back and walk the land once more, could you imagine, just imagine, how they would feel and what they would say about the condominiums and hotels that are built on sacred land. Imagine, imagine how they'd feel about the traffic lights and freeways. . . . Could you imagine yourself watching your King and Queen walk the land today, and all of a sudden they come up to a fence, with a sign upon it that says "Keep Out. No Trespassing." People, how would they feel to walk the land today? The life of this 'āina, this land, is perpetuated in righteousness for you and I, the people . . . would they smile, be content, or would they just cry? Today our generation cries for the gods that passed. They cry out for ourselves. Most of all they cry for the land that was taken away. And, yet they call this land, this 'āina, Hawai'i. (Kamakawiwo'ole 1998, emphasis added)

This song, Sherri Lynn said, helped Hawaiians remember their cultural losses and recognize the lies and distortions of official Hawaiian history. Kamakawiwo'ole's emphasis on the act of *imagining* specifically asks the listener to think beyond Western myths of Hawai'i, to remember a different past and conjure a different present. As Lewis (1991, 55; see also Trask 1993, 179–200) has argued, significant shifts in Hawaiian popular music in the twentieth century clearly demonstrated commercial music's role in ideology building. When the first Hawaiian musicians cut records for the American recording industry, the images evoked by the music were "cartoon[s] . . . of the islands as a lush, vacation playground, populated by smiling natives . . . welcome[ing] of visitors from afar" (Lewis 1991, 56). The images prevalent in the mid-twentieth century also trivialized and ridiculed Hawaiian people, and Hawaiian artists like Alfred Apaka and Don Ho were thoroughly involved in delivering these degrading messages to a largely tourist audience. Apaka sang songs such as "Princess Poo-Pooly" that both debased the cultural heritage of Hawai'i and titillated foreigners with puerile depictions of sexuality.[15]

"Hawaiian soul," the music that helped give birth to the Hawaiian sovereignty movement of the 1970s, was a conscious merging of the traditions of chanting and slack key guitar with music as social protest that both celebrated the culture and traditions of Native Hawaiians and protested the cultural domination of the United States (Lewis 1991, 61, 53).

> The new music, in its choice of lyrics, its use of the Hawaiian language, and its modes of presentation, serve[d] to identify sources of discontent of the local population and to address, to a great extent, three major issues prominent as social concerns in Hawai'i: 1) land use issues; 2) ecological and cultural impacts of mass tourism; and 3) the destruction of traditional culture and the dying out of the Hawaiian race. (Lewis 1985b, 159)

Musicians committed to the movement "refused to continue the tradition of 'cute' names of the past, like the Royal Hawaiian Serenaders or the Wiakiki Beachboys—names that conjured up images of happy-go-lucky brown lackeys of the Hawaiian films and nightclubs" (Lewis 1984, 49). Instead, they created names for themselves that reflected the importance of the 'āina. The Mākaha Sons, for example, were named after the Mākaha area on the Wai'anae Coast, and their music especially captured the attention and loyalty of Wai'anae Hawaiians. First known as a member of the group the Mākaha Sons of Ni'ihau, Israel Kamakawiwo'ole was a greatly beloved figure of Hawaiian resistance and popular culture. The new soul music managed to inspire Hawaiians across generations, and this is one of the keys to understanding what made it soulful in the first place.

> . . . [C]ritics called the Son's music "unspoiled," "pure and simple," and "down home." These qualities captivated Hawaiian elders, and at the same time, the new songs drew young people who were grateful for a group willing to sing songs describing the desecration of their native lands. In one set, the Sons might have combined a traditional Hawaiian hymn from their childhood . . . [with a song] about the pleasure of smoking marijuana . . . or [a song] whose lyrics expressed contempt for a Caucasian plantation boss riding a big white horse ("here comes that son of a bitchin' haole"). (Hartwell 1996, 25)

"It was when I was in high school and . . . [Kamakawiwoʻole] said now you gotta take the Hawaiian language and we was like 'Hey, what'chu mean . . . there was an illegal overthrow of our Queen'" (interview with Sherri Lynn Sussex, 1997). Sherri Lynn was clear that the Hawaiian pride evident in the 1990s was the result of a long struggle with shame and contempt for Hawaiian language and culture that was instilled by a haole-dominated society. "It is a genetic pain," Sherri Lynn said, "that is in your family for so long. What we need now is mourning time, grieving time, healing time, a way for people to grieve their losses and move on."

Like official versions of history, the production of Hawaiian music for the consumption of tourists portrayed Hawaiians as incapable of sovereignty.[16] Haoles were historical agents and absent from the degrading portrayals of happy and promiscuous Natives. Part of leaving behind the shame of being colonized was finding the courage to define culture and politics and to develop agendas for social change. The blossoming of the sovereignty movement in the late twentieth century indicated that, for many, the courage had been found.

DYSFUNCTION

Shame was a corrosive emotion that exacerbated forgetting, and its effects were felt deeply at the level of Hawaiian families and communities. It created distance between parents and children and was passed through generations. Colonialism ideologically debased Hawaiian ways of being and knowing and subverted the transmission of relevant wisdom. Many of the Hawaiians I met and interviewed believed that, in place of viable cultural practices and beliefs, dysfunction was passed through the generations.

Lokomaikaʻi Chung's[17] Hawaiian grandparents also were forced to speak English. Although Chung was not involved in any political organizations and was deeply skeptical about the goal of sovereignty, he was passionately committed to the Hawaiian cultural renaissance and involved in the production of island-wide hula competitions. He learned the Hawaiian language and was teaching it to his nieces and nephews. He believed that colonialism had poisoned generations of Hawaiian families in much the same way as alcoholism and drug addiction. He said that neither he nor his parents were addicted, but that both sets of his grandparents were alcoholics. He had assimilated the logic of Al-Anon,[18] a support organization for the family and friends of alcoholics, into a set of beliefs that helped him deal with issues around self-esteem and feelings of shame about being Hawaiian. The insight that nonalcoholics could exhibit alcoholic behavior was key to Chung's philosophy of life, as was the view that the shame of being colonized reverberated through generations. "We were not raised Hawaiian, we were raised haole [white]," he told me, "because you get ahead if you are haole. Now, since the [Hawaiian cultural] renaissance, since the '70s, everybody is trying to be Hawaiian again" (interview with Lokomaika'i Chung, 1996). Chung described his "quest" to understand his life, his family, and his culture. It was, he said, Al-Anon that finally taught him the dimensions of his loss.

> *So now, we know more about alcoholism. We know that the behavior can be passed on to the next generation even if the next generation does not drink. The behavior is there . . . exhibiting the behavior of an alcoholic, yet not drinking.*
>
> *That was a discovery. And we had to learn not to blame them [the grandparents] because that was the only tools that they had. . . . So what we are trying to do with the next generation is we know where we come from, and people in my line, in my generation, still have the behavior. But when we work ourselves, we are not extending that behavior to the next generation.* (Interview with Lokomaika'i Chung, February 23, 1996)

Alcoholism, in Chung's view, was one of the few survival tools available to the generations being colonized. Reaching out to his keiki (children),[19] Chung was both attempting to repair the damage done to him by his ancestors and modeling behavior that, he believed, would stop the transmission of destructive behaviors stemming from the trauma of being colonized.

In Chung's narrative, alcoholism is the exemplar of a cluster of behaviors introduced to Hawaiians through contact with the West, those behaviors that reflected the self-loathing of being colonized. The Alcoholics Anonymous logic of the intergenerational transmission of alcoholism is appropriated by Chung as an analytic tool to explain the state of Hawaiian culture as a result of Western colonization. The challenge, as Chung articulated it, was to override the influence of commodified Western culture, as transmitted through television, on the present generation. The challenge was to "teach [the children] to be proud of their heritage, to be secure within themselves, and not to be afraid out there" (Chung 1996).

Teaching his children to be Hawaiian was no small challenge. Constantly bombarded with Western culture and values, it was easy for children to ignore the lessons about the importance of knowing Hawaiian history and tradition.

> *The problem is propaganda coming across the TV. We need to get family back into family. . . . But the "babysitter,"—the TV—makes kids think that the things advertised grows on trees. . . . The parents can say, 'no need, no need,' but the TV constantly makes the kids want these things.* (Chung 1996)

Chung said that when he finally got his nieces and nephews to sit down for the Hawaiian language tutor, their "terrible attitude(s)" were "overpowering," since they want "to be cheerleader(s), and . . . do MTV."

> *Every time I get the class going I want to wring their necks. . . . "I don't give a fuck about what you are thinking about, we are going back to how it is." But that is my bad behavior—impatience. So, I think the only thing we can do with our own personal family is repeat, I don't care if it is a broken record. . . . Because subliminally it will stick. So just repeat the information, it will create some basic grounding. You know what? If a person felt confident in who they are and what they are, they can achieve anything they want in life. Nobody can take that away from them, they are grounded, they are secure.* (Chung 1996)

As the proprietor of a hair salon, Chung also made himself responsible for educating his clients in Hawaiian ways. Clients waiting for beautification might browse the salon's collection of books on Hawaiian myth and history, read the Hawaiian language lesson on the chalkboard in the corner, or sit and talk story for the afternoon. While cutting, coloring, and styling hair, Chung might discuss some aspect of "Kahunaism" or the merits of Christian Orthodox theology versus Buddhist philosophy. Aside from discussion on Hawaiian politics, religion, philosophy, and culture, there was always much conversation about alcoholism and codependency. Indeed, many customers identified themselves as part of the Alcoholics Anonymous or Al-Anon fellowship.

The atmosphere of the salon (as both a place of beauty and of learning and debate) was due in large part to the intensity with which Chung did both hair and philosophy. In 1982, he won a prestigious cosmetologists' award that honored his excellence. And although his degree, from the University of Hawai'i-Mānoa, was in outdoor recreation, several years after graduating from college he began to read Hawaiian religion and philosophy and Christian theology. Well read and opinionated, Chung appreciated a good debate. One afternoon, as he colored a client's hair, Chung discussed the importance of the traditional Hawaiian system of land use and its difference from the Western conception of private property. The ahupua'a system, the Hawaiian system of resource distribution in the times of ka po'e kahiko, was based on use rights, and, as Chung argued, it was a manifestation of reciprocity between the ali'i (the ruling elite) and the maka'āinana. After contact with the West, a cash economy replaced the system of reciprocity.

> *The concept of money was hard for us to grasp, when this money t'ing came around. The new ali'i, the white person, never gave us nu'ting. But the*

Hawaiian ali'i, through a system of reciprocity, cared for all the people.
(Field notes)

The conversations in the hair salon and throughout Wai'anae in the 1990s demonstrate the quotidian nature of local discourse on being Hawaiian, and the degree to which the issues surrounding the struggle for Hawaiian cultural integrity were actively being debated. The public reemergence of Native Hawaiian practices and systems of knowing in the 1990s showed that, despite a century of formal American rule, Hawaiian culture was thriving.

By reframing issues of Native Hawaiian social dysfunction away from personal inadequacy and toward notions of cultural trauma, by challenging the assumption that Western lifestyles are the most advantageous, and by centering analysis on the corrosive effects of shame, Wai'anae Hawaiians were contesting the logic of colonialism. What was considered dysfunctional in the view espoused by Chung and others in Wai'anae was land as alienable property, culture as commodity, the suppression of Hawaiian language, and a set of transmissible behaviors that derived from shame, self-loathing, and the fear of being Hawaiian.

MEMORY AND TRANSCENDENCE

The story about Auntie Leilani's experience with the enforcement of the English language is an example of both the transmission of memory and the preservation of tradition. For Auntie Leilani's generation, the fact that these stories are being retold and reinterpreted by young people—who are themselves struggling to (re)learn Hawaiian—is both validation and an invitation to remember.

American hegemony marginalized Hawaiian language and culture. But although nā mea Hawai'i were hidden from sight, they were never really forgotten. Certeau (1997, 129–32) reminds us that memory must be accounted for in any analysis of communication. The circulation of memories and the production of narratives by those who lived during the years when the English language was first enforced by the colonizers made possible the act of remembering. The stories of trauma by schoolchildren attending English-only schools or adapting to Western culture[20] are common, everyday narratives. The telling of these stories across generations—from grandparents to grandchildren—is itself an act of resistance to the official, sanitized stories of the fiftieth state. Certeau posited that the repetitive telling of tales works to "reinscribe the past in the present." The transmission of these life stories from grandparents to grandchildren creates, in Certeau's phrase, a "cultural memory" that establishes an intergenerational link "transmitting to the youngest members fragments of earlier practices and ways of knowing" (1997, 131–32). From the vantage point of official history, these memories are both polyphonic and fragile. But Chung's Hawaiian history lectures in the relaxed atmosphere of a beauty salon demonstrate the quotidian nature of these society-wide debates.

6

DREAMING CHANGE

When I was born my mother gave me three names.
Christabelle, Yoshie, and Puanani

Christabelle was my "english" name.
My social security name,
My school name,
    the name I gave when teachers asked me
    for my "real" name, a safe name.

Yoshie was my home name,
My everyday name,
    the name that reminded my father's family
    that I was Japanese, even though
    my nose, hips, and feet were wide,
    the name that made me acceptable to them
    who called my Hawaiian mother kuroi (black),
    a saving name.

Puanani is my chosen name,
My piko name connecting me to the 'aina
    and the kai and the po'e kahiko
    my blessing; my burden,
    my amulet, my spear.
        (Punanai Burgess n.d.[1])

When Hawai'i was under martial law, after the Japanese attack on Pearl Harbor in 1941, a baby girl was born whose Hawaiian name was concealed between a Christian first and last name. Concealing Hawaiian names was a widespread form of quiet resistance to the colonial law requiring the use of

"Christian names,"[2] and to the imposition of English as the official language of the Islands. In the 1970s, when this girl was a woman, she helped organize a women's support group with a Maryknoll nun in her home community of Waiʻanae, and significant transformations occurred. Her Hawaiian name—Meipala—emerged, and she began to understand herself as a *Hawaiian woman.* This was when she committed her life to the struggles of suffering Hawaiian people, and her priorities immediately changed. Meipala said that before the women's group she would "wake up in the morning, make breakfast, then go outside to warm up the car for [her] husband. But after [the support group began meeting she] wanted to work outside of the home. . . . [So she] told [her husband], 'get your own beer.'"

Meipala was raised in Papakōlea, on lands set aside for Hawaiians under the Hawaiian Homestead Act. In this Honolulu neighborhood, she learned to be Christian and American. She attended Catholic schools and worked stringing and selling leis to tourists at Aloha Tower Market Place. She remembers that her mother resisted teaching her Hawaiian things, and that adopting American ways was considered positive and progressive.

Her own children were born at a time when the Hawaiian sovereignty movement was becoming impossible to ignore, and she wondered what to teach them. Working with the women's group invested her with a sense of her own power to change things for the better, and when her children encountered difficulties in school, she realized that the school system was systematically discriminating against poor Hawaiian children. Meipala became a public school parent activist. She felt shame when she heard people say that Hawaiians could not write, that she could not write (see Hoʻomanawanui 2004, 87), so the women's group asked a local poet to teach them. It was in the writing groups, where she practiced with short poems, that Meipala's "Hawaiian thinking" emerged. "Writing poems," she said, "helped to connect me with my mother and helped me to develop a sense of hope for my children."

The collective process of Hawaiian women writing was also a collective process of uncovering submerged Hawaiian consciousness, a process that helped Meipala understand the powerful links between Hawaiian women in the present and their mothers and grandmothers. She saw that they were connected to their children and through them to the future. She achieved clarity about generational and ancestral connection. "We were only taught about the present, so we were not allowed to know ourselves" she said. "We were not taught that being Hawaiian meant that we did things differently, lived differently, had different concepts about the world." The poetry writing work helped Meipala see that "all of this wonderful knowledge is deep inside of us."

In the late 1970s, Meipala went to her first sovereignty movement protest. She held a sign that said "Stop the Bombing of Kahoʻolawe." But her fears that she would be recognized, that her mother-in-law might be angry with her, led her to hide her face behind her sign. But more and more, Meipala got involved, and when I first met her in 1994, she was a veteran protestor.

SERENDIPITY

At my desk in Philadelphia, I tried to learn through books about Hawaiian history, culture, and the politics of the sovereignty movement. My interest in medical anthropology, and specifically the ways that the body was impacted by histories of colonialism and other oppression, led me to hope that my fieldwork in Hawai'i might be based in some kind of clinical setting in which Hawaiian ways of seeing and knowing challenged Western conceptions of the body and health. I had no idea if such a place existed, and if it did, I doubted that they would allow my prolonged intrusion as a U.S. anthropologist in training. I had read enough to know that there was a great deal of animosity toward Western educated, mainly white anthropologists who had studied and written about Hawaiians.

Haunani Trask excoriated American anthropologists in *From a Native Daughter* (1993, 123–35), pointing with anger and precision at the ways in which anthropologists have ignored indigenous ways of knowing and have "invent[ed] Native Hawaiian culture at an unbelievable rate." In *From a Native Daughter*, Trask calls for a moratorium on all anthropological and archaeological studies of Hawaiians. The "studying, unearthing, slicing, crushing, and analyzing of us," she wrote, must stop (Trask 1993, 171–72). Trask's insistence that anthropologists stay away was part of what drew me to Hawai'i for fieldwork. There, I thought, is an example of a successful struggle against American hegemony in a world sorely in need of such struggles. There, I thought, Native scholars are pushing back, publishing critiques about the relationship between colonialism and Western scholarship and histories that draw on and articulate Native epistemology. I drew on my community organizing networks to locate contacts in Hawai'i. A friend who worked at an international social justice organization recommended that I contact Meipala Silva, a former staff member at a Honolulu anti-nuclear activist organization. When I arrived in Honolulu for a brief period of preliminary research and called Meipala, I was stunned by the serendipity. At the time of my preliminary field research in 1994, Meipala was working at a Native Hawaiian drug treatment center, and during our initial conversation, she agreed to meet with me. I was nervous driving in a rental car to Wai'anae, and as I sat outside her office waiting for our appointment to begin, Haunani Trask's warning words echoed in my head.

When Meipala came out to greet me, she smiled and said, "Thank god you are not a skinny white girl!" She was tall and large, and the flat planes of her broad face reminded me of a Zuniga sculpture that sat in front of a high-rise

apartment building on Park Avenue in New York City when I was an undergraduate at Hunter College. And this made me relax and imagine that I might have a
foot in the door. We met several times during my six-week stay in Honolulu,
and before I left she tentatively agreed to allow me to enter her work and her
community when I returned.

DREAMING

Meipala dreamt often. Her dreams, she said, were important signs. When she
dreamt that she held the moon in her hands she understood that the goddess
Hina was directing her toward leadership, and she knew that she would work
with great women who would change Hawai'i. "This is my calling," she told me,
"to form a society led by women of Hawaiian spirituality and culture on the
Wai'anae Coast."

Meipala dreamed about the moon in her hands while she was still an anti-
nuclear activist working in Honolulu. Even though she was committed to peace
and anti-nuclear activism in the Pacific, she was dissatisfied working in an international context when her own community of Wai'anae was suffering. Although
she traveled every day eighty miles back and forth to her job in the Mānoa section of Honolulu, she began to volunteer for community action and social service agencies in Wai'anae. She was very busy, but as she told me, she "followed her
passion" to local community work while continuing a full-time job in Honolulu.
She served as a co-principal investigator for a women's cancer research project,
and she served on the boards of the local health center and a program for drug-
addicted teen mothers. She was a grandmother, a mother, and a wife.

But the strain on her was great, and she became very ill. To heal herself she
went to see Auntie Rita—a mana-filled elder with a rare gift of prayerful healing.
In her diagnosis, Auntie Rita told Meipala that the only way she would be healed
was to work healing her Hawaiian people. And so Meipala became the first staff
kūpuna at the Pōka'ī Bay Addiction Center, a Wai'anae-based substance abuse
treatment center that was primarily for clients remanded by the courts in lieu of
incarceration. In kinship terms, kūpuna included the generation of grandparents
and all lateral kin. Kūpuna also signified "forbears and related folk who have
died, or distant forbears in genealogy or legend" (Handy and Pukui 1972[1958],
42–45). Kūpuna in late-twentieth-century Hawai'i were understood to be
sources of wisdom and the means of remembering ka po'e kahiko. In organizational terms, the role of staff kūpuna was "to make things more Hawaiian." For
Meipala this meant (re)creating clinical and therapeutic contexts to support
specifically Hawaiian forms of healing.

In its first years of operation, the drug treatment center was more successful
with clients from other ethnic groups and did not attract a majority of Native

Hawaiians. Native Hawaiians, the group identified as the core constituency, had a great deal of trouble completing the program and entering recovery. When Meipala assumed the role of staff kūpuna, things began to change. Meipala, with a cohort of leaders and activists on the Waiʻanae Coast, had moved toward an understanding that healing was a metaphor for decolonization. She and others viewed the multiple diseases that affected Hawaiians as a lack of mana and pono (social harmony) as a result of being colonized and the imposition of Western ways. In the 1990s, drug addiction and alcoholism were major problems that had deep reverberations through families and the entire community. Addiction was perceived as a family and community issue, not as a problem stemming from an individual organic body, or its individual psyche. In order to create a program specifically tailored to the needs of Hawaiians, it was necessary to challenge the view that disease stemmed from individual bodies divorced from colonial oppression. It was necessary to recognize the ways in which individuals existed in complicated webs of family and community and were ultimately impacted by larger social structures.

The disturbing fact that Hawaiians were not successfully completing the program, and that they were not moving into the phase of recovery, caused a period of intense critical and spiritual reflection on what it might mean to successfully heal Hawaiians. As the staff kūpuna, Meipala led this process. She said:

> When [we] confronted the red flag of the fact that the Hawaiians were not completing the program, [we] interviewed the families and the clients. And the question we asked was, "How can we Hawaiians make things more Hawaiian?" (Field notes)

From the interviews, they learned about the need for programs that were not modeled after Western classrooms, and so clients and counselors "went camping for . . . days and things started to change and people were transformed by the stars and the universe." They learned that in order for clients to release their profound emotional pain they needed therapeutic models that specifically addressed issues of shame and self-loathing and the realities of being a colonized people.

They learned that they needed to create processes that facilitated the release of this profound emotional pain and so, Meipala told me, they developed a model called "deep culture therapy" in which the clients enacted Hawaiian legends and myths.

> My first job [as kūpuna] was a fourteenth-century Hawaiian legend that the clients were to enact. In the process something deep was touched. We find that acting brings up deep distresses . . . and they [the clients] can release the pain. There is all this pain . . . that comes up. When the clients enacted the legend . . . it was the first time many of them had been publicly Hawaiian. (Field notes)

Unlike Western psychology, with its insistence that the psyche is only as deep as the self, deep culture therapy was meant to awaken memory of ka poʻe kahiko and to open the possibility that this ancestral connection could heal. They learned also to listen more closely, to challenge the concepts of professional expertise, detachment, and boundaries. Meipala told me that "in their stories their suffering and healing can be shared with the world. They have much to teach about suffering and healing. To work with them, to be near them, is a privilege."

Meipala's job was to create possibilities, to open a path that might allow Hawaiians to transcend their feelings of shame, to develop methods of healing based upon memory, recreations of tradition, and specifically Hawaiian culture. The organization was renamed Hoʻo Mōhala—"to cause to blossom, to recover." The renaming process occurred in consultation with a respected kupuna who was well versed in Hawaiian language and legend. There was kaona in this name, it was layered with multiple meaning. It pointed to the notion that Hawaiians needed to turn away from foreign culture, and it revealed the underlying purpose of the recovery and blossoming of specifically Hawaiian ways of being and knowing. More implicitly, the new name reflected the notion that Western culture, and not Hawaiians, was pathological. When the organization became Hoʻo Mōhala, all staff members who did not already have one were given Hawaiian names.

In her poetic way, Meipala described the process of infusing Hoʻo Mōhala with the powerful tools of memory and dreaming in order to bring the wisdom of ka poʻe kahiko to bear on the struggles of their colonized descendants.

> We need to be a people who can reconcile our hearts, develop past wisdom, be guided by past knowledge and build it with the spirit. We dream it. . . . We pull it out from our naʻau (guts, intestines). . . . We pull it out of our childhood. . . . We remember a moment. . . . (Field notes)

Hoʻo Mōhala's overarching goal, under Meipala's leadership, was to create healing spaces where those who are preyed upon by the influx of foreign substances, such as crystal methamphetamines, could recover. Meipala told me the following:

> My Hawaiian culture is not static and is forever changing as we organize to fight new threats to our being. Our Hawaiian communities are being actively destroyed by a predator that is creating increased paranoia, violent behavior, and criminal activities. This predator is having a heyday in the poor . . . communities we all live in. There is not one family in Waiʻanae who hasn't been touched in some way by the chaos of drug addiction. (Field notes)

The notion that addicted clients were preyed upon by forces outside of the community distinguished Hoʻo Mōhala's model of treatment from those treatment models in which the addicted client was portrayed as preying upon the community. This representation of clients as prey was woven throughout the organization's internal discourse, although it sometimes conflicted with the notion of radical self-responsibility defined by Alcoholics Anonymous, which was also a part of Hoʻo Mōhala's program.

At Hoʻo Mōhala, addiction was understood as a disease affecting ke kino, ka manaʻo, and a me ka ʻuhane (body, mind, and spirit) and as an example of the malaise and dysfunction of Western living. Because Hoʻo Mōhala was a substance abuse treatment facility it operated in the nexus of physical, mental, and spiritual health, and it dealt on a daily basis with connections between addiction, poverty, criminality, and family crisis.

The concern for the recovery of Hawaiians was a guiding principle of the staff. Recovery, in the understanding of Hoʻo Mōhala, involved not only the maintenance of sobriety but also the active recuperation of Hawaiian values and worldviews. Less widely articulated among the clinical staff than among the administrative staff was the desire for decolonization, although at the time of my research both the current and former executive directors expressed their belief that part of Hoʻo Mōhala's mission was decolonization. Since many of Hoʻo Mōhala's clients were men and women coming directly from the state prison system as a condition of parole, Hoʻo Mōhala also had a strong emphasis on "getting Hawaiian[s] . . . out of prison" and keeping them out. Key members of the staff of Hoʻo Mōhala were ex-convicts, and an intake counselor made regular trips to Oʻahu's men's and women's prisons to assess potential clients. The desire to keep Hawaiians out of prison was so strong that in at least one case policies were bent to allow a parolee who had broken the rules to stay in the program rather than being sent back to prison.

A couple of years ago Aunty Leimomi's boy was in treatment. He had come to the program out of Hālawa [an Oʻahu prison facility; treatment was a condition of his parole]. While he was in the program he violated the rules by having sex with one of the women clients. The policy was that clients are not allowed to have sex while they are in the residential program. So we had no choice but to kick him out [and send him back to Hālawa]. [His mother] came to us and cried and cried and begged us not to make her son go back to prison. The staff did not want to send him back, but we wanted to be true to our policies for the residential program. So we sat down and figured out a way [to] let him stay.

CULTURE

A handwritten sign hanging on the wall of the day treatment facility outlined the differences between drug culture and Hawaiian culture, specifically emphasizing the distinction between Kōkua (caring and collective effort) and the paranoia and lack of cooperation in "drug culture." For the clients, Hoʻo Mōhala was a kind of safe haven where they could deal with recovery from drug and alcohol abuse around other people who looked and thought and acted like them. The fact that "book learning" was deemphasized, the fact that kūpuna were available for one-on-one sessions, and the fact that the program emphasized outdoor activities were all reasons cited by the clients for choosing Hoʻo Mōhala. Many clients I interviewed felt that the emphasis on "cultcha" at Hoʻo Mōhala enabled them to learn self-esteem and "to love themselves." Clients also mentioned that they liked the fact that the program stressed family reunification, especially through hoʻoponopono.

For Meipala, who eventually became the organization's executive director, the challenge of the work was to build a community-based program that facilitated the emergence of Hawaiian culture, integrated and synthesized (re)emerging indigenous understandings and practices with Western bio-psycho-social models, and at the same time secured funding from federal, state, and local government sources. The trick for organizations like Hoʻo Mōhala, which relied upon funding streams that did not always recognize the efficacy of "alternative" or "indigenous" medicine, was in the joining of empirical socioeconomic and health data describing the existential condition of Native Hawaiians with a fusion of Hawaiian and Western ways of treating disease and practicing healing, including mythic, sacred, and spiritual solutions.

"DEEP CULTURE"

If success is measured by client popularity, and by the perception of client transformation, then deep culture therapy was one of the most successful activities in Hoʻo Mōhala's clinical program. Although it drew on such traditional practices as chanting, praying, and oral storytelling, deep culture therapy was a unique invention of Hoʻo Mōhala staff that drew on Hawaiʻi's rich oral traditions.

A sign reading "KAPU!" was placed on the door during deep culture therapy, and no one was permitted to leave or enter. Auntie Kēhaulani, the Hoʻokele Huakaʻi i ka Moʻolelo Hoʻōla—in English, the navigator of journeys into the healing power of our stories—walked into the center of the circle of clients. She was dressed in white Levi's and a white cotton T-shirt overlaid with a golden yellow kīhei. The color gold signified that that was part of the clinical staff of Hoʻo Mōhala. Kēhaulani explained to me the meaning of her title, and the reason for the kapu.

The word huaka'i means travel, but also mission. The mission is one of attending to the privilege of spending a few hours with the clients in an exploration of who they are, where they come from, and where they are headed in their life's journey. I tell them that their life stories are the most wonderful stories ever told, simply because it's their story.

I ask the clients to think about the stories of their lives. Where does it begin? Perhaps clues to the answers can be found in deep culture. Hawaiian protocol is observed. A kapu is placed on our gathering. No one else may enter after the opening chant. No one in the group may wander in and out at will. This ensures that clients will focus on me and on each other, that each client will receive the full due of attention and that they will give their attention to each other. But even more than that, once the kapu is in place and observed well, it allows the gift of mana from each client to grow to a kind of multiplied awareness, to a kind of increase in loving and caring energy of thought, word, and action. This is healing, in and of itself, and it has often been called awesome. . . . Something approaching the sacred unfolds. (Interview with Kēhaulani Lee)

Before the session, clients moved all of the furniture out of the room and placed lau hala mats on the floor. Clients sat on the mats, or in folding chairs, in a circle. Kēhaulani asked for permission to join the circle. She often spoke Hawaiian, although few of the clients understood all of her words. "Listen," Kēhaulani told them, "even if you cannot understand all of the words. Listen."

Deep culture therapy often began with an opening chant in Hawaiian. Oli, or chanting, was the means for preserving history and mythology before contact with Europeans and the transformation of Hawaiian into a written language. Chanting is a form of communication between humans and the divine, between humans and the ancestors, and between living humans. As a form of communication between the living, a chant contains information about genealogy and establishes position within a social hierarchy. A chant that opened deep culture therapy was addressed to God and the ancestors and is a prayer for life on behalf of the clients, staff, and families of Ho'o Mōhala.

Ē ke Akua hemolele loa/Oh most sacred God
Ka mea i hana i ke ao holo 'oko'a/Creator of the Universe
A me ko mākou mau kia'i mai ka pō mai/and our Guardians from time
    beginning to now
Ua kū ka hale, ua pa'a ka hale/the house stands, the house is solid
E nānā mai i kēia hale no Ho'o Mōhala/watch over this house for Ho'o
    Mōhala
He hale i kāmauli ola, he hale i ka ho'ōla/a house to revive life, a house
    to extend life

E ola iā mākou, ka pulapula i kēia ao/grant life to us, your descendants in this world

E ola he kanaka pilikia e komo i kēia hale ola/grant life to a person in trouble who enters this house of life

E ola iā mākou e lawelawe i ka hana hoʻōla ʻana/grant life to those of us who attend to the healing work

Ka luna a me ka limahana/the leaders and workers

e lawelawe i ka hana kōkua/who provide supportive services

E ola iā ko mākou ʻohana,/grant life to our families

Nā hoaaloha a me nā malihini kipa/to our friends and to our guests

E hele mai e hāʻawi aku i ke aloha a me ke kōkua/who come to give their love and help

Ke nonoi nei mākou i kou hoʻopōmaikaʻi ʻana mai/we ask your blessing

I kēia hale/of this house

Mai luna a lalo/from top to bottom

Mai kahi kihi a kahi kihi/from one corner to the other

Mai ka hikina a e komohana/from east to west

Mai ke uka a ke kai/from facing the mountain to facing the ocean

Mai loko o waho/from inside to outside

Kiaʻi ʻia mālama ʻia/watch over and protect it

E pale aku ke hoʻopilikia mai i ko mākou nohona/ward off all that may trouble our way of life here

E hō mai iā mākou i ka ʻike/grant wisdom to us

i mea e hoʻomaikaʻi ʻia ai ka mākou hana/so that our deeds and efforts will be good

I ka hoʻomanaʻo ʻana i kou inoa hemolele/in remembrance of your sacred name

mākou i pule aʻe ai/we have just prayed

ʻamama, ua noa./the prayer is finished, it is released.

Clients who had been in treatment for several weeks might know the chant by memory. Others chanted with the aid of a handout of the words in Hawaiian and in English. After the chant, clients remained standing in a circle for pule, or prayer. While the oli is in Hawaiian and addressed to Hawaiian gods and ancestral spirits, the prayer was often in English and addressed to the Christian god. One of the organization's staff kūpuna leads the pule. Following the pule, Auntie Kēhaulani leads the clients in a breathing exercise based on hula. The clients breathe in and out deeply, saying "hā." Kēhaulani told clients that the breathing exercise symbolizes the breath of life and the beginnings of language. According to Pukui, Haertig, and Lee (1972), in the times of ka poʻe kahiko, "Hawaiians . . . invested the 'breath of life' with a spiritual significance that closely parallels Biblical and earlier Hebrew references" (42).

The oli, pule, and breathing exercises were meant to produce a state of readiness within the clients and within Kēhaulani for the deeper journey to follow into awareness of the sacred. Kēhaulani explained to me that she placed great emphasis on the creation of space for Hawaiian clients to tell their stories.

> *We have learned very well the lessons of where and when it is never safe to speak. Creating a culturally safe space for the talk-story of the self is one of the goals of the program. It was a challenge at first, but the how-to became very clear when I simply relied on [Hawaiian] protocol and priority, something we as a people understand very well. Nānā i ke kumu—"look to the source."*
>
> *Protocol means the carefully observed sequence of events. . . . [In standard protocol] honor must first be paid to events in cosmic time . . . to legendary heroes and heroines . . . to the ali'i . . . to the concerns of the people of the recent past and the present. . . .*
>
> *Before I even get to the facility, [the evening before I lead deep culture therapy] I observe a protocol [which involves] my asking for permission to tell a certain story, a quiet time for reflection and setting right of my thoughts. [Before I enter the circle of clients] I seek another permission, one to come from the outside into the group.*
>
> *[Following the oli, pule and breathing] the famous "chicken skin[3]" has already come to many, if not everyone, including me. This is a very valuable experience. I liken it to a state of awe, [preparation] for the deeper journey into . . . the sacred.* (Interview with Kēhaulani Lee, 1997)

The next part of deep culture therapy involved the reading of Hawaiian legends and myths. The legend "The First Breadfruit Tree" was adapted and copied on sheets of paper, which were passed out to the clients. Each client took a turn reading part of the legend.

In ancient times, a god arrived from Kahiki and lived in Hawai'i. His name was Kū. He married a Hawaiian woman, and they had a lot of children. The woman did not know that her husband was a god because he worked at everything like the other men.

At one time, the rain didn't rain for a very long time. The taro and the sweet potato and all the crops died. There wasn't enough food, and Kū and his family were very hungry. Kū looked at his wife and children, and his pity for them was very great. So one day he told his dearly beloved wife, "My beloved wife, I can get food for you all, but if I go I can't come back." His wife didn't agree to this action, but later she heard the crying voices of the children, and she asked her husband to go and get food for them.

The entire family went into the yard, and they expressed their love for each other. Kū said to his family, "I'm going to stand on my head and dig down underneath the dirt. Afterwards, food will emerge. Aloha!" And he stood on his head and disappeared.

His wife sat down at that place, and she cried night and day. After several days, a shoot emerged. This tree grew very quickly, and the family ate the fruit. This was Hawai'i's first breadfruit tree. Only Kū's family could pick the breadfruit; the other people couldn't. If a person tried to pick, the breadfruit turned to dust and the tree returned under the ground.

But later, offspring emerged from the fruit tree, and these other trees were given to all the families to plant in their own gardens. The breadfruit was given to the Hawaiian people by Kū, a sacrifice of love.[4]

After reading the story aloud, clients and counselors volunteered to act out the different roles of Kū, his wife and children, the neighbors, and the breadfruit trees in the legend. The remaining clients participated as the audience. The performance was silly, and clients laughed at each other, but the whole story was finally enacted. Kēhaulani asked clients to reflect on the themes of loss and sacrifice. A woman client said that although in the story it was the man/god who sacrificed, in real life it was usually women who must sacrifice. In this deep culture session, however, the issue that generated the most discussion concerned the breadfruit turning into dust. A client asked if clients who relapse are seen as turning into dust. The discussion was emotional for both clients and counselors. Clients cried, yelled, and withdrew. Over the weekend, a young woman client had been discharged from the program for drinking beer. The woman had not yet been removed and was still in the group. She sat silently and sullenly, while her co-participants expressed anger and sadness. The counselors, who supported the client and did not agree that she should be discharged, were also emotional and turned to Kēhaulani to explain the decision. In the counselor's view, the decision made by the administrative staff was unfair and reflected their distance from the day-to-day realities of the clinical program. The counselors, all women at this time, expressed the view that the administrative staff was "sexist" because they discharged women more frequently than men. Kēhaulani's role in this session was to steer the conversation away from anger toward the administrative staff and toward an understanding of why the question of relapse and discharge was so upsetting. After an hour or so of discussion, the group reformed the circle for the pule pane, or closing prayer. The kapu was lifted, and the clients went to lunch.

The success of deep culture as a therapeutic modality depended in large part on the mana of the facilitator. Kēhaulani was a particularly gifted facilitator whom the clients loved and respected. However, Kēhaulani was a part-time consultant to Hoʻo Mōhala and was hired to conduct deep culture biweekly. During the weeks that Kēhaulani was not present, the deep culture sessions were led by the regular counselors or other kūpuna. In these sessions, the sense of sacred space evoked by Kēhaulani was missing. In some ways, the sessions led by the counseling staff were parodies of sessions led by Kēhaulani. In one session, Uncle Kimo, a counselor, led the clients in the chant, *E Hō Mai Ka ʻIke* but could not remember all of the words. One of the clients jumped up into the middle of the circle and performed a comedic rendition of Hawaiian chanting, mimicking Hawaiian words without knowing them. The clients and counselors all laughed.

Without Kēhaulani there was a lack of focus and concentration and an absence of seriousness. But even in the hilarious chaos, Hawaiian culture emerged as a profound focal point. Uncle Kimo, who was struggling to remember the words to the chant, quietly and continuously chanted.

> E hō mai ka ʻike, mai luna mai e
> O nā mea huna noʻeau o nā mele e
> E hō mai, e hō mai, e hō mai.
> (Grant us knowledge/insight from above,
>   the things of knowledge hidden in the song,
> grant us these things.)

As he remembered the words, Kimo's chanting took on a quiet intensity. At times the clients would drop whatever they were doing to join in the chant, so that the oli became a persistent backdrop to the antics in the center of the circle.

When I questioned Kēhaulani about the efficacy of deep culture when she was not present, she agreed that the role of kumu or facilitator required a high degree of "spiritual power to pull it off." She said that it had taken her a lifetime to gain mastery over her spiritual power, and that in order for deep culture to play a therapeutic role, "the kumu needs to be strong in the culture and to create a space of safety, confidence and trust." But Kēhaulani also told me "that all Hawaiians are in recovery, whether they've ever used drugs or not." She said that at Hoʻo Mōhala that meant that the clients and the counselors were part of a continuum of healing and recovery, and that even without her presence, there were important lessons that clients and counselors were learning together. Furthermore, she said, laughing is an indication that students (or clients) are engaged. "If you hear students laughing," she said, "you know they are learning. It's different from Western society. Using a Western style of teaching with Hawaiian kids puts them to sleep."

HO'OPONOPONO[S]

More than any other of the Hawaiian healing methodologies, ho'oponopono stands out as a preeminent form. It is less as a singular, codified healing ritual than a framework undertaken for the therapeutic purpose of "making things right." While the practice of ho'oponopono dates back to the time of ka po'e kahiko, like other Hawaiian practices and beliefs, it was driven underground. According to Shook (1985), ho'oponopono had fallen from popular usage by the mid-nineteenth century, and it was not until the publication of *Nānā I Ke Kumu* (*Look to the Source*) (Pukui et al. 1972) that a detailed description of one form of ho'oponopono emerged for general use (Shook 1985, 7–8).

The description of ho'oponopono in volume 1 of *Nānā I Ke Kumu* was the result of the work of the "Culture Committee" of the Queen Lili'uokalani Children's Center.[5] The committee was comprised of the highly respected Hawaiian kūpuna, translator, and author, Mary Kawena Pukui, a psychiatrist, Dr. E. W. Haertig, a psychologist, and several Hawaiian and non-Hawaiian social workers, who came together to address culturally specific problems occurring in Hawaiian families. The committee's process involved the social workers presenting case material, followed by "talk story" from Pukui, who told stories about Hawaiian practices and beliefs that seemed relevant to the case at hand. The committee met for seven years, taping all of its sessions, and during that time it gathered enough material for the publication of the two volumes of *Nānā I Ke Kumu*. In the committee's discussions of traditional remedies for family problems, ho'oponopono came to light (Shook 1985, 9; Pukui et al. 1972, vii, ix).

According to *Nānā I Ke Kumu*, ho'oponopono is a ritual of "setting to right," a means of restoring and maintaining good relations among family members and between families and their ancestral spirits. Ho'oponopono required that family members gathered together for "prayer, discussion, confession, repentance, and mutual restitution and forgiveness" (Pukui et al. 1972, 60). Ho'oponopono was meant to be led either by a kahuna or the senior family member, and was believed to be most efficacious when confined to small, immediate family groups rather than extended family or community.

A wide variety of ho'oponopono practices exists. Even within one agency, such as Ho'o Mōhala, ho'oponopono described various practices that led to the eventual goals of family reunification or staff-administration harmony. Ho'oponopono was used at Ho'o Mōhala as both a therapeutic method between clients and their counselors and kūpuna and among staff.[6] As a tool for building staff unity, ho'oponopono sessions were less popular and viewed as flawed. As Boggs and Chun point out, "in ho'oponopono, a superior by means of questions helps a subordinate to express feelings that result in the avoidance of further punishment, instead of eliciting evidence that leads to punishment" (Boggs and Chun 1990, 144). However, for junior staff at Ho'o

Mōhala, hoʻoponopono sessions were viewed with suspicion. Some clinical staff members in particular viewed the staff hoʻoponopono sessions as a means for the senior administrative staff to collect information that would jeopardize their jobs. Although Hoʻo Mōhala self-consciously modeled itself as a family, the reality was an organizational hierarchy. The turnover at Hoʻo Mōhala during my field research was high, particularly among the clinical staff. Attempts to build unity through a staff hoʻoponopono process did not succeed, because not all staff members felt the same degree of job security and thus could not express themselves. According to Pukui, Haertig, and Lee (1972), participants in hoʻoponopono must have "a true intention to correct wrongs. Confession of error must be full and honest. Nothing could be withheld. Prayers, contrition, and [forgiveness] . . . must come from the heart" (62). Furthermore, central to the process is the mana-filled kūpuna, or senior family member, whose role is to mediate both between family members and between family members and supernatural beings. To the leader in this process accrues the exclusive right to interpret and evaluate others statements, and to reprimand (Boggs and Chun 1990, 134–35). In an organizational setting, the exigency of honest confession is subverted by hierarchy, since staff members, unlike family, can be fired.

But for clients, the hoʻoponopono sessions were one of the highlights of program. One of Meipala Silva's first tasks as staff Kūpuna was to conduct hoʻoponopono sessions with clients and their families. When I asked Meipala how she had been "trained" to conduct hoʻoponopono, she told me, with great irritation, that she was never "trained" in the Western sense of the word.

> *I learned hoʻoponopono by watching my mother and my aunties when I was a child. It was something that we did in our family, I remembered what I could, and I reached out to other practitioners for help in implementing the program. When I first came to Hoʻo Mōhala, the staff seemed kind of afraid of starting hoʻoponopono. But when I came in, I said let's just start and see what happens.*

Hoʻo Mōhala's hoʻoponopono sessions were the method most often discussed when the organization's Hawaiian healing methodology was referred to. Eventually, all of the counselors who participated in hoʻoponopono sessions conducted between Meipala (and other kūpuna) and clients learned how to conduct hoʻoponopono sessions themselves. A goal of the clinical program was for each client to participate in hoʻoponopono at least every other week during a twelve-week course of treatment. Although in the strictest sense—outlined by Mary Kawena Pukui and the QLCC Culture Committee—hoʻoponopono was a process that best occurred within families, hoʻoponopono at Hoʻo Mōhala often occurred between the client and her or his counselor. Since family reunification was the goal of ho'oponopono, spouses, significant others, parents, siblings, and children usually participated toward the end of a course of treatment.

George Kohala,[7] a Ho'o Mōhala client, described for me how important ho'oponopono was in his recovery process.

> The ho'oponopono is a session which covers how you feel about yourself, about the past. Things that had hurt you in the past and you didn't wanna explain it to anybody, so you explain it to Auntie Kalani [a Ho'o Mōhala staff Kūpuna], and she goes through a ho'oponopono session with you. And for me, it really hurts, it really helped me a lot because for three years I didn't talk about my deepest feelings that was really bothering me and led me to the drug abuse. I shared it with Auntie Kalani, and after I shared it with her I felt really at ease and I could move forward to the next step in growing. We have four ho'oponopono sessions as you go along, each step. And today was my last step. I wanted my wife to participate in my ho'oponopono and she did and I was very proud of her. It really made me feel good. I brang up issues that was bodderin' me and I felt comfortable about talking it with Auntie Kalani and my wife because she's not there to take any sides, but to help bot' of us understand and grow. (Interview with Client A)

Another client, Kaimi Motes,[8] a recent graduate, described to me the difference between Ho'o Mōhala's program and a haole-run substance abuse treatment program at Tower Medical Center:

> KM: *I had a clinical discharge from Tower too. It was pretty different from this one. This is more like a family here, yeah? So it's more close, you get a little more bonding. But there it was mainly technical things, over heah is like a big family. Majority of the people who come in is Hawaiian too, so you could pretty much relate. This program has taught me to deal with my family too, my kids. In my drug addiction, I kine a put them on the side, so even when I first came in, the first couple of weeks and maybe even the first month, like, [my counselor] she noticed that I was still kind a scared to contact my kids, cause I didn't know how actually. Bein that at that time I was doin the drugs I wasn't really thinkin of my kids. So she helped me really closely to get that bond with my two sons.*
>
> WM: *How old are they?*
>
> KM: *One is eight and one is four. This program actually taught me how to love, how to love myself and my family. I really didn't know how to love people.*
>
> WM: *Did they teach you that at Tower?*

KM: *No. At Tower they just dealt with the drug addiction, my problem.*

WM: *So how is it different here?*

KM: *Here you go t'ru . . . you get help for your addiction and they help you with your family. You get family day, family visits. Help you to be closer to your family, to be reunited with your family. That was something big for me. Learn how to love my children, and to be a better father to my children. It was something I really needed.*

WM: *How does the emphasis on Hawaiian culture connect with treatment and becoming sober?*

KM: *Over here we go t'ru the ho'oponopono process. It actually brings you back to your culture, that's why the majority of the people [in treatment at Ho'o Mōhala are] Hawaiian, it is about getting back to the old Hawaiian ways.* (Interview with Client B)

As Boggs and Chun (1990) discussed, "talk in *ho'oponopono* reinstates by reenactment the social relationships that are to be maintained ideally in the culture. . . . Talk is both expression and enactment of social structure." A result of ho'oponopono is the reestablishment of the hierarchical relationship between the leader and other participants (1990, 144, 147). At Ho'o Mōhala, the reenactment serves to establish the hierarchy between clients and counselors. However, it also plays a significant role in redeeming Hawaiian culture, both by asserting the efficacy of a culturally based intervention and by implicitly challenging clients' (and counselors') feelings of shame about being Hawaiian. Similarly, clients learn how to confront the shame they feel as ex-cons and recovering addicts, and they are supported through a process of asking their family members for forgiveness. Jona Like recalled the impact of his first ho'oponopono session.

My first ho'oponopono that I ever did was with Auntie Kalani. Like before we used to do 'em in groups, now she does it individual. So she sat us down in a circle and got out a ti leaf to put it in the cup in front of us and then she goes to each one of us, she grabs our hands and I guess she meditates and she feels our vibes, yeah? So, I never realized what was happening inside of me. . . . She went around the circle, she came up to me, she grabbed my hand and she went open her eyes and she just started crying. And I was kind a like, hoo, chicken skin, but then she started explaining it to me. She said she feels some kind of anger or fear inside of me. And I brought it to her attention that me and my Dad wasn't really seeing eye to eye. We was havin' problems communicating with each 'utta. And she wen sense that. So that made me kind a feel like, ooh, something is out there, eh? For this lady I don't even know for come up to me and hold my hand and then let me know what's happening in my life. That was a kind of awakening for me.

. . . So, I learned pretty much how to bond with other people, how to, if I stuck on something and I need help, how to ask for help instead of trying to do things on my own. I picked up on a lot of things, not only [about] the drug addiction. The biggest one was how to love people as well as myself. I just thank the lord that God brought me back here instead of turn me back out into the streets. It's giving me a good foundation. (Interview with Client C)

HEALING 'UHANE

Clients and staff also participate in another form of ho'oponopono with a mana-filled kūpuna, Auntie Rita.[9] Auntie Rita was a wehewehe moe 'uhane, or dream interpreter, who used her gift to diagnose imbalances in the 'uhane or soul of her clients. She was particularly adept at the interpretation of persistent bad dreams and of diagnosing a condition known as 'uhane hele, or wandering soul. Auntie Rita interpreted dreams, but she was also gifted at diagnosing spiritual (and sometimes biomedical) conditions through a process of "seeing."

In ho'oponopono sessions with Auntie Rita, a client's (or counselor's) distress from persistent bad dreams would be interpreted according to traditional Hawaiian beliefs, which identify dreams as a dimension of an alternative reality parallel to the reality of the waking world. In this perspective, dreams produce "symbols which have causal or purposive meanings, with some definite relationship to reality [. . .] and are believed to be caused] by the movement of one's 'uhane, or spirit," out of the physical body or through encounters between the 'uhane and 'aumākua or other spiritual entities. Dreams were related to subconscious desires or viewed as the causes of waking psychological reactions. Decoded, dreams revealed the future, remembered the past, posed solutions to problems, located hidden places and lost persons, and warned of impending disaster (Kanahele 1986, 46).

Ho'o Mōhala clients were frequently diagnosed by Auntie Rita with 'uhane hele. In Auntie Rita's understanding, the 'uhane sometimes wanders, causing dreams that, although disturbing, may be beneficial. However, a chronically wandering 'uhane is a sign of trouble. The diagnoses of 'uhane hele, as applied to Ho'o Mōhala's chemically dependent clients struggling for recovery, symbolize both the spiritual and cultural distress of clients. According to Pukui, Haertig, and Lee (1972),

A person who dozed when he should be awake was thought to have a *'uhane hele*, or wandering spirit. . . . For this, prayers were said and treatments were given. One treatment . . . used crushed *ti* leaf (a traditional purifying-protective agent). This was put in water with a pinch of salt. The drowsy person took it every noon when the sun was directly overhead and his shadow had retreated in his body.

Treatment was needed. For fear that a wicked *kahuna poʻi ʻuhane* (spirit catcher) might snatch the wandering spirit and keep it from re-entering the body. This meant death. (193–94).

A "person who dozes when he should be awake" became a metaphor in the Hawaiian realm of substance abuse treatment, both for chemical addiction and for clients' sense of cultural shame.

On some Saturdays, clients and counselors would climb into the Hoʻo Mōhala van and travel to another part of the Oʻahu to visit Auntie Rita. She did not charge a fee for sharing her spiritual talents; rather, people who sought her services brought small gifts, primarily prepared food. Many Saturdays Auntie Rita's front porch was crowded with people waiting their turn. People from all over Oʻahu traveled to see her.

Auntie Rita—who was disabled and sat in a wheelchair—started each session praying in Hawaiian over the bent head of her "clients." After shaking salt water with a ti leaf onto them and asking them to sip from the glass, she lay her hands on their heads and shoulders and spoke—in Hawaiian and English—of what she "saw." Her words did not always form full sentences; much of what she said emerged in fragments, and when she spoke, her eyes were closed, and her face was turned upward. A description of a hoʻoponopono session between Auntie Rita and Marianna, a member of Hoʻo Mōhala's administrative staff, follows. During this session I was permitted to sit quietly and take notes.

> *First Auntie Rita prayed in Hawaiian for about five minutes. . . . Then she sprinkled salt water around Marianna, and asked her to drink from the glass; Auntie Rita put her hands on Marianna's head and silently prayed. After a while she said:*
>
> *I see red up here. Someone huhū [angry, offended, mad]. I see monkey's mouth, somebody trying to be a fool. Monkey with black mouth. ʻŌkole [anus] up near mouth. Extremely negative. Let it go, it's their problem. . . . Be very careful of the budget. Be careful of spending too much. In the waterfall I see red lava—plenty money will come, and yet, somebody huhū. . . . Always ask the Lord for his noʻonoʻo [thought]. Money will come and ideas and people who you never thought would help. . . . I see a black bottle in the air shooting up. Someone negative airing out negative things. I see black eyeglasses. . . . In the big white book, the book of life, there are no real big problems that you cannot settle. . . . Negative cross, charmed gift god gives man.*
>
> *After being quiet for a minute or two, Marianna hugged Auntie Rita and thanked her.*

The following notes are from my session with Auntie Rita, during which a Ho'o Mōhala staff member took notes:

> *I see an unusual waterfall, it is very curved which means that money will come in spurts. Somebody is looking cross . . . be careful of heavy words. . . . I see a pick, but it is a pick of white light instead of iron. White light means purity, righteousness, and gifts. . . . Are you a diabetic? I ask because my eyes are itchy. . . . There is some jealousy coming down towards you— humans are strange . . . I see . . . waterfall . . . cross . . . graduated levels . . . tribulation . . . no big import. . . . What I see is unusual . . . strange, it's like in Kaua'i area not the Grotto, the waterfall is like a pit—that waterfall flows inside of a pit. This means that you have personal things that need to be addressed between you and God, about your commitment to God . . . I am seeing only half of you. We say "uhane hele." . . . When you go home go to sleep, 'uhane will come back. Ask the Lord to return your spirit . . . I see that there are dead spirits here and there. . . . Has anyone passed away recently? Yes, you have personal things to settle between you and God. You are going to succeed. I see a cross and a nun in white regalia who looks like Mother Mary. I see a ring of diamonds which represents no'ono'o-knowledge, thinking, reflection. You'll do very well. I see a gradua- tion cap and gown. But someone is trying to demean you. Never allow it. I see the mouth of a whale, the mouth is black. Life is as you make it. I see a huge platter of Jell-O. Try not to waiver. In Jell-O are the fruits of life.*

Clients were more ambivalent about ho'oponopono with Auntie Rita than they were with the ho'oponopono sessions that occur on site at Ho'o Mōhala. It was not easy to explain what Auntie Rita does. Meipala told me that she was always correcting clients who joked that going to see Auntie Rita was like calling "the Psychic Friends Network.™" But the staff of Ho'o Mōhala took Auntie Rita's gifts very seriously. Meipala tried to see Auntie Rita regularly and relied upon her for dream interpretation.

NARRATIVES OF HEALING AND REDEMPTION

Alaka'i Ono, the clinical director of Ho'o Mōhala, was an ex-convict and a recovering alcoholic and drug addict, and, when I met him, five years sober. When he was a teenager, he told me, he and a group of buddies would travel around O'ahu (or sometimes fly to Maui for the day) with a group of friends to break into tourists' rented cars and steal from them. When he reflects upon his past, he believes that his heavy drug and alcohol use cut off any other viable life options. Alaka'i told me that as a Hawaiian he was angry at all of the "rich tourists" and used that as a justification for his criminal activities. After spending some time in prison, Alakaʻi began the process of recovery—he was one of the first clients at the Hoʻo Mōhala in the first year of operation. In recovery, he said, he "learned other ways of being Hawaiian besides robbing tourists." These other ways included attending rallies and demonstrations supporting the sovereignty movement. But for Alakaʻi, the most profound expression of "being Hawaiian" was his work to assist the recovery process of other Hawaiians.

After a couple of years in recovery from drug addiction and after completing the Alcoholics Anonymous Twelve-Step program, Alakaʻi took a job as a counselor at Hoʻo Mōhala. In the first year of his employment, the organization held a staff immersion in Hawaiian language and culture at Waipiʻo Valley on the island of Hawaiʻi. Waipiʻo is a lush, verdant valley on the windward side of the island, surrounded by the precipitous heights of the Kohala mountain range. The steep, nearly vertical cliffs limit access to four-wheel-drive vehicles and rugged hikers, and therefore Waipiʻo is bypassed by most of the tourist trade.[10] Ten Hoʻo Mōhala staff members traveled in jeeps down the steep slopes of the mountains and met up with a small group of Hawaiians who lived "in the traditional way," speaking only ʻolelo Hawaiʻi (Hawaiian language), tending loʻi kalo (taro patches) and irrigation canals, hunting, pounding poi, and living in thatch hale (houses). The Hoʻo Mōhala staff had to communicate in Hawaiian, although none of the members were fluent. They slept in tents, pulled weeds, and bathed in the ocean. For Alakaʻi, the trip to Waipiʻo was transformative. He explained to me that sleeping under the stars, communicating in Hawaiian, and eating poi made him feel proud to be Hawaiian. He decided then that he would begin to eat poi at home, send his children to Hawaiian language-immersion school, and live his life "as a Hawaiian."

Alakaʻi's transformation narrative became part of the basis of an internal Hoʻo Mōhala discourse about the need for transformative natural spaces for Hawaiians in recovery. By internal discourse, I mean that Alakaʻi's narrative of transformation was not discussed publicly in grant applications or reports to funding agencies. Rather, it was part of an internal conversation among Hoʻo Mōhala staff (particularly clinical staff) and volunteers in which Hawaiian methods for healing addiction were legitimized and purely Western methods were viewed as inadequate. Other staff told similar stories of spaces in nature that facilitated their transformations from drug addicts to recovering Hawaiians. Susan Miller, another graduate of Hoʻo Mōhala, who went on to become the organization's assessment and intake counselor, told me how cynical she was when she was paroled from prison to drug treatment.

And how I got into Hoʻo Mōhala was, at that time they had a contract with the Department of Public Safety [the state's prison bureaucracy]. And

so Public Safety was paying for my treatment. So what the hell, you know.
This is free. And I am going to stay here for t'ree months and clean up little
bit and come back out and [continue using drugs] . . . that's how I thought.
My first week was okay. And I was there my first week and I was up at the
lo'i [at Mt. Ka'ala Cultural Learning Center], and it just overwhelmed
me. . . . I went through some kind of grieving. My first time being clean, I
think. Clear of mind . . . Mt. Ka'ala is so, I don't know how to explain it.
It is so spiritual up there. I felt at ease. I felt comfortable, I felt so relaxed.
And I never felt that way for a long time. And I think that's what it was,
that feeling of being free. (Interview with Susan Miller)

The lo'i at Mt. Ka'ala Cultural Learning Center was a project of the Wai'anae
Coast Alternative Economic Development Association. It was a sprawling series
of taro patches fed by irrigation canals that predate European contact. Located
high up in the valley and surrounded by the Wai'anae range, with a stunning
view of the sea, clients at Ho'o Mōhala volunteered at Mt. Ka'ala as a regular
part of the treatment program. Susan's experience at Mt. Ka'ala was not uncom-
mon; many people who worked or volunteered at the center spoke of its intense
beauty and spirituality.

Clients, as well as staff, learned to describe nature as a powerful healing
place. Kili Simmons[11] was a middle-age Hawaiian woman diagnosed with bipolar disorder and substance addiction. I met Kili in a group called *Ka Maile o*
Ka'ala, a Native Hawaiian women's group for Ho'o Mōhala clients. The stories
Kili told the group about her life were ones of violence and disease, going back
to the time of her grandparents. Sometimes Kili would wail and cry and rock;
her pain was immense. She told stories about incest: she was raped by her grand-
father and molested by her uncle, and she told stories about her father beating
her mother and then turning his anger toward her. As a child, when she felt
threatened, Kili would run away seeking refuge.

In small kid times, I was an abused child. My father fought my mother and
then he fought me. I used to hide in the space under the house to get away
from them, but when I really wanted to get far away, I would run up into
the mountains. Up in the mountains there were birds and guava trees and I
always felt safe. I would lie on the ground and I remember the smell of the
lo'i kalo. It was a certain sweet earthy smell that I always remember. And I
remember the leaves of the taro, which are shaped like a heart, bending as
they were blown by the wind. It was like the taro leaves were waving to me.
(Interview with Client D)

The 'āina as a place of healing and transformation was a major theme in the stories of staff and clients at Ho'o Mōhala. These narratives contradicted Western

notions that treating disease was a process that occurred indoors under professional supervision. In narratives of transformation at Ho'o Mōhala, the 'āina was accorded the status of healing agent and understood as a catalyst for the achievement of health.

The emphasis on healing spaces in nature clearly derives from notions of the power of space in pre-European Hawaiian cosmology. Persistently, Ho'o Mōhala administrators and clinicians expressed a desire for pu'uhonua, or sacred spaces of refuge, beyond the dangers and exigencies of the West. Counselors, most of whom were themselves "in recovery," spoke often of the need for safe spaces where clients in various stages of recovery could practice the Hawaiian culture. Makuakanenui, a Ho'o Mōhala counselor, told me, "We need a treatment village, where [clients] can come get treatment and be away for awhile . . . detoxing Hawaiian style . . . a place where [clients] can come back if they are threatened, a pu'uhonua, a city of refuge."

The expression of a need for pu'uhonua within the contemporary clinical discourse was based on a spiritual and historical understanding of the times of ka po'e kahiko. In that time, the physical and spiritual landscape was infused with many wahi kapu, places and spaces of refuge, sanctuary, and healing. Wahi kapu in ancient Hawai'i included burial sites, hula platforms, ancestral shrines, and heiau, or religious temples. Pu'uhonua were wahi kapu that made manifest the incredible mana of the highest ali'i to grant mercy to the condemned. Pu'uhonua were asylums for the weak avoiding warfare, for defeated warriors escaping their pursuers, and for violators of the kapu. Pu'uhonua were spaces of refuge within the laws and structures of the social order of ka po'e kahiko. But the desire for pu'uhonua and other sacred spaces in the late twentieth century expressed a yearning for space/time beyond the reach of Western modernity, where Hawaiian identity and Hawaiian culture could be healed and nurtured away from the powerful gaze of neocolonial officials.

MEDICALIZATION IN A POSTCOLONIAL CONTEXT

In "The Shaman's Needle," Shane Greene (1998) introduced the concept of intermedicality to discuss and analyze the fusion of Western and indigenous healing methodologies. Greene's concept of intermedicality is useful to explore the fusion of biomedical and Hawaiian healing methodologies, and to bring the concept of intermedicality into dialogue with the notion of medicalization as social control. Greene defined intermedicality as "a contextualized space of hybrid medicines and sociomedically conscious agents" (1998, 641). He argued against the tendency within development discourses to render "ethnomedicine" static and passive. In Greene's analysis, the Aguaruna shaman Yankush practiced a dual diagnostic technique that distinguished between those illnesses that he was able to cure and illnesses that required biomedical treatment, particularly injection. Yankush also identified those imbalances whose etiologies derive from the negative effects of biomedical treatment. Injections do not only cure pain, they may also cause it. Like sorcery, Yankush viewed biomedicine ambivalently but incorporated it into his shamanic discourse, thereby tapping into the source of biomedical power. Greene called the intermedical space of Yankush's healing task the "shamanizing of science."

At Hoʻo Mōhala, clinical practice involved a fusion of biomedical and "ethnomedical" methods for diagnosis and treatment. Working and playing outdoors, hoʻoponopono, ʻike pāpālua, a form of prayerful spirit diagnosis, lomolomi, a massage method, other forms of praying and chanting, and a diet based on traditional foods, such as kalo, sweet potato, and raw and steamed fish, formed the core of Hawaiian methodologies. These were combined with psychotherapy, urinalysis, medical exams, anti-depressant medications, and other biomedical methods as necessary. Clinical practice in this case was intermedical, because the biomedical forms existed within a space defined by the cultural parameters of Hawaiian healing practices. The goal of the clinic was to create a space that would facilitate the healing of patients defined specifically as Native Hawaiian. The space of the clinic was meant to promote the health of ka manaʻo a me ke kino—mind/body—to reunify the ʻuhane, or soul, with ka manaʻo a me ke kino, and in the largest sense to perpetuate Hawaiian values and the achievement of decolonization. In this example of intermedicality, Hawaiian healing formed the epistemological basis for diagnosis: the etiology of disease was not understood as simply organic. Instead, disease was viewed as a symptom of the malaise and dysfunction inherent in Western living, and often as a specific effect of colonization.

Intermedicality, as a hybrid space of sociomedically conscious agents in a neocolonial context, such as Hoʻo Mōhala in Waiʻanae, complicated the notion of medicalization as social control. Politically and culturally conscious Hawaiians, many of whom were trained as physicians, social workers, and psychotherapists, have reinvigorated demoted healing practices and practitioners (and invented new ones) by using Western techniques in the service of Hawaiian political aspirations and culturally defined treatment objectives. Green argued that while biomedical resources are scarce in developing countries, biomedicine manages to proliferate its power and influence nonetheless. In light of this scarcity, development specialists turned toward the very ethnomedicines they had previously demonized and transformed them into biomedical resources. In other words, ethnomedicines served to reinforce the maintenance of biomedical power. But in the case of Hoʻo Mōhala, the situation was somewhat reversed: biomedicine was serving to further the power of Hawaiian cultural and political interests. Policy makers in managed care in late-twentieth-century Hawaiʻi determined that "alternative" methods of treatment might be appropriate because they were much cheaper than standard biomedical care. While, as Green argued, this might be viewed as an attempt to put alternative treatment methods in the service of biomedicine (not to mention the health insurance industry), it also provides a significant space for the staging of Native Hawaiian challenges to the legitimacy of both Western epistemology and Western power.

Greene's exploration of Yankush's shamanizing of science did not include an explicit discussion of the political role of the shaman, or of the political relations between the Aguaruna community and either the development apparatus or the Peruvian government. He defined intermedicality as primarily a sociomedical space. But I would like to inflect the notion of intermedicality with a sense of neocolonial power relations and suggest that, following the example of the Hawaiian clinic, intermedicality has the potential to both challenge the hegemony of biomedicine and to put biomedicine in the service of libratory aspirations for decolonization rather than in the service of Western power. Intermedicality, then, is not merely a neutral fusion of two competing epistemologies but an alibi and a motive for the reinstantiation of notions of healing and health that derive from a cosmology of mana.

CONCLUSION

"Ropes of Resistance" and Alternative Futures

[L]iberation can only come from a praxis committed to the sufferings and hopes of the people. (Martín-Baró 1996, 32)

In legal activist Mililani Trask's view, dispossession was a key metaphor for the experience of colonialism. She wrote:

> Hawaiians were evicted from their land . . . that was genocide. Their ability to fish certain waters and cultivate land so that they could eat and live was taken away at the very time that Western diseases were taking a terrible toll. . . . The appropriate healing practices were almost lost because people who were oral keepers of those traditions died. Genealogies were lost, so people no longer knew who their families were. *They were dispossessed of the land, they wandered, and they were not able to find their own families again."* (M. Trask 1996, 392, emphasis added)

Trask's eloquence regarding the trauma of dispossession makes clear that the colonized were affected at the level of families, and of bodies and souls, and not just in the public domains of politics and economics. Structurally and ideologically, in both formal and intimate realms, colonialism meant the erasure of the history, culture, and cosmology of Kanaka Maoli. The structures of Hawaiian society were dismembered. Dispossession from the land, which in the cosmology of ka po'e kahiko was a familial relation, was a profound trauma that severed cycles of reciprocity that were the basis of mana and the means of achieving a thriving society. When Trask wrote that the people "wandered, and they were not able to find their own families again," she meant that dispossession from the land was a

159

sundering of the familial relations upon which Hawaiian society in the times of ka poʻe kahiko was built. Unbound from the social and spiritual basis of being, the bodies of Kanaka Maoli were further devastated by waves of epidemics introduced by foreigners. And, intellectual traditions of healing, orature, poetry, art, and dance were demoted and dismissed as superstition. Dispossession in Hawaiʻi was dangerous, degrading, and nearly fatal.

POSSESSION AND DISPOSSESSION

I cannot end *Potent Mana* without turning to the question of dispossession in its historical and contemporary iterations. Dispossession was/is an effect of global capitalist economics: the system that shapes the living and dying, and contemporary dispossession of Kanaka Maoli. There is, in fact, no possibility of achieving decolonization without "imagining a future outside of" current economic arrangements (Giroux 2005, 15–16). The story about the struggle to decolonize Hawaiʻi is critical not only because it pushes forward theorizing on overcoming colonialism but also because it demonstrates the urgent relevance of the cosmology of Kanaka Maoli for theorizing and creating alternative, democratic, and sustainable futures in place of capitalism.

In order to understand the cycles of dispossession that both precede and define capitalism, we must briefly examine the role of dispossession in the rise of capitalism as a social order. Karl Marx's description of primitive accumulation— the origins of capitalism—in mid-first millennial Europe anticipates future cycles of dispossession up to the present moment. In *Capital*, Marx wrote that "[i]n actual history, it is a notorious fact that conquest, enslavement, robbery, murder, in short force, play the greatest part" in the origins of capitalism. "[T]he methods of primitive accumulation are anything but idyllic" (Marx 1977[1867], 873, 874). At the end of the fourteenth century, English peasants possessed lands in common, but by the end of the fifteenth century, they were forcibly removed from the land "to which they had the same feudal title as the lords themselves" (878). Driven by the rise of wool manufacturing, land that had been suitable for subsistence farming was transformed into enclosures for sheep—the source of wool (879). During the eighteenth century, in a process that foreshadows the Māhele in Hawaiʻi, "the law itself [became] the instrument by which the people's land [was] stolen" (885). By the end of the eighteenth century, the last traces of common land had disappeared (883), and by the nineteenth century, "the very *memory* of the connection between [peasants] and communal property had . . . vanished" (889, emphasis added). In language similar to Trask's, Marx described how primitive accumulation required the dispossession of the ancestors[1] of the present-day working class (896). They were, he wrote, "forcibly expropriated from the soil, driven from their homes, turned into vagabonds, and then whipped, branded and tortured by grotesquely terroristic laws into accepting the discipline necessary for the system of wage-labor" (899).

The roots of capitalism lie in this dispossession, in the sundering of European people from the means of subsistence and resources held in common. Once seized by private individuals, the land and the people were harnessed for the production of private wealth. Despite the present myth that "globalization" is a new phenomenon, capitalism also derived from the dispossession of non-European others across the globe.[2] Colonial plantation agriculture was a primary means through which forms of production outside of Europe were forced into the orbit of capitalism on an international scale (see Mintz 1985, 51, 54, 61, 64–65).

Primitive accumulation by dispossession remains "powerfully present" within contemporary capitalism (Harvey 2005b, 145). If the theft of indigenous land during the colonial era (or the theft of the land of English peasants in the fourteenth century) can be described as "primitive accumulation," then the continuing process of accumulation by dispossession has grown more sophisticated and is just as crucial to the survival of capitalism in the current neoliberal era (Glassman 2006, 615–18). Neoliberal capitalism carries to an extreme the logic of private property rights, individual liberty, free markets, and open trade across borders (Harvey 2007, 22).[3] In practice, neoliberalism contradicts the theory of free markets. It relies heavily upon state intervention. For example, a largely government-funded military protects global corporate investments and enforces the creation of new consumer markets.[4] And, government bailouts of failing financial markets ensure that loss is absorbed by working- and middle-class taxpayers (see Morgensen 2008; Meyers 2008). The political objective of neoliberalism, as an elite campaign waged in the second half of the twentieth century, was to deregulate powers of wealth extraction (Harvey 2005a, 19). The achievement of neoliberal hegemony, marked by the political ascendancy of Margaret Thatcher and Ronald Reagan in the period 1979–1980, signaled the passing of liberal democracy as the governing mode of Keynesianism, the form of capitalism prior to the onset of neoliberalism.[5]

Neoliberalism has become *the* global organizing principle in political, economic, and cultural spheres. It has "swept across the world like a vast tidal wave of institutional reform and discursive adjustment" (Harvey 2007, 23), and although its effects are unevenly distributed, no place on earth has been unaffected. Global institutions that regulate finance and trade, such as the World Bank, the World Trade Organization, and the International Monetary Fund, "instantiate neoliberalism as a global set of rules" (Harvey 2007, 145). The growing global gap between wealth and poverty is one concrete manifestation of neoliberalization.[6]

While poverty and homelessness are structural issues with, as we have seen, deep historic roots, under the regime of the neoliberal state the social, political, and economic production of inequality is personalized and depoliticized (Brown

2006, 704). Neoliberalism abjures commitment to substantive democracy in everyday life (695) and transforms social issues into individual problems that must be solved through consumption. The political-economic effects of neoliberalism in the United States include the privatization of public services such as housing and education, the explosion of the prison-industrial complex, and the commoditization of health through corporate medicine and the pharmaceutical industry. The abolition of programs such as Aid to Families with Dependent Children (AFDC), under the banner of "welfare reform," allowed the government to avoid responsibility for poverty. Under neoliberalism, poverty has increased, and government responsibility has been dissolved in favor of the private market as a source of solutions. The privatization of welfare includes such "solutions" as underemployment, low-wage jobs without health care benefits, and predatory "pay day" lending (Karger 2005, 24; Stegman 2007; Snarr 2002: CC1; King et al. 2006, 10, 17).⁷ The privatization of other formerly public services has resulted in poorly educated students, homeless families, neighborhoods with crumbling vital infrastructures, and people who are sick and unable to afford medical care. In the global South, neoliberalism subverts the achievement of democracy, sovereignty, and economic self-determination through mechanisms such as the World Trade Organization and the International Monetary Fund, which transfer wealth from poor nations to rich nations and to the international corporate elite (Giroux 2005, 6).

Neoliberalism is more than a set of free-market policies. It is fundamentally a political and cultural ontology, "a specific form of normative political reason organizing the political sphere, governance practices and citizenship" (Brown 2006, 693). It is, as Giroux argues, supported by a set of pedagogical practices that normalizes the conditions it produces. Neoliberalism creates a "social universe and cultural landscape" that depends upon authoritarian notions of market fundamentalism and anti-terrorism, and results in "laws that suspend civil liberties, incarcerate disposable populations, and provide the security forces necessary for capital to destroy those spaces where democracy can be nourished" (Giroux 2005, 13). In fact, the United States held 1.6 million people in its prisons and jails (Liptak 2008), had the highest number of individuals (and the most women) behind bars in the world, and had an incarceration rate four times the world average (Hartney 2006, 1). The massive expansion of the prison-industrial complex, despite a steadily decreasing crime rate (1), has resulted in starkly disproportionate racial incarceration rates among Native Hawaiians, Native Americans, blacks, and other people of color, further straining already deeply distressed communities.

It has never been clearer that alternatives to the dominion over nature and the dispossession of people are desperately needed. As a hegemonic mode of discourse and practice, however, the fundamentals of neoliberalism have become common sense. Neoliberalism colonizes the future, renders capitalism inevitable, and works to extinguish alternative possibilities for social organization. It seeks to destroy and replace other "ways of life, attachments to the land, habits of the heart, [and] ways of thought" (Harvey 2007, 23). And this attempt to destroy other ways of life and to confine the future to the needs of capital is part of the story of colonialism and neocolonialism in Hawai'i. But the process of decolonization in Hawai'i demonstrates that capitalism and colonialism were not able to expunge the roots of, and routes to, alternative indigenous futures. To say that the forces of neocolonialism and neoliberalism are not easily defeated is a gross understatement, and while I do not wish to seem naïve, I know it is certain that the struggle continues.

NEO-DISPOSSESSION

From the times of ka po'e kahiko to the neoliberal present, Native Hawaiians have experienced successive waves of dispossession. This is most evident in the current deadly crisis of Native Hawaiian homelessness. The massive contemporary eviction of Native Hawaiians from their (rented or mortgaged) homes must be understood within a framework of dispossession that can be traced back to the origins of capitalism, the initial encounter with European foreigners, and the alienation of land at the Māhele. The logic of accumulation by dispossession that defined the Māhele in the first century of colonialism continues to govern the crisis of homelessness 230 years later.

Dispossession and homelessness in Hawai'i are facts of history. In 1965, a group of homeless Hawaiians living in tents on a Wai'anae beach was evicted by the state so a film crew could construct elaborate and expensive structures to replicate a "traditional Hawaiian village" for the filming of James Michener's novel *Hawai'i* (Mākua's Storied History 1997; Reyes 1995). In November 1982, when hurricane Iwa struck Wai'anae, many homes were destroyed. A group of homeless families calling themselves "Mākua 'Ohana" (families of Mākua) set up a village on the beach at Mākua. The 'Ohana asserted the right to live on the beach, arguing that since "[t]he [American] government stole [the land] from the Nation and People of Hawai'i in the armed overthrow of Hawai'i's government in 1893" they had no right to evict the homeless families (Mākua Valley Support Committee 1983). The Mākua 'Ohana managed to live on the beach for a year, at which time the state sent "their bulldozers, dogs and armed enforcers" to remove them (Laenui 1983, 1). Other homeless settlements followed. In the early 1990s, a group of Hawaiian activists[8] set up a "village" at Mākua Beach. The U.S. Army, whose use of Mākua Valley included live-fire exercises, first complained to the state in 1992 about the settlement, requesting that it "expedite . . . coordination with the Department of Human Services to determine the 'homeless' status of these people and initiate appropriate measures to relocate them from Makua Beach" (Tummons 1992, 3).

The state evicted the residents of the Mākua Beach settlement at dawn on June 18, 1996. Fifty families remained to conduct civil disobedience in protest of the evictions. While a group of peace and sovereignty movement activists chanted in support, a convoy of state vehicles erected roadblocks on Farrington Highway from Keaʻau Beach Park to Yokohama Bay, preventing access to Mākua Beach. The National Guard handled the heavy equipment used to remove the structures erected on the beach. Two state marine patrol boats were stationed offshore, and a Honolulu Police Department helicopter loomed overhead. The Honolulu Fire Department, armed state public safety officials, sheriff deputies, and conservation law enforcement officers were also present. In a controversial move, the state, citing the possibility of violence, barred the news media from the site of the eviction. The few newspaper and television journalists who managed to access the beach were threatened with arrest and accused of "obstructing justice."[9] A representative of the state justified the action, claiming that the "needs of the media were secondary" to the need for "public safety" (Shapiro 1996).[10]

Before the eviction from their perilous position on the margins of the land, the settlers at Mākua were prescient and prophetic. One settler, captured on video by the producers of "Mākua: To Heal the Nation," said "They are like pushing us off the face of the earth. This is as far at the end of this island that you can get. Where we going next? In the water?" (Mākua: To Heal the Nation 1996). This question—Where are we going next? In the water?—acutely expresses the dire consequences of neoliberal economics for the descendants of ka poʻe kahiko.

NATIVE HAWAIIAN HOMELESSNESS IN THE EARLY TWENTY-FIRST CENTURY

"This is Beirut, Hawaiʻi," a physician at the Waiʻanae Coast Comprehensive Health Center told a reporter from a Honolulu newspaper in 2006. "It's very sad." He was referring to the twenty-first century crisis of homelessness and to a 44 percent increase in the number of homeless patients treated at the health center since 2005 (Perez 2006). By invoking Beirut, the physician was drawing upon a metaphor for the ravages of war and conjuring images of poverty, disease, and hopelessness. In 2006, the fifteen-mile stretch of beach along Farrington Highway in Waiʻanae had become a teeming tent city inhabited by an estimated 3,500 homeless people (Beachfront Tent Cities 2006), some 60 percent of whom were Native Hawaiian (Kelly 2007). The beaches of Waiʻanae in the early twenty-first century reflected a "full-blown epidemic" (Perez 2006) of homelessness.

The dispossession of Native Hawaiians that began with the Māhele in the mid-nineteenth century continues into the early twenty-first century (see Kelly 2003, 1002). The current mass eviction of Native Hawaiians from their homes needs to be understood in the context of this colonial history and of iterating processes of accumulation by dispossession into the neoliberal era. Although Hawaiians comprise 20 percent of the state's population, they comprise half of the state's homeless. While Wai'anae Hawaiians struggled with poverty, political disenfranchisement, and cultural marginalization throughout the twentieth century, the early twenty-first-century upsurge in homelessness marks a harsher reality indexed to economic neoliberalization. It was clear to the Mākua beach settler in 1996 that "welfare reform" would cause an explosion in homelessness. "I like know what they are gon' do with the rest of the people when the welfare get cut?" one settler asked, "'Cause most of them gon' end up down here wit' us" (Mākua: To Heal the Nation 1996).

Indeed, it must have been clear to policy makers and legislators that a lack of funding for social welfare programs would create havoc in the lives of the poor (Welfare Cutbacks 1996). But the neoliberal state abdicates any responsibility for social needs and proffers the market as the site for solutions.[11] In 2000, the community of Wai'anae contained almost 25,000 Native Hawaiians (Family Health Services Division 2005, 14). Key economic indicators for Wai'anae told a story of a community in great distress. Hawai'i guidelines set in 1999 by the U.S. Department of Health and Human Services determined that a family of four earning a pre-tax annual income of $19,210 was officially poor. In Wai'anae, in 1999, nearly 22 percent of the population fell under this designation, and twice that percentage was below 200 percent of the state poverty level. At almost 7 percent, unemployment in Wai'anae was more than twice as high as the statewide rate of slightly less than 3 percent. The infant mortality rate for Wai'anae between 1999 and 2004 was 12.9, nearly twice the state-wide rate of 6.9 (Family Health Services Division 2005, 18, 28, 29, 39). But despite the manifest need in Wai'anae, only 12.6 percent of families were receiving Temporary Aid to Needy Families (TANF) in 2004 (Family Health Services Division 2005, 32).

The housing market put even the most modest housing beyond the reach of most Hawaiians. Median rents in Hawai'i are among the highest in the United States. In 2007, according to a Honolulu housing analyst, the "going rate for a typical two-bedroom apartment [was] about $1,901, up 71 percent , from 2001" (Gerena-Morales 2007). The state office, overseeing public low-income housing in Hawai'i had a $9 million deficit in 2007. There were 6,500 available units of public housing, with a waiting list of 7,000. The Section 8 Program, designed to offer rent subsidies to encourage low-income renters to seek housing in the private market, had a wait of eight years. Also in 2007, a gallon of milk was $6 and gas was $3.50 a gallon (Kelly 2007).

It is not possible to discuss the historic trajectory of dispossession in Hawai'i without considering the role of the U.S. military, which controls a quarter of the land base in the Islands, and post-9/11 began the largest expansion since World War II (Kelly 2003, 1002). In a Free Speech Radio documentary called "On Being Hawaiian and Homeless," Anne Keala Kelly documented the effects of post-9/11 militarism on the skyrocketing problem of Native Hawaiian homelessness. The swelling coffers of the military included a $530 million housing subsidy for military personnel. The influx of personnel strained the military's ability to provide housing on base, and in Hawai'i they were encouraged with a $1,300 monthly stipend to seek housing in the private market. In response, landlords in Hawai'i sharply increased the rent—apartments in Wai'anae that rented for $700 before 9/11 were now up to $1,000 (Kelly 2007). Kelly, who described the scenic beaches of Wai'anae as "refugee camps" and "shanty towns," argued that increased military spending, a $30 million annual budget for the state's tourism department, and a housing boom had driven the cost of housing beyond the reach of most Native Hawaiians. "Six years ago," she said, "there weren't miles and miles of coast line filled with shanty towns, which owe their existence in part to a runaway market that has turned housing into ATM machines and redefined the meaning of the word 'home'" (Kelly 2007).

FORWARD TO DECOLONIZATION

Ashis Nandy wrote that colonialism is a process in which the modern West exceeds its specific geographic and temporal boundedness and is transformed into a generalizable psychological category. In this way, he argued, colonialism has a total impact on the minds and bodies of the colonized and alters their cultural priorities "once and for all" (Nandy 1983, xi). But Nandy's work begs the question of whether the colonized can challenge the neocolonial (neoliberal) grip on bodies and souls, and whether they can again determine political and cultural priorities. It is precisely this project, the creation of the means for healing the physical, mental, and spiritual wounds of colonialism, that was the aim of Native Hawaiians in Wai'anae.

The wounds of colonialism have been explored by the work of such authors as Nandy, Fanon (1963, 1967, 1969) and Memi (1965). While there is certainly a need for further analysis of the ways in which colonialism injures, there is also a need to move forward and beyond with explorations of the means of decolonization. The stories told in *Potent Mana* move forward this conversation about the healing of the colonized by exploring the theories and practices of Native Hawaiians engaged in creating the means to overcome the effects of (neo)colonialism.

The work of Ignacio Martín-Baró (1996; see also Duran and Duran 1995[12]) also moves forward the conversation on overcoming oppression. In the series of essays that comprises *Writings for a Liberation Psychology*, Martín-Baró (1996) launched incisive critiques against the American discipline of psychology. Beginning at the turn of the twentieth century, he argued, psychology "ran so fast after scientific recognition and social status that it stumbled" (20). It became a discipline entangled with the exigencies of the American empire, both at home and abroad, and with both local and global elites. It turned away from its psychoanalytic roots, which at least left open the practice of hermeneutics. It embraced epistemologies based on behaviorism and positivism and codified them in frameworks of oppressive class and cultural relations. The dominant paradigm of twentieth-century American psychology was rooted in theories of individualism and of the pathology of individual behaviors and persons (as we saw in chapter 4 in the discussion of Mauna Ala's insanity). While germ theory in biomedicine obscured the social production of health and disease, the focus on the individual in psychology eclipsed an understanding that humans are fundamentally social beings that cannot exist outside of kinship networks that include the earth.

The epistemology of positivism is at the root of the discipline's entanglement with elite power. According to Martín-Baró, psychology (along with other twentieth-century disciplines) posited that knowledge was limited to positive facts, events, and their "empirically verifiable relations." What could not be explained via scientific method was ignored, and thus the "most important meanings of human existence" were disregarded (Martín-Baró 1996, 21). Positivism recognized nothing beyond the given and refused to concede that alternative futures, under different sociohistorical conditions, were possible. "To consider reality as no more than the given," Martín-Baró wrote, is to believe "that the Salvadoran campesino is just fatalistic, or the black less intelligent." To understand the given as the only possibility was "an ideologization of reality that winds up consecrating the existing order as natural" (1996, 21). In contrast to this ideologization of reality, liberation psychology posited "reality" as that which limited human knowledge and capability. "[O]nly by acting upon [reality], by transforming it," could a new reality emerge. Thus for Martín-Baró the job of the psychologist was to immerse herself in "a new praxis . . . of transforming reality" in order to become oriented toward "what ought to be" (1996, 28). It is not, he admitted, easy to figure out where and how psychologists should be placed, but it is clear that they must enter the process "alongside the dominated rather than alongside the dominator," must deviate from technocratic professional superiority, and must allow for self-transformation in the process of transforming reality.

Although Martín-Baró wrote specifically about the lives and aspirations of the oppressed in El Salvador, his work resonates elsewhere in a globe full of suffering and dominated people. And although his commitment was, first of all, to the people of El Salvador, his intention was to make a contribution to "universal psychology" through the development of a specifically Latin American one (1996, 32). Martín-Baró's essays provide an important framework for interpreting the work of Native Hawaiians engaged in decolonization and healing the wounds of colonialism.

Over the course of many conversations, Kalama Liu (see also chapter 3), a Native Hawaiian social worker, tried to teach me about healing and decolonization. Liu articulated notions of healing and health that reflected the emphasis on developing specifically Native Hawaiian treatment methods, and that viewed the recuperation of Hawaiian culture and memory as the basis for well-being. These conceptions of healing and health were common among the cohort of young Native Hawaiians working as social workers, psychologists, and treatment counselors in Wai'anae in the mid-1990s.

In Liu's articulation of the trauma of colonialism, he continually juxtaposed the short time of Westernization with the eons of pre-haole Hawaiian life. "[I] speak of a primordial soul," he said, "of many years that we were here as Hawaiians before contact with the West. . . . We were connected to everything and that defined who we were" (Liu 1997). In our conversations, Liu sometimes grew frustrated with his inability to explain the ways in which Hawaiians had lived in the eons before the arrival of Westerners. And he often expressed disappointment with my inability to grasp it. "How do I explain to you our Hawaiian universe," he would say. "How do I explain to you how we were as a people, and our connection to everything, and how that connection defined who we were." He pointed to my "Western thinking," and to the "very Western system" of education that had produced me as a scholar as a serious limit to my ability to grasp the impact of colonialism on the bodies and souls of Hawaiians. Liu said:

> We were oppressed and we continue to be oppressed, and we continue to be denied access to those things that brought us fulfillment as Hawaiians. . . . This is post traumatic stress disorder, and that has been experienced by Hawaiians since contact with the West. I don't know how to explain it, but I think the trauma has occurred and the trauma continues to occur. . . . So maybe it isn't PTSD, maybe its TSD—traumatic stress disorder. (Liu 1997)

For Liu, healing Hawaiians meant taking the theories he learned in graduate school and applying them where they seemed appropriate. But it was outside of the classroom where he learned the most valuable lessons. The focus on the individual in traditional psychology was a challenge that those engaged in creating specifically Hawaiian mental health treatment necessarily faced. Liu said that he learned those theories at the university and was expected to use them in treatment. "But, come on," he said, "how much of a success and how much of a benefit are we doing to our clients if we know they are not raised thinking solely of themselves as individual?" The singular focus on the living in traditional psychotherapy was also problematic, and, coupled with the focus on the individual, made the psychotherapeutic tradition problematic for Hawaiians who had been shaped by cultural concepts of reciprocity and obligation. Liu said that Hawaiians in therapy were never solely individuals. Rather, they were connected with families and communities, circumstances and environment (see also Mokuau 1990b, 1995). What Hawaiian clients bring into therapy "is a sense of obligation and responsibility" to their children, to their ancestors, and to the land. This sense of obligation, he argued, "needs to be talked about, as well as talking about our dead, our ancestors. . . . It doesn't have to stop because they are dead . . . because for us they are still with us, and we still have an obligation to take care of them and them to take care of us . . . they are still entities that we can deal with." He described his primary role as helping clients with cultural restoration and overcoming shame. Liu said:

> *For me there is restoration when I talk to a client, [a project of helping them] find that center in themselves, of digging deep to find [it]. . . . [M]y work with Hawaiian clients is removing all that shame-based stuff that's there, that we have put on ourselves, that we have accepted. . . . What we talk about behind closed doors . . . , though we are not supposed to, is religion and spirituality. But damn it, damn it, we're Hawaiian. We live and look and spirituality is all around us. How can we not talk about it? How can we not bring it up in a session with a client? How can we not help them realize that their culture, their Hawaiian being, is strength.* (Liu 1997)

In conceptualizing "cultural curricula and approaches to healing," Native Hawaiian health practitioners distinguished between a Western biomedical notion of "treatment" and a Hawaiian notion of "healing." The biomedical focus on the individual as the unit for treatment is displaced by an approach that locates the family and community as the ultimate target of healing. Liu said that he was opposed to the word "treatment" or "therapy" as a description of method because it ignored the tangled roots of the problem to focus on the individual's symptoms of disease.

Native Hawaiian practitioners in the mid-1990s had also mastered the art of cultural translation with funding sources. As one young practitioner put it:

> *Clinical is definitely a Western thing. But I think the challenge for administrators . . . especially living in today's society and applying for funding, I think it is important that we sort of learn how to play the game, to be active players. . . . Like I can tell you that I am practicing family conflict*

resolution or family mediation therapy . . . and then on another level, I can tell you that simply the whole structure is ho'oponopono [a specifically Native Hawaiian method of resolving family conflict]. I can tell you that what I am doing is cognitive behavioral therapy, or the restructuring of negative thoughts, and the development of self-esteem. Another way of saying it is basically I am teaching the person spiritual aspects of ways to cope with his identity. . . . That is a cognitive behavioral model, a Western model; I'm just doing it in a cultural context, you understand. (Chung 1997, interviewed by author)

The careful analyses and learned ability to conduct cultural translation of Native Hawaiian mental health care workers in 1997 is one example of changes that have occurred since the founding of the first Native Hawaiian-run health centers (see chapter 4). While the earlier experiments were beset by administrative and funding crises, they also suffered from an inability to translate Hawaiian methods into the language of Western health care bureaucracies. Native Hawaiian practitioners in the mid-1990s had mastered the art of cultural translation with funding sources.

Native Hawaiians have a long history of resistance to the imposition of Western systems of being and knowing. They have harbored Hawaiian names in the middle, between first and last names that were "Christian." They wrote songs obscure to haole listeners that contained messages of solidarity, pride, and expressions of kinship with the land. They fought continued dispossession by protesting the eviction of Hawaiians from land slated for resort development (Trask 1987). They saved a sacred island from bombardment by the U.S. Navy (Blackford 2004). Native Hawaiians realized that in order to counter the consciousness of colonialism, they had to create methods that would lead to decolonization. And so they remembered the potency of ancestral knowledge and conceived of it as a guide for contemporary well-being. They relearned ʻōlelo Hawaiʻi and realized that through the medium of their own language an alternative worldview reemerged. They found the strength to overcome the shame inherent to being colonized, and the wisdom to doubt the social-scientific knowledge that rendered them diseased and pathological. They rewrote their own history and challenged the self-interested politics of colonial knowledge production.

Native Hawaiians in the late twentieth century grasped the concept that decolonization was based upon healing, and they revived ways of understanding health and disease that had been outlawed and suppressed by colonial rule. Most significantly, they understood that decolonizing and healing meant recovering historical and ancestral memory (Martín-Baró 1996, 31) and reasserting the primacy of mana, love, and dependence between humans, the environment, and the divine. But the assertion of ancestral and historical memory in Hawaiʻi was not simply about understanding the past, it was about creating the means for a different, decolonized future.

"ROPES OF RESISTANCE" AND ALTERNATIVE FUTURES

The writer Kuʻualoha Hoʻomanawanui (2004, 89) posited that the renaissance in Kanaka Maoli writing in the last several decades was an important political act of cultural empowerment that "enable[d] us to leave a record . . . for future generations, as our ancestors have left a record of their manaʻo [beliefs] and experiences." Hoʻomanawanui cited a line from Haunani-Kay Trask's poem *Sons* to underscore the importance of writing as resistance. In *Sons*, Trask (1994, 55–56) wrote:

> But, I have no sons
> to give, no line of
> immortality.
> I am slyly
> reproductive: ideas
> books, history
> politics, reproducing
> the rope of resistance
> for unborn generations.

It is my hope that this book will contribute to the "ropes of resistance" by telling the story of late-twentieth-century Native Hawaiians who were learning how to be decolonized. As a Western-educated anthropologist, there was much I had to overcome in order to perceive the integrity of Hawaiian aspirations for decolonization. I had to approach much Western scholarship on the colonized with an intense hermeneutic of suspicion. I had to confront the imbrication of Western scholarship and Western power not only as theory but as practice that distorts through endless cycles of (intellectual, material, and spiritual) dispossession. Grasping the meaning of decolonization enabled me to see the potent mana of Hawaiʻi, and to imagine a very different global trajectory. My hope is that readers will also grasp the relevance of these lessons and will see how crucial they are—in Hawaiʻi and beyond.

NOTES

INTRODUCTION

1. According to Nkrumah, "A colonialist country can in fact offer independence to a people, not with the intention which such an act might be thought to imply, but in the hope that the positive and progressive forces thus appeased and quietened (*sic*), the people might be exploited with greater serenity and comfort (1970, 102).

2. Kwame Nkrumah was a mid-twentieth-century anti-colonial and Pan-Africanist movement leader, who in 1952 became the first prime minister of independent Ghana. *Consciencism: Philosophy and Ideology for Decolonization* is both a critique of Western philosophy and an extended meditation on the relevance of philosophy to African socialism and decolonization.

3. Mana was misinterpreted as a "dynamic impersonal force," which is "tapped to produce magic" (Elbert 1957, 268), or as a "supernatural power" (Oliver 1989[1961], 72).

4. I use quotation marks around "ancient Hawai'i" to point to the use of the term to instantiate decisive junctures between pre-haole Hawai'i, the colonial era, and the neocolonial present. While many scholars have accepted the politics of this periodization, fieldwork in Hawai'i made it clear to me that the past is in the present for many Hawaiians engaged in decolonizing.

5. 'Ai signifies eating, food, consumption, and rule (see chapter 2) and forms the root of 'āina, the Hawaiian word for ancestral land.

6. For a discussion of the meaning of mana in contemporary Fijian society, see Tomlinson (2006, 2007).

7. Critics claim that histories like the one produced by Kame'eleihiwa celebrate "golden myths of origin" and deny the existence of oppression and inequality in Hawaiian society before the coming of Europeans. But to make an analysis of history based on Hawaiian metaphors and to grasp the centrality of serving and caring as a dominant social ethos is not to deny

oppression but, rather, to pose a contrast with Western meanings and metaphors centered on land as a commodity and as a source of private wealth. The work of Samuel Kamakau, a nineteenth-century Hawaiian scholar, whose historical research was published in a Hawaiian language newspaper, makes clear that this ethos of serving and caring was aspirational, a high standard that when met increased the fecundity of the land and the people. For example, Kamakau describes the celebrated chief Kalamakua-a-Kaipūhōlua who "was noted for cultivating, and . . . [for constructing] the large pond fields," and for traveling "about . . . to cultivate the land and [give] the produce [to] the commoners" (Kamakau 1991, 45). This reign is contrasted with the rule of Haka, who was "a bad chief and a stingy one . . . [who] did not take care of the chiefs and the people" (Kamakau 1991, 53–54).

8. "Pre-haole Hawai'i" is Stannard's phrase to indicate the time before the arrival of Europeans (Stannard 1989, 70).

9. "Talk-story is a relaxed, rambling, sometimes intense commentary or conversation. This form of communication most likely derives from the vast and rich oral tradition of Hawaiian culture" (Ito 1999, 12).

10. The "rope of resistance" is a phrase from *Sons*, a poem by Haunani-Kay Trask (1994, 55–56).

CHAPTER 1. KA PO'E KAHIKO

1. Nineteenth-century Hawaiian scholar Samuel Kamakau delineated the classes of kāhuna and their responsibilities. Kāhuna read omens, understood the means of selecting appropriate sites for building, mastered knowledge of the configurations of the earth and the sky, controlled knowledge of deep sea fishing, designed and constructed implements for tapa (cloth made from bark) work, and mastered the arts of 'anā'anā—a "means of absolution . . . and of dispelling troubles" (Kamakau 1991, 27, 119). Specialist knowledge pertaining to healing and health was controlled by kāhuna lapa'au. This knowledge included the treatment of pregnancy, labor, and delivery; the treatment of childhood ailments; diagnosis by a "table of pebbles" and finger tip palpitation; diagnosis by "insight" or "critical observation"; treatment with 'anā'anā ("to remove the grounds for offense within the victim, and so remove . . . the affliction"); treatment to counteract sorcery; and treatment "of the spirits of illness." Kamakau noted that kāhuna 'anā'anā were the most powerful healers, as they controlled both the ability to use prayer to heal people and to pray people to death (Kamakau 1991, 98, 119, 122).

2. The word ahupua'a refers to an ahu (stone heap), which supported an image of the head of a pua'a (pig). This heiau, or shrine to the god Lono, marked the boundaries of the land division for purposes of taxation under the control of a konohiki (overseer in the service of the ali'i, or chiefly class), who supervised planting, harvesting, and the maintenance of irrigation and mediated water and fishing rights. The konohiki also enforced the "seasonal kapu that protected various kinds of fish during seasons of spawning" (Handy, Handy, and Pukui 1991, 48, 321–22, 323).

3. Most writing about this subversion refers to "the abolition" of the 'aikapu, as if it were a custom, like slavery in the United States, whose end was wholly positive. While it may not be possible to imagine how the 'aikapu would have evolved without the intrusions of foreigners, it is certain that its end was of great benefit to Euro/Americans. The abolition of this structural order furthered the economic and political goal of colonizing the Islands. Because the 'aikapu had features that disturbed political ideologies of individualism, gender equality, and democracy, its discursive production as a custom in need of abolition has been unproblematically reproduced. However, since European enlightenment practice lags far behind its philosophical ideals, it is not a trustworthy basis for critiquing the pre-contact Hawaiian religious system.

4. A full discussion of the events surrounding the abolition of the kapu system and its political ramifications is beyond the scope of this book. See Davenport (1969) for an analysis of the political and economic issues that defined this dramatic cultural shift, and for an argument that the "abolition of the *kapu* was . . . a deliberate political response to political crises" triggered by "social and economic intercourse with Europeans" (18); see Kame'eleihiwa (1992, ch. 4) for an excellent discussion of the genealogical and political issues defining the abolition of the kapu in terms relevant to the present-day struggle for sovereignty and Kamakau (1992, chapters 22 and 23) for a view of these historical changes through the eyes of a late-nineteenth-century Christianized Hawaiian.

5. Kame'eleihiwa (1992) posited that the other attraction of Christianity was based upon the great enthusiasm with which Hawaiians embraced palapala (reading and writing). Missionaries organized Christian schools for both the elite and commoners, but it was learning to read and write and not the gospel that attracted them. Following Benedict Anderson (1991), Ohnuma (2008, 369) argued that "it was the advent of a written language and the flowering of a Hawaiian-language press beginning in the 1830s more than Christianity itself that filled the void after the kapu system was abandoned."

6. In "Speaking 'Truth' to Illness," Scheper-Hughes and Lock (1986) posit that while sickness is embodied and material, it is also symbolic and metaphori-

cal. While their analysis attended primarily to the experience of individual patients in biomedical settings, it is also relevant to the ideology of infirmity through which the diseases of Hawaiians were understood in the nineteenth and twentieth centuries. According to Scheper-Hughes and Lock, "The societal and cultural responses to disease create a second illness in addition to the original affliction, what we are calling the 'double': the layers of stigma, rejection, fear, and exclusion that attach to particularly dreaded diseases" (137; see also Sontag 1990).

7. Kirch and Sahlins (1994, 44), citing Schmitt (1970a, 363; cf. 1970b), doubt the veracity of memories of the impact of this epidemic. Sahlins, who is concerned with "the economic upsurge that began at O'ahu in 1804," argued that the impact of the epidemic was not so great as to effect an increase of population on O'ahu. Kuykendall argued that "native accounts [which] say the disease . . . carried off more than half the population [are] probably the result of legendary exaggeration" (Kuykendall 1965[1938], 49ff.).

8. According to McNeill (1989[1976]), widespread inoculation became possible in England in the 1740s and was used particularly in rural communities and small towns. In France, opposition to the smallpox vaccine as "interference with God's will" abated, and use of the technique became widespread in the early nineteenth century. In the English colonies of America, smallpox inoculations were introduced early in the eighteenth century. However, "[W]hite settlement along the frontier was assisted also by the fact that destruction of Indian populations by infectious diseases, of which smallpox remained the most formidable, continued unabated. The ravages of smallpox among Indians may in fact have been assisted by deliberate efforts at germ warfare. In 1763, for instance, Lord Jeffrey Amherst ordered that blankets infected with smallpox be distributed among enemy tribes, and the order was acted on. Whether the result was as expected seems not recorded." In Spanish America, inoculations of the indigenous population occurred beginning in 1803, shortly after the method was approved in metropolitan Spain. Significantly, a medical mission from Spain departed for the Philippines in 1807 to provide inoculations to the population of that colony (McNeill 1989[1976], 221–23).

9. The 'Ahahui Lā'au Lapa'au found that the majority of traditional kāhuna practiced several forms of healing. According to Chun, the kāhuna interview by the 'Ahahui were "trained in Hāhā (to diagnose by palpation) and Pā'ao'ao (childhood illness) and some specialized forms of diagnosis such as au maka (observation), moe (dreams), and 'uhane (spirits), but several also knew what late-nineteenth-century translators and ethnographers called sorcery or black magic, such as 'Anā'anā, Kuni, Kuehu kapa, and Ho'opi'opi'o" (Chun 1994, viii).

10. A leader of the European Protestant Reformation, Calvin was obsessed with sin. In the institutes, Calvin's work of systematic theology, first published in 1536, he dwelled at length on the notion of original sin.

> This is that hereditary corruption which the fathers called original sin: meaning by sin, the depravation of a nature previously good and pure. . . . From a putrefied root, therefore, have sprung putrid branches, which have transmitted their putrescence to remoter ramifications. . . . Original sin, therefore, appears to be an hereditary pravity and corruption part of our nature, diffused through all the parts of the soul, rendering us obnoxious to the Divine wrath. . . . [W]e derive from [Adam], not only the punishment, but also the pollution to which the punishment is justly due. (cited in Manschreck 1964, 90)

In other work, Calvin spelled out the most serious sins, and the punishments to be meted out to the most serious sinners. Anyone who practiced idolatry or otherwise lapsed into "papistical" worship, blasphemy, or any contradiction of the Word of God was to be "admonished." Drunkenness, singing "unworthy" songs, "spin[ning] wildly around in the dance," and fornication should be punishable by imprisonment (93–95). Clearly, Hawaiian culture from the point of view of the Calvinists was a vivid example of rampant, unrepentant sin.

11. "Regrettably but obviously, Liholiho drank too much—so much, in fact, that foreigners who kept diaries at Honolulu found it simplest to note the days when the king was sober. In his cups he might limit himself to ordering some feux de joie from the battery at the fort in the harbor, or he might set off on a long carouse and be unmanageable for weeks on end" (Daws 1968, 68).

CHAPTER 2. WAI'ANAE

1. The second biggest obstacle to organizing in Harlem in the late 1980s was the burden of poor health and the lack of affordable, accessible, relevant health care.

2. "A limit situation is a personal or political obstacle perceived by humans to restrict their freedom and ability to carry out their goals. . . . To challenge a limit situation requires a sense of hope and confidence; submission to its restrictions is an act of hopelessness" (Benesch 2001, 51).

3. Kama'āina, according to Pukui and Elbert's Hawaiian dictionary, means "Native-born, one born in a place, host" (Pukui and Elbert 1986, 124).

However, the term was commonly used by haole (white) longtime residents, or haoles born in the Islands, to indicate their sense of belonging and to distinguish themselves from tourists and other malihini newcomers.

4. I encountered a similar story later in my fieldwork, according to which Filipinos were traveling around the island and stealing black dogs in order to eat them. Roderick Labrador (2008) has analyzed Filipino jokes that circulate on the kanaka comedy circuit (local comedy for local audiences). According to Labrador, "Filipino dog eating jokes are widely disseminated, in public and in private" and serve both as entertainment and as enactments "of social hierarchy and order" (293).

5. There is a large literature exploring the historical, cultural, and socioeconomic experiences of groups imported as plantation labor in Hawaii and of their subsequent labor struggles. Most of the laborers brought to Hawaii were Asians from Japan, China, the Philippines, and Okinawa. However, imported plantation laborers also included workers from Portugal and Puerto Rico (see Okihiro 1991; Takaki 1983).

6. In contrast to the literature examining the presence of haoles in Hawai'i, much less is written about the status of the relatively small population of blacks in Hawai'i. See Lee (1948, 419–37) for a discussion of negative attitudes by especially middle-class Native Hawaiians toward Negroes, the tendency of especially Negro men to "pass" into the "local" community, and the acceptance of Negroes as individuals but not as a group in Hawai'i from the late nineteenth to the early twentieth centuries.

7. Rohrer's (2008) essay also explores the "local" as a recent staging ground for haole claims of reverse racism and attacks on Native Hawaiian entitlements, culture, and sovereignty movement politics (1116).

8. According to Pukui and Elbert (1986), aloha translated into English means "love, affection, compassion, mercy, sympathy, pity . . . sentiment, grace, charity" and can be used as a greeting, salutation, or indication of kind regard (21). The "aloha" brand, as a marketing tool, abstracts the meaning of the Hawaiian word for the purposes of attracting tourists.

9. Kamana'opono Crabbe (2002) studied the degree of acculturation and ethnic identity among Native Hawaiian adults with an instrument he developed called the "Hawaiian Ethnocultural Inventory of Cultural Practices" (HEI). The HEI measured involvement with Native Hawaiian cultural practices and knowledge of Native Hawaiian culture (9) among a sample of 427 adults (55.7 percent of whom were Native Hawaiians and 44.3 percent of whom were non-Native Hawaiians). Ethnicity and blood quantum (for the Native Hawaiians in the sample) were determined by self-report (11). Crabbe found that "individuals of Native Hawaiian heritage possess[ed] significantly greater knowledge of and belief in culturally relevant practices, and engage[d] in these practices more often compared to individuals of non-

Hawaiian heritage" (20). Respondents with higher blood quantum scored "significantly higher on the Knowledge of Hawaiian Cultural Practices than those with lower blood quantum" (21). Noting that it was not possible to establish a causal relationship between blood quantum and knowledge of cultural practices, Crabbe hypothesized that "Native Hawaiians with a higher blood quantum have greater exposure to Hawaiian customs and practices within their families because they are modeled by parents and other family members who value and promote culturally relevant practices" (21). He further posited that "biological predisposition," coupled with interests in perpetuating cultural practices within families and across generations, might account for the higher scores of Native Hawaiians with higher blood quantum on the HEI measure. Crabbe posited that "the likelihood of ethnic folklore, facts and data surviving from one generation to the next is greatly enhanced" by higher blood quantum. My ethnographic data indicated that those involved in decolonization efforts in Waiʻanae in the late 1990s were ethnically mixed *and* strongly identified as Native Hawaiian. A goal of my study was to examine how decolonization efforts were both theorized and practiced. I did not ask questions about blood quantum, and my unit of analysis was the community rather than the individual. Therefore, I do not believe that my data contradict Crabbe's findings in regard to the relationship between higher blood quantum and greater knowledge of cultural practices for individuals. Rather, I would argue that as the largest "ethnic" group in Waiʻanae, Native Hawaiians (across the blood quantum spectrum) exerted a great deal of cultural influence, and that the history of Waiʻanae as a harbor of Hawaiian traditions made the transmission of Native Hawaiian culture possible across generations (see chapter 5). On a metaphorical level, the "blood quantum" of the community of Waiʻanae in the late twentieth century could be characterized as high.

10. "Reports circulating in the mainland press of riots, race hatreds and acute danger to women in Honolulu . . . [are] viciously false, and utterly misrepresent the people and spirit of Honolulu among all races and all classes" (Farrington 1932, 4).

11. A *Los Angeles Times* article that decried the "lurid tabloid" coverage of the Massie Case argued that since there were "ten crimes against native women to one against white women," race was surely irrelevant to the case. The same article then contradicted this point about raced and gendered violence by curiously arguing that the trial "threaten[ed] to disturb race harmony for the first time in the history of the islands" (Carr 1932).

12. One of the complaints lodged against Boki and Liliha was that they were never married in the Christian sense.

13. According to Kamakau (1992), the regent Kaʻahumanu traveled about the Islands in order "to turn" the common people "to the word of God" and

proclaim new laws: 1. Murder is prohibited, also robbery, cheating, and stealing. 2. Adultery (moekolohe) is prohibited, also prostitution (hoʻoka-makama); a man must not persuade away another's wife or a woman another's husband. Each is to have but one husband or one wife, and all must [from this time] be legally married, but those who were married before the word of God became known are to be regarded as legally married. 3. (*sic*) Worshipping of idols such as sticks, stones, sharks, dead bones, ancient gods, and all untrue gods is prohibited. There is one God alone, Jehovah. He is the God to worship. 4. The hula is forbidden, the chant (olioli), the song of pleasure (mele), foul speech, and bathing by women in public places. 5. The planting of ʻawa is prohibited. Neither chiefs nor commoners are to drink ʻawa. 6. The manufacture of liquor is prohibited, such as distilling ti plant and fermenting potatoes, mountain apples, and other such foods. 7. Let us seek after truth and keep the words of God. I am traveling in my old age with my chief (the king) in order to turn you to the word of God, which has come to me in my old age and which I prize (298–99).

14. In my use of the term "culture," I draw from the work of Freire (1989), as well as from Rosaldo (1993), Fanon (1968), and Nandy (1983). I am arguing that, for the oppressed, culture is less a unified, formal set of static customs than informal, improvisational, heterogeneous practices; in Waiʻanae in the 1990s, such practices were linked with the desire to create and sustain a viable Hawaiian community in the twentieth and twenty-first centuries.

15. Walter Rodney (2005) posited that colonial capitalism introduced technological backwardness in African agriculture. According to Rodney:

> On the reserves of South Africa, far too many Africans were crowded onto inadequate land, and were forced to engage in intensive farming, using techniques that were suitable only to shifting cultivation. In practice, this was a form of technical retrogression, because the land yielded less and less and became destroyed in the process. Wherever Africans were hampered in their use of their ancestral lands . . . the same negative effect was to be found. Besides, some of the new cash crops . . . were very demanding on the soil. In countries like Senegal, Niger, and Chad, which were already on the edge of the desert, the steady cultivation led to soil impoverishment and encroachment of the desert. (2005, 113)

16. de Certeau put it this way: "Every group lives by the compromises it invents and by the contradictions that it manages (all the way up to the thresholds beyond which it can no longer assume them). To identify it as a stable and homogenous totality is already to treat it as a dead body" (Certeau 1997, 160).

17. According to the 2000 U.S. Census, Native Hawaiians and other Pacific Islanders comprised 27 percent of the total Wai'anae population. Nearly 42 percent of Wai'anae was counted as "two or more races," which of course would include many Native Hawaiians.

18. I use italics to distinguish interviews and field notes from citations taken from written sources.

CHAPTER 3. MANA

1. "Be fruitful and multiply, and fill the earth and subdue it; and have dominion over the fish of the sea and over the birds of the air, and over every living thing that moves upon the earth" (New Revised Standard Version, 2).

2. Abulafia (2008) described the development of an official policy by Spain regarding the treatment of newly conquered people. Twenty years after the mission of Columbus, Spain proclaimed the Doctrine of Submission (known as *El Requerimiento*). The conquered would "do well" if they acknowledged the primacy of the Roman Catholic pope and the rule of the king and queen of Spain. If not, *El Requerimiento* specified that Spain would "powerfully enter your country, and . . . make war against you . . . and subject you to the yoke and obedience of the Church and of their Highnesses," including taking wives and children and making slaves of them, and taking away all goods. *El Requerimiento* blamed the conquered for all death and losses (2008, 294–97). While the Doctrine of Submission was specific to Spanish conquest, it clearly influenced the conquest experience of other European countries and the people they colonized.

3. Abulafia argues that the history of violent conquest is not yet over, since "[a]trocities continue in remote parts of Brazil, where native tribes live lives not so very different from what was described by" sixteenth-century Europeans who arrived to conquer Brazil (Abulafia 2008, 312)

4. See http://www.dictionary.reference.com/search?q=commensality (accessed March 26, 2009).

5. See http://www.dictionary.reference.com/browse/eat (accessed March 26, 2009).

6. Philosopher John Patterson's (2000) exploration of the meaning of mana in Maori culture argues for the possibility of mana as the ontology of an environmental philosophy suitable to Western cultures. He says that in order to understand mana, Westerners must grasp the "web of relationships" between the natural and the supernatural, between the past and the present, and between Oceania and the rest of the globe (233). The relational web implied in the concept of mana, the notion that kinship encompasses all things living and divine, however, has not been grasped in the power centers

of global capitalism. Western adoption of mana as a basis of environmental philosophy would require a thorough understanding of the theological, sociocultural, and political-economic implications of the vast epistemological difference between the concept of 'ai and the concept of "eat." Deleuze's (2006) concept of incompossibility articulates the skepticism with which we might view Patterson's desire for the Western adoption of mana as ontology. Deleuze (2006, 60) cited Leibniz's notion that the Christian God chooses from an "infinity of possible worlds." God, Deleuze wrote, chooses the world "that has the most possible reality." Alternative worlds are "incompossible." Dimakopoulou (2006, 81–82) elucidates Deleuze's notion of incompossibility with reference to the transition from the European baroque period to the neo-baroque era, and from modernity to post-modernity. According to Dimakopoulou,

> Deleuze writes that the transition from the baroque to the neo-baroque is marked by the absence of the principle of convergence according to principles of pre-established harmony and the incompossibles enter the arena of fragmentation. . . . The dissonant coexistence of incompossible "events" can be read as an allegory of the transition from modernity onto postmodernity: a cultural and historical condition in which more than one [virtuality is] actualized . . . a world that witnesses the transition from "harmonic closure" to . . . "polyphony of polyphonies." (2006, 81–82)

7. Cesairé (1990, xlviii) argued that poetry "calls upon the receptacle of original relationships that bind us to nature." Although mana is a Polynesian, and not a Caribbean, concept, Cesairé's words are relevant to the meaning of mana and the cluster of concepts formed around the Hawaiian word 'ai.

8. Lo'i refers to irrigated ponds for growing taro.

9. Jonathan Okamura (1990) has argued that demographic studies of Hawai'i (see Adams 1925; Lind 1955) support discourses of racial harmony that hide the history of colonialism, along with contemporary structural inequality and racial hierarchy. Okamura argued that the emphasis on demographic populations, rather than on social structure, "masks the monopoly for political and economic power wielded by haoles (whites) as an oligarchy of planters, merchants, and politicians during much of Hawai'i's history" (1990, 276).

10. The Pacific Islander population is comprised of Native Hawaiians, Guamanians or Chamorros, Samoans, and Tongans and includes those who wrote in entries such as Tahitian, Marianna Islander, Chuukese, or "other Pacific Islander" (UCB 2007, 1)

11. During the years of my field research in the late 1990s, homelessness in Wai'anae was a significant problem. But by 2006, the state of Hawai'i esti-

mated that there were as many as one thousand homeless people living on the fifteen-mile stretch of Wai'anae beaches (Magin 2006, n.p.).

12. My conception of the awakened, knowing, Hawaiian body is influenced by the work of Nancy Scheper-Hughes and Margaret Lock (1987). In their conception of the mindful body, they explore Western conceptions of the mind/body. My analysis of a knowing body in Hawai'i is influenced by this work. However, while the three bodies (individual, social, and political) explored by Scheper-Hughes and Lock are all temporally rooted in the present, the awakened, knowing, Hawaiian body transcends the present and incorporates the future and the past.

13. Poi is prepared by cooking the starchy root of the taro plant and then pounding it into a paste that is kneaded with water to form a pudding-like substance. It is sometimes fermented for sour poi.

14. Schlosser (2001) noted that during the economic boom of the 1990s, the real wages of 3.5 million fast food industry workers declined, and that the only Americans consistently earning lower wages than fast food industry workers were migrant farm workers. Both fast food workers and migrant farm workers occupy low-wage rungs in the sprawling fast food industrial complex (6).

15. During my field research in Wai'anae in the late 1990s, I encountered several community members who had been study participants. One of these participants became a key informant.

16. Other epidemiological and demographic studies based on similar causal hypotheses and potential critiques of colonialism include Blaisdell 1993, Braun et al. 2002, Casken 2001, Gotay et al. 2000, Hughes et al. 1996, Look and Braun 1995, and Mau et al. 2001.

17. For discussion of a 1995 summit of Hawaiian healers, see Hartwell 1996, chapter 8.

18. The organizations with representation on Papa Ola Lōkahi Board include E Ola Mau, Alu Like (a nonprofit social service agency), State of Hawai'i Office of Hawaiian Affairs, State of Hawai'i Department of Health Office of Hawaiian Health, and the University of Hawai'i Mānoa.

19. Land division extending from the uplands to the sea.

20. Interview with Hokulani Sussex, Wai'anae, Hawai'i, January 7, 1997.

CHAPTER 4. THE STENCH OF MAUNA ALA, COLONIALISM, AND MENTAL HEALTH

1. The Kumulipo, a two-thousand-line genealogical prayer chant, links the highest ranking ali'i to the first humans, to all other creatures of the land and sea, and to the spiritual world. Similar to creation stories in other Polynesian cultures, the Kumulipo was passed orally across generations and

became text in the late nineteenth century. A German anthropologist, Adolf Bastian, first called scholarly attention to the document in the 1880s and published a book comparing Polynesian, Asian, and European cosmogonies. The Kalākaua text was translated into English by Queen Liliu'okalani and published in Boston in 1897.

2. Both Daws (1968) and Fuchs (1961) dispense with a discussion of Native Hawaiians in the years between annexation and statehood in one chapter. The majority of their work is devoted to a detailed analysis of the rise to power of Asian immigrant communities and to the relationship of these groups to the haole elites.

3. The Hawaiian Homes Commission Act of 1920 was one of the programs designed to rehabilitate Native Hawaiians.

4. In 1930, the Legislature of the Territory created the Department of Institutions, which took over many of the functions previously administered by the Board of Health, including the Territorial Prison, leprosy institutions, institutions for the care of children of leprous patients, boys' and girls' training schools, and the Territorial Hospital.

5. Note that there are contemporary scholars who hold these beliefs.

6. According to Galton, "the ancient Greeks" were the absolute nadir (Galton 1892, 340).

7. "More recent attempts have been made to gain by way of the enactment of laws as a means to curb the number of the so-called physical misfits in the islands. The increasing number of mentally handicapped as public charges have been called continually to the attention of the legislators, and recent attempt[s] to reduce the number of mentally handicapped have been made by the introduction of sterilization bills into the legislature. The latest bill, which met its defeat with an indefinite postponement, was based on the reasoning that sterilization would eliminate large families which could not be cared for adequately and would also eliminate the weaker stock of the race" (Leong 1933, 122–23).

8. Prefrontal lobotomy involved a neurosurgeon poking holes in front of the ear canals and plunging a flat knife, a leucotome, into the frontal lobes "to a depth of about two inches. By sweeping the leucotome up and down within the brain, the . . . anterior tips of the frontal lobes" were amputated (Vertosick 1997). Surgeon Walter Freeman popularized and modified the procedure. Freeman, who traveled across the U.S. demonstrating his modified procedure, "inserted an ice pick . . . under the . . . eye lid and drove it . . . into the frontal lobe with a few sharp raps of a mallet. The pick was then twisted and jiggled about, thus scrambling the anterior frontal lobes. . . . A cheap outpatient procedure, the ice pick lobotomy became a common psychosurgical choice in state hospitals across the country" (Vertosick 1997). There were few contemporary long-term studies of lobotomy patients, and

those that were conducted failed to establish a scientific basis for the procedure. The tranquilizer chlorpromazine, introduced in 1954, proved to be effective and soon replaced lobotomy as the primary means of treating severely disturbed patients.

9. Hoʻopākōlea, translated into English, means "[t]o train to grow straight . . . to train to grow in a desired shape, as a plant" (Pukui and Elbert 1986, 306). "Ola" means life.

10. See the QLCC Web site at http://www.qlcc.org/ (accessed July 20, 2007).

CHAPTER 5. KA LEO

1. Pseudonym.

2. Kolekole Pass is the gap in the mountain range that enabled the Japanese Air Force to fly undetected from the east to bomb Pearl Harbor in 1941.

3. McGrath et al. (1973, 132) record a similar story.

4. According to Pukui, the ability of akua and ʻaumākua to inhabit plants, animals, and rocks meant that the misuse of these things could result in illness or even death. See Pukui et al. 1972, 37–38.

5. Shortly after Kupau called for a work cessation, the construction site was blessed by the Reverend Abraham Akaka of Kawaiahaʻo Church. In response to Native Hawaiian demands, the construction site had been so blessed several times over the course of construction (Gordon, Mike 1996. "H3 Dynamite Sends Workers to Hospitals." *Honolulu Star Bulletin.* August 4: A19).

6. As Okamura (2008, 189) makes clear, "fissures in ethnic relations" are "deep and persisting" and "the gap between . . . dominant and subjugated ethnic groups" grows wider into the twenty-first century.

7. The current cohort of Native Hawaiian scholars stands upon the shoulders of many scholarly ancestors whose work resisted colonialism. According to Goodyear-Kaʻōpua (2005, 326), "[I]n the nineteenth century, Kanaka Maoli debated the genealogies of our aliʻi in political struggles between themselves, and they recorded and published genealogies as a hedge and a weapon against colonial encroachment."

8. According to Pukui et al., "Hawaiʻi had yet another classification of sorcerer *kāhuna* whose arts could be applied to help or to hurt. These included the kāhuna hana aloha who cast "love spells," either to make someone fall in love—or to forget a loved one" (1972, 162).

9. Hawaiian language classes, which were funded by the federal Administration for Native Americans, required proof of 50 percent Hawaiian blood quantum for participation.

10. Pseudonym.

11. Horizontal oppression refers to oppression that comes from within the group rather than from above or outside of it.
12. According to Warner (2001, 135), "Some Hawaiians educated during this period recall being physically punished or humiliated for speaking Hawaiian in school. Ironically, many teachers who meted out this punishment were also Hawaiian. At this time, the illusion of future prosperity resulting from the abandonment of Hawaiian in favor of English was inculcated into the Hawaiian people."
13. Pseudonym.
14. Pseudonym.
15. Holt's writing is reminiscent of a passage in DuBois's *Souls of Black Folks.* DuBois wrote:

> A people thus handicapped ought not to be asked to race with the world, but rather allowed to give all its time and thought to its own social problems. But alas! While sociologists gleefully count his bastards and his prostitutes, the very soul of the toiling, sweating black man is darkened by the shadow of vast despair. But the facing of so vast a prejudice could not but bring inevitable self-questioning, self disparagement, and lowering of ideal which ever accompany repression and breed in an atmosphere of contempt and hate. Whisperings and portents come borne upon the four winds: Lo! We are diseased and dying, cried the dark hosts; we cannot write, our voting is in vain; what need of educations since we must always cook and serve? And the Nation echoed and enforced this criticism, saying: Be content to be servants, and nothing more; what need of higher culture for half-men? Away with the black man's ballot, by force or fraud—and behold the suicide of a race! (DuBois 1999, 14–15).

16. "The Princess Poo-Poo-ly has plenty papaya, She loves to give them away, for all the neighbors they say . . . oh me, oh my, you really should try a little piece of Princess Poo-Poo-ly's papaya" (Lewis 1991, 56).
17. George Lewis (1985a, 193) pointed to the fact that while "soul music" was flourishing, the largest commercial market for music in Hawai'i was still the tourist industry.
18. Pseudonym.
19. Al-Anon is an international support organization for the family of alcoholics. It stresses that alcoholism is a family disease, and that nonalcoholic family members express alcoholic dysfunction through rage, fear, and irrationality (Alcoholics Anonymous 2002, 26–27).

20. The Hawaiian language does not distinguish between ego's own biological children and the offspring of ego's siblings and collateral siblings. All children are keiki. While Chung has no biological offspring, he plays an important role in the lives of his siblings' and cousins' children. In addition, Chung has a keiki hānai, a troubled child from a biologically unrelated family, whom he informally "adopted." Hānai means to raise, rear, feed, nourish, sustain as a verb, and it indicates a foster child or an adopted child as a noun.

21. See, for example, "An Interview with Katherine Maunakea," in *He Alo ā He Alo: Hawaiian Voices on Sovereignty*, ed. Roger MacPherson Furrer, 27. Honolulu: American Friends Service Committee.

CHAPTER 6. DREAMING CHANGE

1. Puanani Burgess, n.d., "Choosing My Name," Choosing My Name Assignment, http://www.teamalakai.com/ChoosingMyNameAssignment.doc?attre directs=0 (accessed on January 13, 2010).

2. A law was passed in 1860 that required the giving of "Christian names" and in 1898, when the American coup ended the Hawaiian monarchy and English became the official language of the colony.

3. People speak of feeling "chicken skin," or goose bumps, when they believe that supernatural spirits are present, for example when they see an extraordinary performance of hula. "Chicken skin" came to clients and staff of Ho'o Mōhala when they evoked a sense of the sacred or felt the presence of ancestors or other spirits (Pukui et al. 1972, 92–94).

4. The legend of the first breadfruit tree is an expression of the love and solidarity between the people, the gods, and the land. It expresses the cosmological relationship of mana.

5. Queen Lili'uokalani Children's Center is a nonprofit child social welfare agency with offices scattered throughout the Islands. The initial funds for the center came from a bequest of Queen Lili'uokalani to provide services to children of Hawaiian and part-Hawaiian ancestry.

6. As a volunteer in Ho'o Mōhala's administrative program, I participated in some staff ho'oponopono sessions. Because of the private nature of ho'oponopono between individual clients and counselors, I was never permitted to observe these sessions. I was allowed to participate in one group ho'oponopono session in 1995.

7. Pseudonym.

8. Pseudonym.

9. Pseudonym.

10. In Kiana Davenport's 1994 novel *Shark Dialogues*, Waipiʻo valley is repre-
    sented as a refuge for armed sovereignty movement revolutionaries who are
    waging guerilla warfare against the tourist industry.
11. Pseudonym.

CONCLUSION

1. Rather than "ancestors," Marx referred to "[t]he *fathers* of the present working class" (1977[1867], 896).
2. According to Marx:

   > The discovery of gold and silver in America, the extirpation,
   > enslavement and entombment in mines of the indigenous popula-
   > tion of the continent, the beginnings of the conquest and plunder
   > of India, and the conversion of Africa into a preserve for the com-
   > mercial hunting of black skins are all things which characterize the
   > dawn of the era of capitalist production. These idyllic proceedings
   > are the chief moments of primitive accumulation. (1977[1867],
   > 915)

3. As a political economic theory, neoliberalism is the historic response of the
   finance sector of the international capitalist class to the restraints on profit
   imposed by Keynesianism—the reigning Western economic theory
   throughout most of the twentieth century. A mediating force between capital and labor (Harvey 2005a, 10), Keynesianism was a political, economic,
   and cultural response to the real threat of anti-capitalist mass movements in
   the West during the Great Depression. The logic of Keynesianism continued as a response to anti-colonial movements that embraced socialism as a
   just alternative to capitalism in Asia, Africa, and Latin America after World
   War II (Harvey 2005a, 15). The United States adopted Keynesianism as an
   economic policy to protect capitalism by ameliorating its worst abuses. It
   was both a socioeconomic and moral economy (11) in which the authority
   of the state was expanded to oversee market processes (to regulate growth
   and investment) and to ensure high rates of employment. The state inter-
   vened by setting standards for a "social wage" and by creating systems of
   welfare in health care, housing, and education (11). What we think of as the
   "welfare state" was the product of Keynesian economic theory, which held
   that government intervention was desirable in order to provide a "social
   safety net" for (some [see n. 5 below]) workers against poverty, unemployment, disease, disability, old age, and the death of a family's primary earner
   (Skocpol and Amenta 1986, 132).
4. As Magdoff (2002, 1) noted, the exigency to accumulate capital in a world
   with limited productive capabilities and heavily saturated consumer markets

fosters "endless gimmicks" to persuade working people to spend money through the consumption of needless items, on usurious interest rates on credit cards, car loans, and mortgages. In the corporate sector, the need to accumulate leads to "speculation (just another word for gambling), and outright fraud."

5. The Keynesian welfare state and the circle of liberal democracy in the United States did not extend much farther than the boundaries of its white citizenry (Gilmore 1998–1999, 178; Gilmore 2007, 52–53; also see Allen 2002, 472; Leonardo 2002, 30). Mourning the passing of liberal democracy from a perspective that privileges the well-being of poor communities of color is complicated by the reality of the color line observed under the Keynesian regime. Social welfare legislation passed during the depression era, for example, excluded domestic servants, farm workers, and part-time employees (Jones 1992, 3–4), categories of workers that in an agricultural state like Hawaii disproportionately included Native Hawaiians (and in the continental United States excluded many African Americans). Still, for people of color in the United States, the passing of the Keynesian state, and the instantiation of neoliberalism, has been an excruciating process.

6. In 1996, the net worth of the world's 358 richest people was equivalent to the combined incomes of the 2.3 billion people who were the poorest on earth. Between 1994 and 1998, the 200 richest people in the world doubled their net worth to more than $1 trillion, and the top three billionaires were worth more than the combined GNP of the least developed nations and their 600 million people (Harvey 2005a, 34–35, emphasis added).

7. Kameʻeleihiwa famously noted that beginning in the 1800s economic imperialism "seduced" the Hawaiian elite "into capitalist cycles of never-ending debt" (1992, 170). The neoliberal form of this seduction involves "payday lending," whereby middle-income consumers (Stegman 2007, 173–74) receive small, short-term loans using future wages as collateral. Payday lending is predatory; it is financially detrimental and exploitative of borrowers (2007, 170). Charges associated with payday loans range from $15 to $30 per $100 advanced. Translated into annual percentage rates, payday loans range between 400 and 1000 percent (Snarr 2002). In Hawaiʻi usurious rates of payday lending cost families (not broken down by race/ethnicity) some $3 million annually. Translated into annual percentage rates, this type of lending in Hawaiʻi generated interest rates of 460 percent (King et al. 2006, 10, 17).

8. Beach occupations, a tactic of Hawaiian activists, were particularly threatening to the state because such action had the potential to impact the tourism industry and sully Hawaiʻi's reputation as paradise. The state acted quickly to evict the occupiers, especially on the beaches of the windward side of Oʻahu, described by tour books as the most beautiful of the Islands. In 1994, two sovereignty groups, the Nation of Kū and the ʻOhana Council,

"reclaimed" land at Makapuʻu Beach, on the windward side of the island. Only days after setting up a camp near an ancient heiau on the beach, they were evicted by the state (Magaoay 1994). On the leeward side of Oʻahu, the state did not act as quickly, because tourists rarely ventured beyond Ko Olina, the golf resort that borders Waiʻanae.

9. Although Honolulu *Star-Bulletin* editorial writers tended to support the eviction, other members of the mainstream press were outraged at being barred. One reporter argued that "the governor barred news coverage of the evictions because he didn't want you—the voting public—to see his little army pushing around Hawaiian squatters. . . . [Governor] Cayetano didn't want the squatters demonstrating in front of the cameras and possibly winning public sympathy. He wanted to make sure only his side of the story got out. . . . The governor's troops didn't only keep journalists away from Mākua; they threatened to arrest them. 'This is a government operation,' sniffed state spokesman Gregg Takayama. Wrong, island guys. It's Cuba where they arrest journalists for covering the news. Here, we actually encourage the public and the press to take an interest in government operations" (Shapiro 1996).

10. Sixteen of the protesting beach people were arrested and booked on misdemeanor charges of obstruction of government operations. Many of the families who chose to leave the beach rather than face arrest purchased permits to camp at Keaʻau Beach, a mile down the road. Others were housed in temporary homeless shelters provided by a nonprofit social service agency as the date of the eviction grew near (Kakesako 1996; Omandam 1996; Shapiro 1996).

11. The private market does not even pretend to address the need of affordable housing. Jared Bernstein, a senior economist at the Economic Policy Institute, was interviewed by a reporter for the Pittsburgh Post-Gazette. Bernstein said that the housing boom had passed by many of the working poor. "They've missed a critical opportunity to begin building housing wealth," he said. In this discourse, homelessness is transformed into a "missed opportunity" for "building wealth" (Gerena-Morales 2007).

12. Eduardo Duran and Bonnie Duran (1995, 6) argued that:

> The generation of healing knowledge from the land of the colonist . . . will no longer suffice. Our communities' indigenous forms of knowledge were and continue to be relevant as we face the task of overcoming the colonial mind-set that so many of us have internalized. For this reason . . . we must address the colonial attitude of [the discipline of psychology]. We cannot continue to reward knowledge that reifies the thought of western Europeans above all others.

GLOSSARY

Definitions are cited directly from Mary Kawena Pukui and Samuel Elbert's *Hawaiian Dictionary* (1986), unless otherwise noted.

ahupua'a	land division that extended from the uplands to the ocean, "land division usually extending from the uplands to the sea, so called because the boundary was marked by a heap (ahu) of stones surmounted by an image of a pig (pua'a), or because a pig or other tribute was laid on the altar as tax to the chief. The landlord or owner of an ahupua'a might be a konohiki."
'ai	"food or food plant," "to eat," "to rule, reign"
'aikapu	"to eat under taboo, to observe eating taboos," basis of the social order (Ohnuma 2008, 368); marked distinctions between genders and between those of high and low rank. Women and men did not eat together, and women were forbidden from eating foods ritually offered to the gods.
'āina	land, land and resources
'ainoa	"to eat freely, without observance of taboos"
akua	god, specifically in reference to gods who comprised Hawaiian cosmogony prior to Western contact
ali'i	chiefly class, ruling chief
aloha	love, affection, compassion, kindness, grace, greeting, salutation, regards
aloha 'āina	"love of the land or of one's country . . . aloha 'āina is a very old concept, to judge from the many sayings (perhaps thousands) illustrating deep love of the land," "expresses a duty to care for the earth from which the people originate, to reciprocate its support of the people" (Ohnuma 2008, 379)

191

'anā'anā	"evil sorcery by means of prayer and incantation"
au maka	specialized form of diagnosis practiced by kāhuna; diagnosis based on observation
'aumakua, 'aumākua (pl.)	ancestral guardian spirits, ancestral deity, "a symbiotic relationship existed; mortals did not harm or eat 'aumākua (they fed sharks), and 'aumākua warned and reprimanded mortals in dreams, visions, and calls"
'awa	Piper methysticum, a shrub, the roots of which are prepared to make a mildly narcotic drink that is used ceremonially, medicinally, and socially
hāhā	specialized form of diagnosis practiced by kāhuna, diagnosis by palpitation
haku mele	composers of music
hānai	to feed, to raise, to rear, foster child, adopted child
haole	white person, "formerly, any foreigner"
heiau	temple, pre-Christian place of worship
ho'okamakama	prostitution
ho'omōhala	to cause to blossom, "to open, unfold, spread, recover, develop, evolve"
ho'opākōlea	"to train to grow straight . . . to train to grow in a desired shape, as a plant"
ho'opi'opi'o	a form of imitative magic in which the practitioner, while concentrating, touched a part of his own body, thereby causing injury to his victim's body in the same place, as a chest pain or headache. If the intended victim saw the gestures, he might imitate them and thereby send the black magic back to the original practitioner.
ho'oponopono	family conflict resolution, form of therapy used in cultural-based clinical setting
hula	Hawaiian dance; types include hula kahiko, traditional Hawaiian dance
kahuna, kāhuna (pl.)	ritual experts and practitioners whose training was rigorous and demanded superior intellect; various types of kāhuna were classified as such ex: kahuna lā'au lapa'au—traditional medical practitioner
kalo	taro

kamaʻāina	lit. land child, "native-born, one born in a place, host"
Kanaka Maoli	lit. native person, Hawaiian native, important term after colonization to distinguish between Native Hawaiian and non-Native Hawaiian populations
kaona	"hidden meaning, as in Hawaiian poetry; concealed reference, as to a person, thing, or place; words with double meanings that might bring good or bad fortune"
kapu	taboo, forbidden, prohibited, sacred
kī	ti plant, a native woody plant; the leaves have many uses in Hawaiʻi and are still believed to offer protection from spirits
kīhei	cape, "rectangular tapa garment worn over one shoulder and tied in a knot"
kīpuka	"variation or change of form (puka, hole), as a calm place in a high sea, deep place in a shoal, opening in a forest, openings in cloud formations, and especially a clear place or oasis within a lava bed where there may be vegetation"; metaphorically: to describe those spaces within neocolonial society in which Native Hawaiian culture has survived, and as an analogy for how such traditional culture can be revitalized elsewhere
konohiki	overseer of an ahupuaʻa, an overseer in the service of the aliʻi, or chiefly class
kuehu kapa	"to shake a tapa in a way that seems innocent but that will bring a curse upon the person to whom the motion is directed"
kuʻi a lua	traditional Hawaiian martial arts
kuni	"type of black magic that results in the death of a sorcerer, achieved by burning an object taken from the corpse of the sorcerer's victim; to practice kuni"
kupuna, kūpuna (pl.)	elders, ancestors
lā ʻau	medicine, medical
lā ʻau lapaʻau	medicine, lit. curing medicine
lapaʻau	"medical practice; to treat with medicine, heal, cure; medical, medicinal"
lau hala	Pandanus leaves, used in plaiting

lo'i (kalo)	taro patch, irrigated ponds for growing taro
lōkahi	practice of spiritual, cultural, and natural balance with the elemental forces of nature, "unity, accord, unison"
lomilomi	a type of massage
lua	a Hawaiian martial art using hand-to-hand fighting and focusing on breaking bones
lū'au	young taro tops
māhele	portion, division, section, when capitalized refers to the land division that took place in 1848
ma'i 'ōku'u	variously identified as cholera, the bubonic plague, typhoid fever, bacillary dysentery, or yellow fever in a biomedical lexicon
ma'i Pākē	leprosy, lit. Chinese disease
maka'āinana	"commoner, populace, people in general; citizen, subject"
mālama 'āina	to care for the land, a reciprocal intimate relationship between humans and the land, where humans serve one another and care for the land, a concept that is a critical distinction between the worldview of Hawaiians and those who came to colonize the islands
malo	loincloth
mana	a relationship productive of a healthy society
mele	"song, anthem, or chant of any kind"
mele lāhui	protest song moe to sleep, lie down
moekolohe	adultery
moe 'uhane	dream, to dream, lit. soul sleep
mo'olelo	story, tale
na'au	guts, intestines, also mind, heart, affections
nā mea Hawai'i	Hawaiian culture, language, spirituality, lit. Hawaiian things
'ōlelo Hawai'i	Hawaiian language
oli	chant
'ōpelu	Mackerel scad
'opihi	limpet
pā'ao'ao	"latent childhood disease, with physical weakening; a general term for ailments"

pae ʻāina	the islands of Hawaiʻi, archipelago, group of islands
piha	pure, full
poʻe kahiko	lit. people of old, ancestors of Native Hawaiians, Native Hawaiians who lived before contact with the West
poi	staple food of Hawaii made by cooking the starchy root of the kalo plant and then pounding it into a paste that is kneaded with water to form a pudding-like substance
poʻi ʻuhane	soul catcher, "soul snatching; to snatch or capture the souls of either the dead or of living persons, as by sorcery"
pono	necessity, goodness, morality and perfect order, a central metaphor for ka poʻe kahiko; (social) harmony that derives from the reciprocal relationship between elder siblings and younger siblings to love, protect, and feed (Kameʻeleihiwa 1992, 25)
pule	prayer, to pray, worship, say grace
pule pane	lit. closing prayer
ʻuhane	soul, spirit
wahi kapu	places and spaces of refuge, sanctuary, and healing

References

Abulafia, David. 2008. *The Discovery of Mankind: Atlantic Encounters in the Age of Columbus*. New Haven, CT: Yale University Press.

Adams, Romanzo C. 1925. *The Peoples of Hawai'i: A Statistical Study*. Honolulu: Institute of Pacific Relations.

"A Hawai'i Way of Life: Statistics Show More People Are Holding Multiple Jobs to Make Ends Meet, Spice up Life." 1996. *Honolulu Advertiser*, December 12.

Akina, S.K. Letters. *Honolulu Advertiser*. November 5, 1996. A9.

Alcoholics Anonymous. 2002. *Twelve Steps and Twelve Traditions*. Alcoholics Anonymous World Service.

Allen, Ricky Lee. 2002. "The Globalization of White Supremacy: Toward a Crucial Discourse on the Racialization of the World." *Educational Theory* 51, no. 4: 467–85.

Allende, Isabel. 1986. *The House of the Spirits*. New York: Bantam.

Alu Like. 1979. "A Report on Mental Health and Substance Abuse among the Native Hawaiian Population." Research and Statistics Office, Honolulu, HI.

Andersen, Johannes C. 1995[1928]. *Myths and Legends of the Polynesians*. New York: Dover.

Anderson, Benedict. 1991. *Imagined Communities*. New York: Verso.

Anderson, Ian, Sue Crangle, Martina Leialoha Kamaka, Tai-Ho Chen, Neal Palafox, and Lisa Jackson-Pilver. 2006. "Indigenous Health in Australia, New Zealand, and the Pacific." *The Lancet* 367 (May 27): 1775–85.

Anderson, Rufus D. D. 1865. *Hawaiian Islands: Their Progress and Condition*. Boston, MA: Gould and Lincoln.

Andrade, Jr., Ernest. 1996. *Unconquerable Rebel: Robert W. Wilcox and Hawaiian Politics, 1880–1903*. Niwot: University of Colorado Press.

"An Interview with Katherine Mauanakea." 1993. In *He Alo ā He Alo: Hawaiian Voices on Sovereignty*, ed. Roger MacPherson Furrer. Honolulu: American Friends Service Committee, 25–32.

Appel, L. J., T. J. Moore, E. Obarzanek, W. M. Vollmer, L. P. Svetkey, F. M. Sacks, G. A. Bray, T. M. Vogt, J. A. Cutler, M. M. Windhauser, P. H. Lin, and N. Karanja. 1997. "A Clinical Trial of the Effects of Dietary Patterns on Blood Pressure. DASH Collaborative Research Group." *The New England Journal of Medicine* 337, no. 9: 637–38.

Arakawa, Lynda. 2004. "Dollar's Slide May Boost Hawai'i's Tourist Economy." *Honolulu Advertiser*, December 6.

Ascherio, Alberto, Charles Hennekens, Walter C. Willett, Frank Sacks, Bernard Rosner, JoAnn Manson, Jacqueline Witteman, and Meir J. Stampfer. 1996. "Prospective Study of Nutritional Factors, Blood Pressure, and Hypertension among US Women." *Hypertension* 27: 1065–72.

Banner, Stuart. 2005. "Preparing To Be Colonized: Land Tenure and Legal Strategy in Nineteenth-Century Hawai'i." *Law and Society Review* 39, no. 2: 274–314.

Barrére, Dorothy B. 1975. *Kamehameha in Kona: Two Documentary Studies.* Pacific Anthropological Records No. 23. Honolulu: Bishop Museum Press.

Barthes, Roland. 1972. *Mythologies.* New York: The Noonday Press.

"Beachfront Tent Cities a Shameful Catalyst." 2006. *Honolulu Advertiser*, June 15. Accessed online at the.honoluluadvertiser.com on March 13, 2008.

Beaglehole, J. C. 1966. *The Exploration of the Pacific.* Palo Alto, CA: Stanford University Press.

Beckwith, Martha Warren. 1942. "A Reply to the Review of Hawaiian Mythology." *The Journal of American Folklore* 55, no. 218: 254–56.

———. 1951. *The Kumulipo: A Hawaiian Creation Chant.* Chicago, IL: The University of Chicago Press.

Benesch, Sarah. 2001. *Critical English for Academic Purposes: Theory, Politics and Practice.* New York: Routledge.

Benham, Maenette Kape'ahiokalani Padeken Ah Nee, and Ronald H. Heck. 1998. *Culture and Educational Policy in Hawai'i: The Silencing of Native Voices.* Mahwah, NJ: Lawrence, Erlbaum Associates, Publishers.

Benjamin, Walter. 1968. *Illuminations: Essays and Reflections.* New York: Schocken Books.

Bingham, Hiram. 1855. *A Residence of Twenty-one Years in the Sandwich Islands.* Rutland, VT: Charles E. Tuttle.

Bird, Isabella L. 1906. *The Hawaiian Archipelago: Six Months amongst the Palm Groves, Coral Reefs, and Volcanoes of the Sandwich Islands.* London: John Murray, Albemarle Street.

Black, John. 2006. "The Dominion of Man." In *Environmental Stewardship: Critical Perspectives—Past and Present*, ed. R. J. Berry, 92–96. New York: T. and T. Clark Publishers.

Blackburn, James. 2000. "Understanding Paulo Freire: Reflections on the Origins, Concepts, and Possible Pitfalls of His Educational Approach." *Community Development Journal* 35, no. 1: 3–15.

Blackford, Mansel G. 2004. "Environmental Justice, Native Rights, Tourism, and Opposition to Military Control: The Case of Kahoʻolawe." *The Journal of American History* 91, no. 2. http:// www.historycooperative.org/ journals /jah/91.2/blackford.html (accessed April 9, 2009).

Blaisdell, Richard Kekuni. 1992. "Afterword." In *To Steal a Kingdom: Probing Hawaiian History*, ed. Michael Dougherty, 182–84. Waimanalo, HI: Island Press.

———. 1993. "The Health Status of Kanaka Maoli (Indigenous Hawaiians)." *Asian American and Pacific Islander Journal of Health* 1, no. 2: 117–60.

———. 1995. "1995 Update on Kanaka Maoli (Indigenous Hawaiian) Health." Revised Abstract of Paper presented at Asian American and Pacific Islander Health Summit. San Francisco, CA, June 21–24.

———. 1996. "Kekuni Blaisdell." In *Autobiography of Protest in Hawaiʻi*, ed. Robert H. Mast and Anne B. Mast, 363–73. Honolulu: University of Hawaiʻi Press.

Boggs, Stephen T., and Malcolm Nāea Chun. 1990. "Hoʻoponopono: A Hawaiian Method of Solving Interpersonal Problems." In *Disentangling: Conflict Discourses in Pacific Societies*, ed. Karen Ann Watson-Gegeo and Geoffrey M. White, 122–60. Stanford, CA: Stanford University Press.

Boswell, Terry. 1989. "Colonial Empires and the Capitalist World-Economy: A Time Series Analysis of Colonization, 1640–1960." *American Sociological Review* 54, no. 2: 180–96.

Bourdieu, Pierre. 1977. *Outline of a Theory of Practice.* New York: Cambridge University Press.

Bourgois, Philippe. 1995. *In Search of Respect: Selling Crack in El Barrio.* New York: Cambridge University Press.

Bowen, John. 1998. *Religions in Practice: An Approach to the Anthropology of Religion.* Boston, MA: Allyn and Bacon.

Brantlinger, Patrick. 2003. *Dark Vanishings: Discourse on the Extinction of Primitive Races.* Ithaca, NY: Cornell University Press.

Braun, Kathryn L., Noreen Mokuau, G. Haunani Hunt, Momi Kaanoi, and Carolyn Gotay. 2002. "Supports and Obstacles to Cancer Survival for Native Hawaiian People." *Cancer Practice* 10:1:4: 192–200.

Briggs, Charles L. 1996. "The Politics of Discursive Authority in Research on the 'Invention on Tradition.'" *Cultural Anthropology* 11, no. 4: 435–69.

Brown, Wendy. 2006. "American Nightmare: Neoliberalism, Neoconservatism, and De-Democratization." *Political Theory* 34, no. 6: 690–714.

Burgess, Puanani. 1993. "He Alo ā He Alo (Face to Face)." In *He Alo ā He Alo: Hawaiian Voices on Sovereignty*, ed. Roger MacPherson Furrer. Honolulu: American Friends Service Committee.

———. 1998. "Choosing My Name." In *Bamboo Ridge: Growing Up Local: An Anthology of Poetry and Prose from Hawaiʻi*, ed. Eric Chock, James Harstad, Darrel H. Y. Lum, and Bill Teeter. Honolulu: University of Hawaiʻi Press.

Burrows, Edwin G. 1970[1947]. *Hawaiian Americans: An Account of the Mingling of Japanese, Chinese, Polynesian, and American Cultures*. Hamden, CT: Archon Books.

Bushnell, O. A. 1993. *The Gifts of Civilization: Germs and Genocide in Hawaiʻi*. Honolulu: University of Hawaiʻi Press.

Campos, Mailelani. 1997. Interview by author, Waiʻanae, Hawaiʻi.

Caraway, Nancy. 1996. "Pulp Fiction: Local Exiles and the Politics of Fiction." *Honolulu Weekly*, November 20–26.

Carr, Harry. 1932. "Blow Dealt to Hawaiʻi: Baseless Yarns Ruin Business." *Los Angeles Times* (1886–current file). February 28. http://www.proquest.com (accessed March 19, 2009).

Casken, John. 1996. Testimony before the Unrepresented Nations and People's Organization Hearings, July 3.

———. 2001. "Improved Health Status of Native Hawaiians: Not Just What the Doctor Ordered." *Wicazo Sa Review* (Spring): 75–89.

Celis, William III. 1994. "In School, a Language May Yet Live on As Long As Children Can Cay 'E ʻōlelo Hawaiʻi wale no ma ʻaneʻi.'" *New York Times*, August 17. Accessed at http://www.select.nytimes.com on July 23, 2006.

Center on the Family. 2007. University of Hawaiʻi. "Homeless Service Utilization 2006." Honolulu, Hawaiʻi. http://www.uhfamily.hawaii.edu/publications/brochures/HomelessServiceUtilization2006.pdf (accessed April 3, 2010).

Certeau, Michel de. 1988[1984]. *The Practice of Everyday Life*. Berkeley: University of California Press.

———. 1997. *Culture in the Plural*. Translated by Tom Conley. Minneapolis: University of Minnesota Press.

Cesairé, Aimé. 1990. "Poetry and Knowledge." In *Lyric and Dramatic Poetry, 1946–1982*, ed. James Arnold, trans. Clayton Eschleman and Annette Smith, xliii–lvi. Charlottesville: University of Virginia Press.

Chapin, Helen Geracimos. 1996. *Shaping Hawaiian History: The Role of Newspapers in Hawaiʻi*. Honolulu: University of Hawaiʻi Press.

Chatterjee, Partha. 1986. *Nationalist Thought in the Colonial World: A Derivative Discourse*. Minneapolis: University of Minnesota Press.

———. 1993. *The Nation and Its Fragments: Colonial and Postcolonial Histories*. Princeton, NJ: Princeton University Press.

Christensen, Jean. 1996. "Union Asks Hawaiian Rites at H3." *Star Bulletin*. July 31: A5.

————. 1997. "Drug Use Up among Isle Children." *Honolulu Advertiser*, April 9.

Chun, Malcolm Nāea. 1986. *Hawaiian Medicine Book*. Honolulu: Bess Press.

Chun, Malcolm Nāea, ed. and trans. 1994. *Must We Wait in Despair: The 1867 Report of the ʻAhahui Lāʻau Lapaʻau of Wailuku, Maui on Native Hawaiian Health*. Honolulu: First Peopleʻs Productions.

Chung, Lokomaikaʻi. 1996. Interview by author, Waiʻanae, Hawaiʻi.

Cohen, Mark Nathan. 1989. *Health and the Rise of Civilization*. New Haven, CT: Yale University Press.

Comaroff, Jean. 1993. "The Diseased Heart of Africa: Medicine, Colonialism, and the Black Body." In *Knowledge, Power & Practice: The Anthropology of Medicine and Everyday Life*, ed. Shirley Lindenbaum and Margaret Lock, 305–29. Berkeley: University of California Press.

"Compendium of Cultural Competence Initiatives in Health Care." 2003. Menlo Park, CA: Henry J. Kaiser Family Foundation.

Conklin, Beth A. 1997. "Body Paint, Feathers, and VCRs: Aesthetics and Authenticity in Amazonian Activism." *American Ethnologist* 24, no. 4: 711–37.

Cook, Bud Pōmaikaʻi, Kelley Withy, and Lucia Tarallo-Jensen. 2003. "Cultural Trauma, Hawaiian Spirituality and Contemporary Health Status." *California Journal of Health Promotion* 1 (Special Issue): 10–24.

Crabbe, Kamanaʻopono M. 2002. "Initial Psychometric Validation of He ʻAna Manaʻo O Nā Moʻomeheu Hawaiʻi: A Hawaiian Ethnocultural Inventory (HEI) of Cultural Practices." PhD dissertation, University of Hawaiʻi.

Cruz, Lynette. 1996. "Lynette Cruz." In *Autobiography of Protest in Hawaiʻi*, ed. Robert H. Mast and Anne B. Mast, 374–88. Honolulu: University of Hawaiʻi Press.

Davenport, Kiana. 1994. *Shark Dialogues*. New York: Penguin Books.

Davenport, William. 1969. "'The Hawaiian Cultural Revolution': Some Political and Economic Considerations." *American Anthropologist* 71, no. 1: 1–20.

Daws, Gavan. 1968. *Shoal of Time: A History of the Hawaiian Islands*. Honolulu: University of Hawaiʻi Press.

Day, A. Grove. 1960. *Hawaiʻi: Fiftieth Star*. New York: Dell, Sloane and Pearce.

DeCambra, Hoʻoipo. 1995. "Activism Is Empowerment." In *Hawaiʻi Journeys in Nonviolence: Autobiographical Reflections*, ed. G. D. Paige, L. A. Guanson, and G. Simson, 254–62. Honolulu: University of Hawaiʻi Press.

DeCambra, Hoʻoipo, Rachelle Enos, Doris Segal Matsunaga, and Ormond Hammond. 1992. "Community Involvement in Minority Health Research: Participatory Research in a Native Hawaiian Community." Cancer Control Research Reports for Public Health (October).

DeCambra, Hoʻoipo, Wende Elizabeth Marshall, and Mari Ono. 1999. Hoʻo Mau Ke Ola: "To Perpetuate Life As It Was Meant To Be." In Responding to Pacific Islanders: Culturally Competent Perspectives for Alcohol and Other Drug Abuse Prevention, ed. Noreen Mokuau, 73–96. Volume 6, CSAP Cultural Competence Series. Center for Substance Abuse Prevention/Substance Abuse and Mental Health Services Administration.

Deleuze, Giles. 1992. *The Fold: Leibniz and the Baroque.* Minneapolis: University of Minnesota Press.

———. 2006. *The Fold.* New York: Continuum.

Dening, Greg. 1980. *Islands and Beaches: Discourse on a Silent Land: Marquesas 1774–1880.* Chicago, IL: The Dorsey Press.

———. 1995. *Mr. Bligh's Bad Language: Passion, Power, and Theatre on the Bounty.* New York: Cambridge University Press.

———. 1996. "The History in Things and Places." In *Prehistory to Politics: John Mulvaney, The Humanities, and the Public Intellectual,* ed. T. Bonyhady and T. Griffiths, 85–97. Melbourne: Melbourne University Press.

Department of Business, Economic Development and Tourism (DBEDT). 1995. *State of Hawaiʻi Data Book.* Honolulu, Hawaiʻi.

Department of Institutions. 1943. Territory of Hawaiʻi. *Department of Institutions Report.* Territory of Hawaiʻi.

Dimakopoulou, Stamatina. 2006. "Remapping the Affinities between the Baroque and the Postmodern: The Folds of Melancholy and the Melancholy of the Fold." *Revue électronique d'études sur le monde anglophone* 4, no. 1: 75–82. http://www.e-rea.org.

Dixon, Roland B. 1932. "The Problem of the Sweet Potato in Polynesia." *American Anthropologist* 34, no.1: 40–66.

Doll, R., and R. Peto. 1981. "The Causes of Cancer: Quantitative Estimates of Avoidable Risks of Cancer in the United States Today." *Journal of the National Cancer Institute* 66: 1192–1308.

Donnelly, Christine. 1997. "Hawaiʻi Second-Worst in Funding Public Education." *Honolulu Star Bulletin,* January16.

Dougherty, Michael. 1992. *To Steal a Kingdom: Probing Hawaiian History.* Waimānalo, HI: Island Style Press.

DuBois, W. E. B. 1999. *The Souls of Black Folk.* Edited by Henry Louis Gates and Terri Hume Oliver. New York: W. W. Norton & Company.

Duran, Eduardo, and Bonnie Duran. 1995. *Native American Postcolonial Psychology.* SUNY series in Transpersonal and Humanistic Psychology. Albany: State University of New York Press.

Durkheim, Emile. 1965[1915]. *The Elementary Forms of Religious Life.* New York: The Free Press.

Ebron, Paulla. 1998. "Enchanted Memories of Regional Difference in African

American Culture." *American Anthropologist* 100, no. 1 (new series): 94–105.

Elbert, Samuel H. 1957. "The Chief in Hawaiian Mythology." *The Journal of American Folklore* 70, no. 278: 306–22.

Ellis, William. 1979[1825]. *Journal of William Ellis*. Rutland, VT: Charles E. Tuttle Company.

Emerson, Eva. 1996. "The End of the Road." *Honolulu Weekly*, November 6.

Errington, Joseph. 2001. "Colonial Linguistics." *Annual Review of Anthropology* 30: 19–39.

Faber, Alyda. 2004. "Eros and Violence." *Feminist Theology* 12: 319–42.

Family Health Services Division. 2005. "State of Hawaiʻi Primary Care Needs Assessment Data Book." Hawaiʻi Department of Health, Honolulu, Hawaiʻi.

Fanon, Frantz. 1963. *The Wretched of the Earth*. New York: Grove Press.

———. 1967. *Black Skins, White Masks*. New York: Grove Press.

———. 1969. *A Dying Colonialism*. New York: Grove Press.

Farrington, Wallace B. 1932. "Farrington Denies Hawaiʻi is Race Mad." *New York Times*, January 15, p. 4.

Finney, Ben. 1991. "Myth, Experiment, and the Reinvention of Polynesian Voyaging." *American Anthropologist* 93, no. 2: 383–404.

Firth, Raymond. 1940. "An Analysis of Mana: An Empirical Approach." *Journal of the Polynesian Society* 49, no. 196: 482–510.

———. 2004[1936]. We, the Tikopia. New York: Routledge.

Flint, John. 1983. "Planned Decolonization and Its Failure in British Africa." *African Affairs* 82: 390.

Foreman, Gabrielle P. 1992. "Past-on Stories: History and the Magically Real, Morrison and Allende on Call." *Feminist Studies* 18, no. 2: 369–88.

Fox, Richard G., ed. 1990. *Nationalist Ideologies and the Production of National Cultures*. American Ethnological Society Monograph Series, No. 2. Washington, DC: American Anthropological Association.

Franz, Marion J., John P. Bantile, Christine A. Beebe, John D. Brunzell, Jean-Louis Chaisson, Abhimanyu Garg, Lea Ann Holzmeister, Byron Hoogwerf, Elizabeth Mayer-Davis, Arshag D. Mooradian, Jonathan Q. Purnell, and Madelyn Wheeler. 2002. "Evidence-Based Nutrition Principles and Recommendations for the Treatment and Prevention of Diabetes and Related Complications." *Diabetes Care* 25, no. 1: 148–98.

Freidel, Frank. 1943. "A Whaler in Pacific Ports, 1841–42." *The Pacific Historical Review* 12, no. 4: 380–90.

Freire, Paulo. 1989. *Pedagogy of the Oppressed*. Translated by Myra Bergman Ramos. New York: Continuum.

Fuchs, Lawrence. 1961. *Hawaiʻi Pono: An Ethnic and Political History*. Honolulu: Bess Press.

Fullilove, Mindy. 2005. *Rootshock: How Tearing Up City Neighborhoods Hurts America, and What We Can Do About It.* New York: One World/Ballantine.

Galton, Francis. 1892. *Hereditary Genius: An Inquiry into Its Laws and Consequences.* New York: MacMillan and Company.

———. 1909. "Eugenics: Its Definition, Scope and Aim." In *Essays in Eugenics.* London: The Eugenics Education Society, 32–43.

Gaventa, John. 1980. *Power and Powerlessness: Quiescence and Rebellion in an Appalachian Valley.* Chicago: University of Illinois Press.

Geertz, Clifford. 1983. *Local Knowledge: Further Essays in Interpretive Anthropology.* New York: Basic Books.

Gerena-Morales, Rafael. 2007. "Hawai'i's Housing Boom Takes Toll on the Homeless." *The Pittsburgh Post-Gazette,* January 11. Accessed online at http://www.post-gazette.com on March 13, 2008.

Gilman, Sander L. 1992. *Jewish Self-Hatred: Anti-Semitism and the Hidden Language of the Jews.* Baltimore, MD: Johns Hopkins University Press.

Gilmore, Ruth Wilson. 1998–1999. "Globalization and US Prison Growth: From Military Keynesianism to Post-Keynesian Militarism." *Race & Class* 40, no. 2–3: 171–88.

———. 2007. *Golden Gulag: Prison, Surplus, Crisis, and Opposition in Globalizing California.* Berkeley: University of California Press.

Giroux, Henry A. 2005. "The Terror of Neoliberalism: Rethinking the Significance of Cultural Politics." *College Literature* 32, no. 1: 1–19.

Gittlesohn, Joel, Thomas A. S. Wolever, Stewart B. Harris, Robert Harris-Giraldo, Anthony J. G. Hanley, and Bernard Zinman. 1996. "Specific Patterns of Food Consumption and Preparation Are Associated with Diabetes and Obesity in a Native Canadian Community." *The Journal of Nutrition* 128, no. 3: 541–47.

Glanz, Karen, Robert T. Croyle, Veronica Y. Cholette, and Vivian Pinn. 2003. "Cancer-Related Health Disparities in Women." *American Journal of Public Health* 93, no. 2: 292–98.

Glassman, Jim. 2006. "Primitive Accumulation, Accumulation by Dispossession, Accumulation by 'Extra-Economic' Means." *Progress in Human Geography* 30, no. 5: 608–25.

Goffman, Erving. 1973. "The Medical Model and Mental Hospitalization: Some Notes on the Vicissitudes of the Tinkering Trade." In *Asylums: Essays on the Social Situation of Mental Patients and Other Inmates,* 301–62. Chicago, IL: Aldine.

Goodyear-Ka'ōpua, Jennifer Noelani. 2005. "Kū i ka Mana: Building Community and Nation through Contemporary Hawaiian Schooling." PhD dissertation, University of California, Santa Cruz.

Gordon, Mike. 1996. "H3 Dynamite Sends Workers to Hospitals." *Honolulu Star Bulletin.* August 4: A19.

Gotay, Carolyn Cook. 2000. "Impact of Culturally Appropriate Intervention on Breast and Cervical Screening among Native Hawaiian Women." *Preventive Medicine* 31: 529–37.

Gotay, C. C., R. O. Banner, D. S. Matsunaga, N. Hedlund, R. Enos, B. F. Issell, and H. DeCambra. 2000. "Impact of a Culturally Appropriate Intervention on Breast and Cervical Screening among Native Hawaiian Women." *Preventive Medicine* 31, no. 5: 529–37.

Governor's Advisory Committee on Industrial Schools. 1935. "Report on Waialee Training School for Boys." Territory of Hawai'i.

Greene, Shane. 1998. "The Shaman's Needle: Development, Shamanic Agency and Intermedicality in Aguaruna Lands, Peru." *American Ethnologist* 25, no. 4: 634–58.

Grimshaw, Patricia. 1983. "'Christian Woman, Pious Wife, Faithful Mother, Devoted Missionary': Conflicts in Roles of American Missionary Women in Nineteenth-Century Hawai'i." *Feminist Studies* 9, no. 3: 489–521.

Haas, Michael. 1981. "Institutional Racism in Mental Health Care in Hawai'i." Second International Philippine Studies Conference, Honolulu, HI, June.

Hale Ola Ho'opākōlea, Inc. Internal Evaluation Team. 1989. "Ke Kino, Ka Mana'o, a me Ka 'Uhane/In Mind, Body and Spirit: An Internal Evaluation of Hale Ola Ho'opākōlea, Inc." Wai'anae, HI.

Handler, Richard, and Jocelyn Linnekin. 1984. "Tradition, Genuine or Spurious." *Journal of American Folklore* 97, no. 385: 273–90.

Handy, E. S. Craighill, Elizabeth Green Handy, and Mary Kawena Pukui. 1991. *Native Planters in Old Hawai'i: Their Life, Lore and Environment.* Honolulu: Bishop Museum Press.

Handy, E. S. Craighill, and Mary Kawena Pukui. 1972[1958]. *The Polynesian Family System in Ka'ū, Hawai'i.* Tokyo: Charles E. Tuttle Company.

Hartney, Christopher. 2006. "Fact Sheet: U.S. Rates of Incarceration: A Global Perspective." National Council on Crime and Delinquency. November. http://www.   nccdcrc.org /nccd/pubs/2006nov_factsheet_incarceration.pdf (accessed April 9, 2009).

Hartwell, Jay. 1996. *Hawaiian People Today.* Honolulu: 'Ai Pōhaku Press.

Harvey, David. 2005a. *A Brief History of Neoliberalism.* New York: Oxford University Press.

———. 2005b. *The New Imperialism.* New York: Oxford University Press.

———. 2007. "Neoliberalism as Creative Destruction." *Annals of the Academy of Political and Social Sciences* 610, no. 1: 22–44.

Hereniko, Vilsoni. 2001. "David and Goliath: A Response to the 'Oceanic Imaginary.'" *The Contemporary Pacific* (Spring): 163–68.

Hereniko, Vilsoni, and Rob Wilson, eds. 1999. *Inside Out: Literature, Cultural Politics, and Identity in the New Pacific*. New York: Roman & Littlefield.

Herman, RDK. 1999. "The Aloha State: Place Names and the Anti-Conquest of Hawai'i." *Annals of the Association of American Geographers* 89, no. 1: 76–102.

Holt, John Dominis. 1971. "Monarchy in Hawai'i." In *Aspects of Hawaiian Life and Environment: Commentaries on Significant Hawaiian Topics by Fifteen Recognized Authorities*. Honolulu: The Kamehameha Schools Press.

———. 1974. *On Being Hawaiian*. Honolulu: Topgallant.

Honolulu Chamber of Commerce. 1941. Mental Hygiene Committee. Survey of the Feebleminded in the Territory of Hawai'i.

Ho'omanawanui, Ku'ualoha. 2004. "Hā, Mana, Leo (Breath, Spirit, Voice): Kanaka Maoli Empowerment through Literature." *American Indian Quarterly* 28, no. 1–2: 86–91.

Howard, Alan. 1974. *Ain't No Big Thing: Coping Strategies in a Hawaiian-American Community*. Honolulu: University of Hawai'i Press.

Hu, Frank B., Eric B. Rimm, Meir J. Stampfer, Alberto Ascherio, Donna Spiegelman, and Walter C. Willett. 2000. "Prospective Study of Major Dietary Patterns and Risk of Coronary Heart Disease in Men." *The American Journal of Clinical Nutrition* 72: 912–21.

Hughes, Claire Ku'ulelani, Jo Ann Umilani Tsark, and Noreen Kehulani Mokuau. 1996. "Diet-Related Cancer in Native Hawaiians." *Cancer* 78, no. 7: 1558–63.

Hyams, B. K. 1985. "School Teachers as Agents of Cultural Imperialism in Territorial Hawai'i." *Journal of Pacific History* 20, no. 3–4: 202–19.

Igler, David. 1994. "Review Forum by Greg Denning, Lilikalā Kame'eleihiwa, and Atholl Anderson of Anahulu: The Anthropology of History in the Kingdom of Hawai'i." *The Contemporary Pacific* 6, no. 1: 212–20.

———. 2004. "Diseased Goods: Global Exchanges in the Eastern Pacific Basin, 1770–1850." *The American Historical Review* 109, no. 3: par. 45. http://www.historycooperative.org/journals/ahr/109.3/igler.html (accessed April 3, 2010).

'I'i, John Papa. 1993[1959]. *Fragments of Hawaiian History*. Translated by Mary Kawena Pukui. Honolulu: The Bishop Museum Press.

Inglis, Kerri A. 2005. "A Land Set Apart": Disease, Displacement, & Death at Makanalua, Moloka'i. PhD dissertation, University of Hawai'i.

Ito, Karen. 1999. *Lady Friends: Hawaiian Ways and the Ties That Define*. Ithaca, NY: Cornell University Press.

Jackson, Fatimah C. 2000. "Anthropological Measurement: The Mismeasure of African Americans." *The Annals of the American Academy* 568: 154–71.

Jackson, Fatimah L. C. 2004. "Human Genetic Variation and Health: New Assessment Approaches Based on Ethnogenetic Layering." *British Medical Bulletin* 69: 215–35.

Jackson, John L. 2001. *Harlem World: Doing Race and Class in Contemporary Black America*. Chicago, IL: University of Chicago Press.

Johnson, Greg. 2003. "Ancestors before Us: Manifestations of Tradition in a Hawaiian Dispute." *Journal of the American Academy of Religion* 71, no. 2: 327–46.

Johnson, Rubellite Kawena. 1981. *Kumulipo: Hawaiian Hymn of Creation*. Volume 1. Honolulu: Topgallant.

Jolly, Margaret. 2007. "Oceanic Hauntings?: Race-Culture-Place between Vanuatu and Hawai'i." *Journal of Intercultural Studies* 28, no. 1: 99–112.

Jones, Jacqueline. 1992. *The Dispossessed: America's Underclass from the Civil War to the Present*. New York: Basic Books.

Kakesako, Gregg K. 1996. "Bulldozers Raze Mākua Campsites." *Honolulu Star-Bulletin*. June 18. Internet archives.

Kamakau, Samuel Mānaiakalani. 1991. *Ka Po'e Kahiko: The People of Old*. Honolulu: Bishop Museum Press.

———. 1992 (rev. ed., 1961]. *Ruling Chiefs of Hawai'i*. Honolulu: The Kamehameha Schools Press.

Kamakawiwo'ole, Israel. 1998. "Hawai'i `78." Iz in Concert. BigBoy Records.

Kame'eleihiwa, Lilikalā. 1992. *Native Land and Foreign Desires: Ko Hawai'i 'Āina a me Nā Koi Pu'umake a ka Po'e Haole: A History of Land Tenure Change in Hawai'i from Traditional Times until the 1848 Māhele, including an Analysis of Hawaiian Ali'i Nui and American Calvinists*. Honolulu: Bishop Museum Press.

———. 1994. "Review Forum by Greg Denning, Lilikalā Kame'eleihiwa, and Atholl Anderson of Anahulu: The Anthropology of History in the Kingdom of Hawai'i." *The Contemporary Pacific* 6, no. 1.

"Kame'eleihiwa Transcript." 1996a. Kame'eleihiwa 1996 girder.

1996b. "H-3 Story: 'A Great Injustice.'" *Honolulu Advertiser*, November 8.

Kanahele, George Hu'eu Sanford. 1986. *Kū Kanaka/Stand Tall: A Search for Hawaiian Values. A Kolowalu Book*. Honolulu: University of Hawai'i Press.

Kana'iaupuni, Shawn Malia, Nolan J. Malone, and Koren Ishibashi. 2005. "Income and Poverty among Native Hawaiians: Summary of the Ka Huaka'i Findings." Honolulu: Kamehameha Schools-Policy Analysis & System Evaluation.

Kaomea, Julie. 2006. "Nā Wāhine Mana: Postcolonial Reading of Classroom Discourse on the Imperial Rescue of Oppressed Hawaiian Women." *Pedagogy, Culture & Society* 14, no. 3: 329–48.

Kardiner, Lionel, and Abraham Ovesey. 1972. *The Mark of Oppression: Explorations in the Personality of the American Negro.* New York: W.W. Norton and Company.

Karger, Howard. 2005. *Short Changed: Life and Debt in the Fringe Economy.* San Francisco, CA: Berrett-Koehler.

Kaser, Tom. 1997. "Hawai'i's Salary Skid." *Honolulu Advertiser,* January 19.

Kashay, Jennifer Fish. 2008. "Competing Imperialisms and Hawaiian Authority: The Cannonading of Lāhainā in 1827." *Pacific Historical Review* 77, no. 3: 369–90.

Kauanui, J. Kēhaulani. 1999. "'For Get' Hawaiian Entitlement: Configurations of Land, 'Blood', and Americanization in the Hawaiian Homes Commission Act of 1921." *Social Text* 59:17, no. 2: 123–44.

———. 2002. "The Politics of Blood and Sovereignty in Rice v. Cayetano." *PoLAR: Political and Legal Anthropology Review* 25, no. 1: 110–28.

Kay, Jeanne. 1989. "Human Dominion over Nature in the Hebrew Bible." *Annals of the Association of American Geographers* 79, no. 2: 214–32.

Keesing, Roger M. 1984. "Rethinking 'Mana'." *Journal of Anthropological Research* 40, no. 1: 137–56.

———. 1985. "Conventional Metaphors and Anthropological Metaphysics: The Problematic If Cultural Translation." *Journal of Anthropological Research* 42, no. 2: 201–17.

———. 1989. "Creating the Past: Custom and Identity in the Contemporary Pacific." *The Contemporary Pacific* 1, no. 1–2.

———. 1991. "Reply to Trask." *The Contemporary Pacific* 3, no. 2.

Kelly, Anne Keala. 2003. "A Kingdom Inside: The Future of Hawaiian Political Identity." *Futures* 35: 999–1099.

———. 2007. "On Being Homeless and Hawaiian." Free Press Radio, December 31.

Kent, George. 2003. "Hunger in Hawai'i." Accessed online at http://www2:Hawaii.edu/~KENT/HUNGER%20IN%20Hawaii%202.doc on January 27, 2008.

Kent, Noel J. 1993[1983]. *Hawai'i: Islands under the Influence.* Honolulu: University of Hawai'i Press.

Kimmich, Robert A. 1956. "100 Years of Hawaiian Psychiatry." *Hawai'i Medical Journal* 15, no. 4: 345–47.

King, Uriah, Leslie Parish, and Ozlem Tanik. 2006. "Financial Quicksand: Payday Lending Sinks Borrowers in Debt with $4.2 billion in Predatory Fees Every Year." Center for Responsible Lending, March 22. http://www.responsiblelending.org/news _headlines/032205release.cfm (accessed April 9, 2009).

Kirch, Patrick Vinton, and Marshall Sahlins. 1994. *Anahulu: The Anthropology of History in the Kingdom of Hawai'i. Volume 2: The Archeology of History.* Chicago, IL: University of Chicago Press.

Kolb, Michael J., and Boyd Dixon. 2002. "Landscapes of War: Rules and Conventions of Conflict in Ancient Hawai'i (and Elsewhere)." *American Antiquity* 67, no. 3: 514–34.

Kroeber, A. L. 1921. "Observations on the Anthropology of Hawai'i." *American Anthropologist* 23, no. 2 (new series): 129–37.

———. 1948. *Anthropology: Race, Language, Culture, Psychology, Pre-History.* New York: Harcourt Brace.

Kromhout, D., E. B. Bosschieter, C. de Lezenne. 1985. "The Inverse Relation between Fish Consumption and 20-Year Mortality from Coronary Heart Disease." *New England Journal of Medicine* 312, no. 19: 1205–1209.

Kuykendall, Ralph S. 1965[1938]. *The Hawaiian Kingdom: Volume I, 1778–1854: Foundation and Transformation.* Honolulu: University of Hawai'i Press.

———. 1967. *The Hawaiian Kingdom, Volume III, 1874–1893: The Kalākaua Dynasty.* Honolulu: University of Hawai'i Press.

———. 1982[1953]. *The Hawaiian Kingdom: Volume II: Twenty Critical Years.* Honolulu: University of Hawai`i Press.

Labrador, Roderick. 2009. "'We Can Laugh at Ourselves': Hawaiian Ethnic Humor, Local Identity, and the Myth of Multiculturalism." In *Beyond Yellow English: Toward a Linguistic Anthropology of Asian Pacific America,* ed. Angela Reyes and Adrienne Lo, 288–308. New York: Oxford University Press.

Ladefoged, Thegn N. 1993. "Hawaiian Dryland Agricultural Intensification and the Pacific Economy." *Pacific Studies* 16, no. 2: 119–31.

Laenui, Pōkā. 1983. "Mākua Rally Talk." Unpublished manuscript from the private papers of Pōkā Laenui (Hayden Burgess).

———. 1993a. "Colonization and Decolonization: A Few Thoughts." Wai'anae: Institute for the Advancement of Hawaiian Affairs.

———. 1993b. "Imagine a New Day in Wai'anae." Wai'anae: Institute for the Advancement of Hawaiian Affairs.

Lal, Brij V. 1994. "The Passage Out." In *The Tides of History: The Pacific Islands in the Twentieth Century,* ed. K. R. Howe, Robert C. Kiste, and Brij V. Lal, 435–61. Honolulu: University of Hawai'i Press.

Lee, Kēhaulani. 1997. Interview, Wai'anae, Hawai'i.

Lee, Lloyd L. 1948. "A Brief Analysis of the Role and Status of the Negro in the Hawaiian Community." *American Sociological Review* 13, no. 4: 419–37.

Lee, William. 1847. Letter to J. S. Emerson. 23 December. Supreme Court Letter Book of Chief Justice William Little Lee, 1847–54. Series 240. Box 1. Hawai'i State Archives.

Leonardo, Zeus. 2002. "The Souls of White Folk: Critical Pedagogy, Whiteness Studies, and Globalization Discourse." *Race, Ethnicity and Education* 5, no. 1: 29–50.

210 REFERENCES

Leong, Elizabeth Yuentsin. 1933. "A Study of the Public Social Services in the Hawaiian Islands." MA thesis, University of Chicago.

Levy, Neil M. 1975. "Native Hawaiian Land Rights." *California Law Review* 63, no. 4: 848–85.

Lew, Rod, and Sora Park Tanjasiri. 2003. "Slowing the Epidemic of Tobacco Use among Asian Americans and Pacific Islanders." *American Journal of Public Health* 93, no. 5: 764–68.

Lewis, George H. 1984. "Da Kine Sounds: The Function of Music as Social Protest in the New Hawaiian Renaissance." *American Music* 2, no. 2: 38–52.

———. 1985a. "Beyond the Reef: Role Conflict and the Professional Musician in Hawai'i." *Popular Music* 5: 189–98.

———. 1985b. "The Role of Music in Popular Social Movements: A Theory and Case Study of the Island State of Hawai'i, USA." *International Review of the Aesthetics and Sociology of Music* 16, no. 2: 153–62.

———. 1991. "Storm Blowing from Paradise: Social Protest and Oppositional Ideology in Popular Hawaiian Music." *Popular Music* 10, no. 1: 53–67.

Lewontin, Richard and Richard Levins. 2007. *Biology Under the Influence: Dialectical Essays on Biology, Agriculture and Health*. New York: Monthly Review Press.

Lind, Andrew. 1955. *Hawaii's People*. Honolulu: University of Hawai'i Press.

Lind, Ian. 1983. "The Captive Valley of Mākua: 42 Years of Military Occupation." *Ka Hukilau ("The Turning Point)* 1, no. 5.

Linnekin, Jocelyn. 1983a. "Defining Tradition: Variations on the Hawaiian Identity." *American Ethnologist* 10: 241–52.

———. 1983b. "The Hui Lands of Keanae: Hawaiian Land Tenure and the Great Mähele." *The Journal of Polynesian Society* 93, no. 2.

———. 1985. *The Children of the Land*. New Brunswick, NJ: Rutgers University Press.

———. 1987. "Statistical Analysis of the Great Mahele: Some Preliminary Findings." *Journal of Pacific History* 22, no. 1–2: 15–33.

———. 1990. *Sacred Queens and Women of Consequence: Rank, Gender, and Colonialism in the Hawaiian Islands*. Ann Arbor: University of Michigan Press.

———. 1991. "Cultural Invention and the Dilemma of Authenticity." *American Anthropologist* 93, no. 2: 446–49.

Linton, Ralph, and A. Irving Hallowell. 1943. "Nativistic Movements." *American Anthropologist* 45, no. 2: 230–40.

Liptak, Adam. 2008. "US Imprisons One in 100 Adults, Report Finds." *New York Times*, February 29. Accessed online at NYT.com on March 20, 2008.

Liu, Kalama. 1997. Interviews with author, Wai'anae, Hawai'i.

Look, Mele A., and Kathryn L. Braun. 1995. *A Mortality Study of the Hawaiian People: 1910–1990*. Honolulu: Queen's Health Systems.

Magaoay, Sandi. 1994. "Hawaiian Campers Leave Makapuʻu." *Honolulu Star Bulletin,* July 27.

Magdoff, Fred. 2002. "Capitalism's Twin Crises: Economic and Environmental." *Monthly Review* 54, no. 4: 1–15.

Magin, Janice L. 2006. "For 1,000 or More Homeless in Hawaii, Beaches Are the Best Option." *New York Times,* December 5. http://www.nytimes.com/2006/12/05/us/05hawaii.html (accessed April 8, 2010).

"Mākua's Storied History." 1997. *Honolulu Star-Bulletin,* June 6, Internet archives.

"Mākua: To Heal the Nation." 1996. Video documentary. Produced by Nā Maka o Ka ʻĀina, Nāʻālehu, HI. Transcription by author.

Mākua Valley Support Committee. 1983. "Support Our Traditional Use of Mākua Valley." Pamphlet announcing Rally at Mākua Beach Park on Sunday, January 2, 1983. From the private papers of Pōkā Laenui (Hayden Burgess).

Malo, David. 1992[1951]. *Hawaiian Antiquities*. Honolulu: Bishop Museum Press.

Manschreck, Clyde L. 1964. *A History of Christianity: Readings in the History of the Church. Volume 2: The Church from the Reformation to the Present*. Grand Rapids, MI: Baker Book House.

Martín-Baró, Ignacio. 1996. *Writings for a Liberation Psychology*. Edited and translated by Adrianne Aron and Shawn Corne. Cambridge, MA: Harvard University Press.

Marx, Karl. 1977[1867]. *Capital*. Vol. 1. Translated by Ben Fowkes. New York: Vintage.

Massey, Linda K. 2001. "Dairy Food Consumption, Blood Pressure and Stroke." *The Journal of Nutrition* 131, no. 7: 1875–78.

Matsunaga, Mark. 1994a (April 24). "Dreams Have Been Dashed." *Honolulu Advertiser*.

———. 1994b (May 19). "Hawaiian Language Reawakens." *Honolulu Advertiser*.

———. 1994c (July 10). "The Shape of Sovereignty to Come." *Honolulu Advertiser*.

———. 1994d (July 17). "Leader to Miss Restoration Day." *Honolulu Advertiser*.

———. 1994e (July 30). "Speakers Link Health to Sovereignty Issue." *Honolulu Advertiser*.

———. 1994f (August 6). "Makapuʻu Seizure If Threatened." *Honolulu Advertiser*.

Mau, Marjorie M., Karen Glanz, Richard Severino, John S. Grove, Bruce Johnson, and J. David Curb. 2001. "Mediators of Lifestyle Behavior Change in Native Hawaiians." *Diabetes Care* 24, no. 10: 1770–75.

Mauna Ala's Daughter. 1997. Interview by author. Wai'anae, Hawai'i.

Mauss, Marcel. 1990[1925]. *The Gift*. New York: W. W. Norton & Company.

McCulloch, Jock. 1995. *Colonial Psychiatry and the African Mind*. New York: Cambridge University Press.

McGrath, Edward J., Kenneth M. Brewer, and Bob Krauss. 1973. *Historic Wai'anae: "A Place of Kings."* Honolulu: Island Heritage Limited.

McGregor, Davianna Pōmaika'i. 1996. "An Introduction to the Hoa'āina and Their Rights." *The Hawaiian Journal of History* 30: 1–27.

McMullin, Juliet. 2005. "The Call to Life: Revitalizing a Healthy Hawaiian Identity." *Social Science and Medicine* 61: 809–20.

McNeill, William H. 1989[1976]. *Plagues and Peoples*. New York: Anchor Books.

Memi, Albert. 1965. *The Colonizer and the Colonized*. Boston, MA: Beacon Press.

Menotti, Alessandro, Daan Kromhout, Henry Blackburn, Flaminio Fidanza, Ratko Buzina, and Aulikki Nissinen. 1999. "Food Intake Patterns and 25-Year Mortality from Coronary Heart Disease: Cross-cultural Correlations in the Seven Countries Study." *European Journal of Epidemiology* 15, no. 6: 507–15.

Merry, Sally Engle. 2000. *Colonizing Hawai'i: The Cultural Power of Law*. Princeton, NJ: Princeton University Press.

Meskin, Kelli. 1997. "Native Hawaiian Inmates: They are the Majority in Hawai'i Prisons, a Minority in the State." *Ka Wai Ola O OHA (The Living Water of OHA)* 14, no. 1 (January).

Meyer, Katie A., Lawrence H. Kushi, David R. Jacobs Jr., Joanne Slavin, Thomas A. Sellers, and Aaron R. Folsom. 2000. "Carbohydrates, Dietary Fiber, and Hidden Incident Type 2 Diabetes in Older Women." *American Journal of Clinical Nutrition* 71: 921–30.

Meyer, Manu Aluli. 1998a. "Native Hawaiian Epistemology: Exploring Hawaiian Views of Knowledge." *Cultural Survival Quarterly* 22, no. 1: 38–40.

———. 1998b. Native Hawaiian Epistemology: Sites of Empowerment and Resistance. *Equity & Excellence in Education* 31, no. 1: 22–28.

———. 2001. "Our Own Liberation: Reflections on Hawaiian Epistemology." *The Contemporary Pacific* (Spring): 124–48.

Meyers, Steven Lee. 2008. "Bush Backs Fed's Actions, but Critics Quickly Find Fault." *New York Times*, March 18. Accessed online at http://www.nytimes.com/2008/03/18/business/18bush.html?ref=us on March 18, 2008.

Mignolo, Walter D., and Madina V. Tlostanova. 2006. "Theorizing from the Borders: Shifting to Geo- and Body-Politics of Knowledge." *European Journal of Social Theory* 9, no. 2: 205–21.

Miller, Angela. 1995a. "O'ahu on Ice: Drug Fueling Crime Wave, Police Say." *Honolulu Advertiser*, October 1.

———. 1995b. "The Savior: His Own Confessions Build Their Trust." *Honolulu Advertiser*, October 1.

———. 1995c. "Suspect High on Crystal Meth Is High Risk for Police Safety." *Honolulu Advertiser*, October 1.

———. 1995d. "The User: Paranoia, Exhaustion, Nightmarish Sleep." *Honolulu Advertiser*, October 1.

Miller, Elizabeth Ruley. 1938. "A Follow-Up Study of Fifty Former Waiale'e Training School Boys." MA thesis, University of Hawai'i.

Mills, George H. 1994. "Hawaiians and Medicine." *Hawai'i Medical Journal* 53, no. 12: 272–76.

Minerbi, Luciano. 1994. "Sanctuaries, Places of Refuge, and Indigenous Knowledge in Hawai'i. In *Science of Pacific Island Peoples*, ed. John Morrison et al., 89–129. Honolulu: Institute of Pacific Island Studies.

Minerbi, Luciano, Davianna McGregor, and Jon Matsuoka, eds. 1993. "Natural Environment, Cultural and Ecological Resources." In *Native Hawaiian and Local Cultural Assessment Project*. Honolulu: Cultural Action Network for Developing Options and the Hawai'i Environment Risk Ranking Project.

Mintz, Sidney. 1985. *Sweetness and Power: The Place of Sugar in Modern History*. New York: Viking.

———. 1996. *Tasting Food, Tasting Freedom: Excursions into Eating, Culture and the Past*. Boston, MA: Beacon Press.

Mokuau, Noreen. 1990a. "A Family-Centered Approach in Native Hawaiian Culture." *Families in Society: The Journal of Contemporary Human Services* 71, no. 10.

———. 1990b. "The Impoverishment of Native Hawaiians and the Social Work Challenge." *Health and Social Work* 15, no. 3.

———. 1995. "Health and Well-Being for Pacific Islanders: Status, Barriers and Resolutions." *Asian American and Pacific Island Journal of Health* 4, no. 1–3.

Moment, David. 1957. "The Business of Whaling in America in the 1850s." *The Business History Review* 31, no. 3: 261–91.

Morgensen, Gretchen. 2008. "Rescue Me: A Fed Bail Out Crosses a Line." *New York Times*, March 18. Accessed online at http://www.nytimes.com/2008/03/16/business/16gret.html on March 18, 2008.

Morrison, Toni. 1990. "The Impoverishment of Native Hawaiians and the Social Work Challenge." *Health and Social Work* 15, no. 3: 235–42.

———. 1993. *Playing in the Dark: Whiteness and the Literary Imagination*. New York: Vintage.

———. 1995. "Health and Well-being for Pacific Islanders: Status, Barriers, and Resolutions." *Asian American and Pacific Island Journal of Health* 4, nos. 1–3: 55–67.

———. 2004. *Beloved*. New York: Vintage.

Morse, Harold. 1996. "Visitors Tour Army's Mākua Area." *Honolulu Star Bulletin*, November 25.

Mueller-Dombois, Dieter, and Nengah Wirawan. 2005. "The Kahana Valley Ahupuaʻa, a Pacific Asia Biodiversity Transect Study Site on Oʻahu, Hawaiian Islands." *Pacific Science* 59, no. 2: 293–314.

Mullings, Leith. 1996. *On Our Own Terms: Race, Class, and Gender in the Lives of African American Women*. New York: Routledge.

Murakawa, Kim. 1996. "H3 Girder Collapse Attributed to Heat." *Honolulu Advertiser*, August 19, A1.

Murphy, Kim. 2002. "In Hawaiʻi, a Lesson in Racial Disharmony." *Los Angeles Times*, August 18. Accessed online at http://www.moolelo.com/ks-disharmony.html on February 1, 2008.

Nā Maka o ka ʻĀina. *Mākua: To Heal the Nation*. 1996. Videocassette (32 minutes). Nāʻālehu, Hawaiʻi.

Nandan, Satendra. 1991. "Higher Education in the South Pacific: Diversity and the Humanities." In *A South Pacific Critique*, ed. David Jones et al., 133–48. Center for the Study of Higher Education, University of Melbourne.

Nandy, Ashis. 1983. *The Intimate Enemy: Loss and Recovery of Self under Colonialism*. Delhi: Oxford University Press.

National Community Reinvestment Coalition (NCRI). 2006. *The Opportunity Agenda and Poverty & Race Research Action Council. Homeownership and Wealth Building Impeded: Continuing Lending Disparities for Minorities and Emerging Obstacles for Middle-Income and Female Borrowers of All Races*. Washington, DC. Accessed online at http://www.ncrc.org/policy/analysis/policy/2006/2006-04-20_NCRC-OA-PRRACReport.pdf on February 2, 2008.

Native Hawaiian Health Research Conference. 1994. Kamehameha Schools, Honolulu, July 29. Personal notes.

Naya, Seiji. 2007. Presentation at the 2nd Annual Hawaiian Business Conference. Hawaiʻi Convention Center, May 22–23. Accessed online at http://www.oha.org/pfd/eco/2007/expo/naya_slides.ppt on February 2, 2008.

Naylor, Gloria. 1989. *Mama Day*. New York: Vintage.

Ngugi wa Thiongʻo. 1986. *Decolonizing the Mind: The Politics of Language in African Literature, Studies in African Literature, New Series*. London: James Currey.

Niles, Geddes. Letters. *Honolulu Advertiser*. August 1996. A21.

Nkrumah, Kwame. 1970. *Consciencism: Philosophy and the Ideology for Decolonization.* New York: Monthly Review Press.

Obeyesekere, Gananath. 1992. *The Apotheosis of Captain Cook: European Mythmaking in the Pacific.* Princeton, NJ: Princeton University Press.

O'Brien, Patty. 2006. "'Think of Me as a Woman': Queen Pomare of Tahiti and Anglo-French Imperial Contest in the 1840s Pacific." *Gender & History* 18, no. 1: 108–29.

O'Cadiz, Maria del Pilar, and Carlos Alberto Torres. 1994. "Literacy, Social Movements, and Class Consciousness: Paths for Freire and the Sao Paulo Experience." *Anthropology & Education Quarterly* 25, no. 3: 208–25.

Office of Minority Health (OMH). 2007. "Health Status of Asian American and Pacific Islander Women." Washington, DC: U.S. Department of Health and Human Services. http://www.minorityhealth.hhs.gov/templates/content.aspx?ID=3721 (accessed April 4, 2010).

Office of Native Hawaiian Affairs (OHA). 2002. *Statistical Portrait of the Hawaiian Population in Hawai'i: State of Hawai'i Data Book.* Honolulu: Office of Native Hawaiian Affairs.

Ohnuma, Keiko. 2008. "'Aloha Spirit' and the Cultural Politics of Sentiment as National Belonging." *The Contemporary Pacific* 20, no. 2: 365–94.

Okamura, Jonathan Y. 1990. "Ethnicity and Stratification in Hawai'i." Operation Manong Resource Papers No. 1. Honolulu: Operation Manong: 1–11.

———. 2008. *Ethnicity and Inequality in Hawai'i.* Philadelphia, PA: Temple University Press.

Okihiro, Gary Y. 1991. *Cane Fires: The Anti-Japanese Movement in Hawai'i, 1865–1945.* Philadelphia, PA: Temple University Press.

Oliver, Douglas L. 1989[1961]. *The Pacific Islands.* Honolulu: University of Hawai'i Press.

Omandam, Pat. 1996. "Mākua Folks Make Camp at Kea'au Beach Park." *Honolulu Star Bulletin,* June 19. Internet archives.

'Ōpelu Project 'Ohana. 1996. *From Then to Now: A Manual for Doing Things Hawaiian Style.* Wai'anae, HI: Wai'anae Coast Alternative Economic Development Corporation.

Osorio, Jonathan Kay Kamakawiwo'ole. 2002. *Dismembering Lāhui: A History of the Hawaiian Nation to 1887.* Honolulu: University of Hawai'i Press.

Oxendine, Jean. 2000. "Diabetes Programs Have Local Style." *Closing the Gap: Pacific Islander Health.* Washington, DC: Office of Minority Health Resource Center. U.S. Department of Health and Human Services.

Oyama, Kaikilani. 1996. Personal communication.

Patterson, John. 2000. "Mana: Yin and Yang." *Philosophy East and West* 50, no. 2: 220–41.

Perez, Rob. 2006. "Health Neglect Strains Main Medical Facility." *Honolulu Advertiser*, October 21. Accessed online at the.honoluluadvertiser.com on March 13, 2008.

Perrett, Roy W., and John Patterson. 1991. "Virtue Ethics and Maori Ethics." *Philosophy East and West* 41, no. 2: 185–202.

Pierce, Lori. 2004. "The Whites Have Created Modern Honolulu: Ethnicity, Racial Stratification, and the Discourse of Aloha." In *Racial Thinking in the United States: Uncompleted Independence*, ed. Paul Spickard and G. Reginald Daniel, 125–54. Notre Dame, IN: University of Notre Dame Press.

"Plans for Hawaiian Highway Hit Snag Over Ancient Burial Ground." 1985. *New York Times*, November 25.

Porteus, Stanley D. 1948. Territory of Hawai'i. Department of Institutions. The Institutions of the Territory of Hawai'i and Their Policies, Plans and Needs for Sound Institutional Practices.

———. 1965. *Porteus Maze Test*. Palo Alto, CA: Pacific Books.

Program Evaluation: Honolulu Model Cities (HUD) Project. 1971 (April). Wai'anae Rap Center. Honolulu: Honolulu City Demonstration Agency.

———. 1979. *Nānā I Ke Kumu (Look to the Source)*. Volume 2. Honolulu: Hui Hānai.

Pukui, Mary Kawena, and Samuel H. Elbert. 1986. *Hawaiian Dictionary*. Honolulu: University of Hawai'i Press.

Pukui, Mary Kawena, Samuel H. Elbert, and Esther T. Mookini. 1974. *Place Names of Hawai'i*. Honolulu: University of Hawai'i Press.

Pukui, Mary Kawena, E. W. Haertig, and Catherine A. Lee. 1972. *Nānā I Ke Kumu (Look to the Source)*. Volume 1. Honolulu: Hui Hānai.

Radin, Paul. 2008[1926]. *Primitive Man as Philosopher*. Hicksville, NY: Maudsley Press.

Ralston, Caroline. 1984. "Hawai'i 1778–1854: Some Aspects of Maka'āinana Response to Rapid Cultural Change." *The Journal of Pacific History* 19, no. 1: 21–40.

Ramires, Tino. 1996. "Highway Chief Says H3 Will be Safe." *Star Bulletin*. July 27: A1.

Rappaport, Nigel, and Joanna Overing. 2000. *Social and Cultural Anthropology: The Key Concepts*. New York: Routledge.

Ravussin, E., M. E. Valencia, J. Esparza, P. H. Bennet, and L. O. Schulz. 1994. "Effects of a Traditional Lifestyle on Obesity in Pima Indians." *Diabetes Care* 17, no. 9: 1067–74.

Redfield, Robert. 1959. "Anthropological Understanding of Man." *Anthropological Quarterly* 32, no. 1: 3–21.

Reeves, Jimmie, and Richard Campbell. 1994. *Cracked Coverage: Television News, The Anti-Cocaine Crusade, and the Reagan Legacy*. Chapel Hill, NC: Duke University Press.

Reyes, Luis I. 1995. *Made in Paradise: Hollywood's Films of Hawai'i and the South Seas*. Honolulu: Mutual Publishing.

Rezentes, William C., III. 1993. "Nā Mea Hawai'i: A Hawaiian Acculturation Scale." *Psychological Reports* 73: 383–93.

Rodney, Walter. 2005. "How Europe Underdeveloped Africa." In *Beyond Borders: Thinking Critically about Global Issues*, ed. Paula S. Rothenberg, 107–25. New York: Worth.

Rohrer, Judy. 2008. "Disrupting the 'Melting Pot': Racial Discourse in Hawai'i and the Naturalization of Haole." *Ethnic and Racial Studies* 31, no. 6: 1110–25.

Romaine, Suzanne. 1994. "Hawai'i Creole English as a Literary Language." *Language in Society* 23, no. 4: 527–54.

Rosaldo, Renato. 1993. *Culture and Truth: The Remaking of Social Analysis*. Boston, MA: Beacon Press.

Ruane, Marie. 1996. Hawaiian consultant, personal communication, June 14.

Sahlins, Marshall. 1968. *Tribesmen*. Upper Saddle River, NJ: Prentice Hall.

———. 1972. *Stone Age Economics*. Hawthorne, NY: Aldine de Gruyter.

———. 1981. *Historical Metaphors and Mythical Realities: Structure in the Early History of the Sandwich Islands Kingdom*. Association for Social Anthropology in the Oceania Publications. No. 1. Ann Arbor: The University of Michigan Press.

———. 1985. *Islands of History*. Chicago, IL: The University of Chicago Press.

———. 1994. "Cosmologies of Capitalism: The Trans-Pacific Sector of the World System." In *Culture/Power/History: A Reader in Contemporary Social Theory*, ed. Nicholas B. Dirks, Geoff Eley, and Sherry B. Ortner, 413–55. Princeton, NJ: Princeton University Press.

Said, Edward W. 1989. "Representing the Colonized: Anthropology's Interlocutors." *Critical Inquiry* 15, no. 2: 205–25.

Saunders, James Robert, and Renae Nadine Shackelford. 1998. *Urban Renewal and the End of Black Culture in Charlottesville, Virginia*. Jefferson, NC: McFarland & Company.

Scheper-Hughes, Nancy, and Margaret M. Lock. 1986. "Speaking 'Truth' to Illness: Metaphors, Reification, and a Pedagogy for Patients." *Medical Anthropology Quarterly* 17, no. 5: 137–40.

———. 1987. "The Mindful Body: A Prolegomenon to Future Work in Medical Anthropology." *Medical Anthropology Quarterly* 1, no. 1: 6–41.

Schlosser, Eric. 2001. *Fast Food Nation*. New York: Houghton Mifflin.

Schmitt, Robert C. 1970a. "Famine Mortality in Hawaii." *Journal of Pacific History* 5: 109–15.

———. 1970b. "The 'Oku'u: Hawaii's Greatest Epidemic." *Hawaii Medical Journal* 29, no. 5: 359–64.

Scott, James C. 1990. *Domination and the Arts of Resistance: Hidden Transcripts.* New Haven, CT: Yale University Press.

———. 1999. *Seeing Like a State: How Certain Schemes to Improve the Human Condition Have Failed.* New Haven, CT: Yale University Press.

Seaton, S. Lee. 1974. "The Hawaiian 'Kapu' Abolition of 1819." *American Ethnologist* 1, no. 1: 193–206.

Shapiro, David. 1996. "Why News Media Were Barred from Mākua." *Honolulu Star-Bulletin*, June 22. Internet archives.

Shapiro, Laura. 1993. "Do Our Genes Determine Which Foods We Should Eat?" *Newsweek*, August 9.

Shintani, Terry T., Claire K. Hughes, Sheila Beckham, and Helen Kanawaliwali O'Connor. 1991. "Obesity and Cardiovascular Risk Intervention through the ab libitum Feeding of Traditional Hawaiian Diet." *American Journal of Clinical Nutrition* 53: 1647S–1651S.

Shook, E. Victoria. 1985. *Ho'oponopono. An East-West Center Book.* Honolulu: Institute of Culture and Communication.

Shore, Bradd. 1989. "Mana and Tapu." In *Developments in Polynesian Ethnology*, ed. Alan Howard and Robert Borofsky, 137–74. Honolulu: University of Hawai'i Press.

Silva, Noenoe K. 2004. *Aloha Betrayed: Native Hawaiian Resistance to American Colonialism.* Durham, NC: Duke University Press.

Skocpol, Theda, and Edwin Amenta. 1986. "States and Social Policies." *Annual Review of Sociology* 12: 131–57.

Smedley, Audrey, and Brian D. Smedley. 2005. "Race as Biology Is Fiction, Racism as a Social Problem Is Real: Anthropological and Historical Perspectives on the Social Construction of Race." *American Psychologist* 60, no. 1: 16–26.

Smith, Linda Tuhiwai. 1999. *Decolonizing Methodologies: Research and Indigenous Peoples.* New York: Zed Books.

Snarr, Robert W., Jr. 2002. "No Cash 'til Payday: The Payday Lending Industry." Compliance Corner, 1st Quarter. Supervision, Regulation and Credit Department of the Federal Reserve Bank of Philadelphia. http://www.phil.frb.org/src/srcinsights/srcinsights/q1cc1.html (accessed April 9, 2009).

Sontag, Susan. 1990. *Illness as Metaphor and AIDS and Its Metaphors.* New York: Anchor Books.

Spitz, Allan. 1967. "The Transplantation of American Democratic Institutions: The Case of Hawai'i." *Political Science Quarterly* 82, no. 3: 386–98.

Spivak, Gayatri. 1988. "Can the Subaltern Speak?" In *Marxism and the Interpretation of Culture*, ed. Cary Nelson and Lawrence Grossman, 271–313. Urban: University of Illinois Press.

Stannard, David E. 1989. *Before the Horror: The Population of Hawai'i on the Eve of Western Contact.* Honolulu: Social Science Research Institute, University of Hawai'i.

———. 1993. *American Holocaust: Conquest of the New World.* New York: Oxford University Press.

———. 1997. "Why Porteus Hall Must Be Renamed." *Honolulu Star-Bulletin,* December 12, Internet archives.

———. 1999. "Honoring Racism: The Professional Life and Reputation of Stanley D. Porteus." In *The Ethnic Studies Story: Politics and Social Movements in Hawai'i. Essays in Honor of Marion D. Kelley,* ed. Ibrahim G. Aoudé. Social Process in Hawai'i 39: 85–125.

State of Hawai'i, Office of Hawaiian Affairs. 1991. *Hui 'Imi: Task Force for Hawaiian Services. Volume 1: A Collective Search (Current Services/Critical Needs).* Honolulu: Author.

Stegman, Michael A. 2007. "Payday Lending." *Journal of Economic Perspectives* 21, no. 1: 169–90.

Stillman, Amy Ku'uleialoha. 1989. "History Represented in Song: The Case of the Hawaiian Counterrevolution." *The Hawaiian Journal of History* 23: 1–30.

———. 1999. "'Aloha 'Āina': New Perspectives on 'Kaulana Nā Pua.'" *The Hawaiian Journal of History* 33: 83–99.

Sussex, Hokuokalani. 1997. Interview by author, Wai'anae, Hawai'i.

Sussex, SherriLynn. 1997. Interview by author, Wai'anae, Hawai'i.

Szasz, Thomas S. 1958a. "Politics and Mental Health: Some Remarks Apropos of the Case of Mr. Ezra Pound." *American Journal of Psychiatry* 115: 508–11.

———. 1958b. "Psychiatry, Ethics, and the Criminal Law." *Columbia Law Review* 58. no. 2: 183–98.

Takaki, Ronald. 1983. *Pau Hana: Plantation Life and Labor in Hawai'i, 1835–1920.* Honolulu: University of Hawai'i Press.

Tatar, Elizabeth. 1981. "Toward a Description of Pre-contact Music in Hawai'i." *Ethnomusicology* 25, no. 3: 481–92.

Tate, Merze. 1962. "Decadence of the Hawaiian Nation and Proposals to Import a Negro Labor Force." *The Journal of Negro History* 47, no. 4: 248–63.

Taussig, Michael. 1991. *The Nervous System.* New York: Routledge.

Tengan, Ty P. Kāwika. 2005. "Unsettling Ethnography: Tales of an 'Ōiwi in the Anthropological Slot." *Anthropological Forum* 15, no. 3: 247–56.

———. 2008. "Re-membering Panalā'au: Masculinities, Nation and Empire in Hawai'i and the Pacific." *Contemporary Pacific* 20, no. 1: 27–53.

Territory of Hawaii. 1930. Bureau of the Budget. A Plan for the Organization of a Department of Institutions (or a Department of Public Welfare) within the Territorial Government.

"The New King of Hawai'i." 1873. *New York Times,* March 15, p. 9.

"The Uprising in Hawai'i." 1895. *New York Times*, January 20.

Thompson, Myron Bennet. 1953. "A Study of the Growth of the Boy's Training School in Hawai'i (1865 to 1959) from an Historical Standpoint." MA thesis, University of Hawai'i.

Thurston, Lucy G. 1921[1882]. *Life of Lucy G. Thurston: Pioneer Missionary.* Ann Arbor, MI: S. C. Andrews.

Tomlinson, Matt. 2006. "Retheorizing Mana: Bible Translation and Discourse of Loss in Fiji." *Oceania* 76, no. 2: 173–85.

———. 2007. "Mana in Christian Fiji: The Interconversion of Intelligibility and Palpability." *Journal of the American Academy of Religion* (October): 1–30.

Trask, Haunani-Kay. 1987. "The Birth of the Modern Hawaiian Movement: Kalama Valley, O'ahu," *The Hawaiian Journal of History* 21: 126–53.

———. 1991. "Natives and Anthropologists: The Colonial Struggle." *The Contemporary Pacific* 3, no. 2.

———. 1993. *From a Native Daughter: Colonialism and Sovereignty in Hawai'i.* Monroe, ME: Common Courage Press.

———. 1994. *Light in the Crevice Never Seen.* Corvallis, OR: Calyx Books.

———. 1996. "Feminism and Indigenous Hawaiian Nationalism." *Signs* 21, no. 4: 906–16.

———. 1999. "The New World Order." In *From a Native Daughter: Colonialism and Sovereignty in Hawai'i,* 58–64. Honolulu: University of Hawai'i Press.

———. 2000. "Writing in Captivity: Poetry in a Time of De-Colonization." In *Navigating Islands and Continents: Conversations and Contestations in and around the Pacific,* ed. Cynthia Franklin, Ruth Hsu, and Suzanne Kosanke, 51–55. Honolulu: University of Hawai'i Press.

Trask, Mililani. 1996. "Mililani Trask." In *Autobiography of Protest in Hawai'i,* ed. Robert H. Mast and Anne B. Mast, 389. Honolulu: University of Hawai'i Press.

Trouillot, Michel-Rolph. 1995. *Silencing the Past: Power and the Production of History.* Boston, MA: Beacon Press.

Trumbull, Robert. 1980. "Native Hawaiians Feel the Squeeze: Resort Boom Is One Reason for Frayed Race Relations." *New York Times,* October 19.

Tummons, Patricia, ed. 1992. "Army's Application for EPA Permit Is Long, but Not Informative." *Environment Hawaii* 3, no. 5.

U.S. Census Bureau (UCB). 2007. *The American Community—Pacific Islanders: 2004.* Washington, DC: U.S. Department of Commerce.

Valenstein, Elliot S. 1986. *Great and Desperate Cures: The Rise and Decline of Psychosurgery and Other Radical Treatments for Mental Illness.* New York: Basic Books.

Valeri, Valerio. 1985. *Kingship and Sacrifice: Ritual and Society in Ancient Hawai'i*. Chicago, IL: The University of Chicago Press.

Vertosick, Frank T. 1997. "Lobotomy's Back." Discover (October 1).

Wagner, Roy. 1975. *The Invention of Culture*. Chicago, IL: University of Chicago Press.

Wai'anae Coast Comprehensive Health Center. 1995. *Wai'anae Diet Cookbook 'Elua*. Vol. 2. Wai'anae, Hawai'i.

Wallace, Anthony. 1957. *The Death and Rebirth of the Seneca*. New York: Vintage.

Warner, Sam L. No'eau. 2001. "The Movement to Revitalize Hawaiian Language and Culture." In *The Green Book of Language Revitalization in Practice*, ed. Leanne Hinton and Kenneth Locke Hale, 133–44. New York: Academic Press.

"Welfare Cutbacks Will Backfire, Researchers Say." 1996. *Honolulu Advertiser*, April 7.

Whitaker, Mark P. 1996. "Ethnography as Learning: A Wittgensteinian Approach to Writing Ethnographic Accounts." *Anthropological Quarterly* 69, no. 1: 1–13.

White, Geoffrey M., and Ty Kāwika Tengan. 2001. "Disappearing Worlds: Anthropology and Cultural Studies in Hawai'i and the Pacific." *The Contemporary Pacific* 13, no. 2: 381–416.

Willett, Walter C. 1995. "Diet, Nutrition and Avoidable Cancer." *Environmental Health Perspectives* 103 (Supplement 8): 165–200.

———. 2005. "Diet and Cancer: An Evolving Picture." *JAMA* 293, no. 2: 233–34.

Wise, Henry Augustus. 1849. *Los Gringos: Or, An Inside View of Mexico and California, with Wanderings in Peru, Chili, and Polynesia*. New York: Baker and Scribner.

Wright, Theon. 1966. *Rape in Paradise*. Honolulu: Mutual Publishing.

Yuen, Mile. 1997. "Open Road: After Decades of Controversy, the 16.1-Mile Highway Will Soon Open for Business." *Honolulu Star Bulletin*, December 3.

Zola, Irving. 1978. "Medicine as an Institution of Social Control." In *The Cultural Crisis of Modern Medicine*, ed. John Ehrenreich, 81–100. New York: Monthly Review Press.

Zuberi, Tukufu. 2001. *Thicker Than Blood: How Racial Statistics Lie*. Minnesota: University of Minnesota Press.

INDEX

223